# HIDDEN SONG OF THE HIMALAYAS

MEMOIR OF A GOSPEL SEED SOWER IN THE
MOUNTAINS OF INDIA

ABIGAIL FOLLOWS

WHATSOEVER
PRESS

ISBN 978-1-7369415-0-8

All Scripture quotations, unless otherwise indicated, are taken from the (NASB®) New American Standard Bible®, Copyright © 1960, 1971, 1977, 1995, 2020 by The Lockman Foundation. Used by permission. All rights reserved. www.lockman.org

Scripture quotations marked (NIV) are taken from the Holy Bible, New International Version®, NIV®. Copyright © 1973, 1978, 1984, 2011 by Biblica, Inc.® Used by permission of Zondervan. All rights reserved worldwide. www.zondervan.com The "NIV" and "New International Version" are trademarks registered in the United States Patent and Trademark Office by Biblica, Inc.®

Scripture quotations marked (KJV) are taken from The Authorized (King James) Version. Rights in the Authorized Version in the United Kingdom are vested in the Crown. Reproduced by permission of the Crown's patentee, Cambridge University Press.

Whatsoever Press

www.whatsoeverpress.com

*To the women of India*
*who dream of safe and happy homes.*
*And to the ones who give up that dream*
*for the sake of the cross.*

# AUTHOR'S NOTE

It has been written that everything said about India is both true and false at the same time. That is a testament to the diversity of the country. What is noted in this book about cultural practices will sometimes be universally true of Hindu Indians of any caste or residents of India in general, regardless of religious or ethnic background. Other times, customs will be unique to the setting of this book, a place where the caste is almost entirely Brahmin and the people almost exclusively rural middle-class. Cultural insights in this book are not meant to be an exhaustive and complete portrait of Hinduism or Indian culture, but a glimpse of the author's experience of them.

This book is a work of memoir. The events described are written from the memory and perspective of the author.

To protect privacy and ensure safety, names of people and places have been changed.

# CONTENTS

# ACKNOWLEDGMENTS

Special thanks to:

Joshua, my husband and best friend, for listening to me talk about this project non-stop for three years. Thank you for being a living parable of Christ to me.

Ashi and Arav, for sharing your mommy with the computer so she could write this book. I'm so glad Jesus gave you to me!

My parents for teaching me, loving me, and believing in me. For supporting my decision to be a missionary. Mom, for giving me permission to share part of your story, and for supporting my faith journey even thought it's different from yours. Dad, for reading every chapter of this book, offering solid advice, and reminding me this story was important when I wanted to quit.

Mr. and Mrs. Follows, for loving me like a daughter. I could write another book about all the times we talked and prayed together while Joshua and I lived in India. The sacrifices you make are not only noticed but deeply appreciated.

Margie, Nathan, Andrew, and Alina, true friends with whom we experienced many stories that didn't find space in this book. Your friendship and hospitality over the years have meant the world to us. Let's try to live in the same country again someday!

Anne, for visiting India with me years later and for being one of the women I strive to emulate.

My beta readers and proofreaders, who read either all or part of this book, and gave suggestions to improve it: Dad, Anne, Sarah, David, Margie, Nathan, Erin, Matthew, Heidi, Joshua, Wanangwa, Mike, Kate, Holly, Sammi. Thank you!

Jeanette Windle, whose honest and encouraging critique and copyedit were invaluable in the process of polishing this book. Thank you for everything!

Doug, for your helpful advice regarding the many versions of the book cover.

Darshika, who gave me permission to share her story and who I consider one of my closest friends.

Our angel dispatchers, whose prayers were instrumental in each of these stories. Thank you for bringing our names and the names of the Parvata people before the throne of grace.

Other people who helped guide along the way: Deborah S., Peggy H., Vio and Lily, Jason W., Terrie A. (may you rest in peace), Michael and Aquarius, the staff and missionaries of our organization, the staff and faculty of Walla Walla University. Thank you for letting God use you to bless and encourage a fellow believer.

Jesus Christ, my Savior and the One who turns our broken lives into beautiful stories. Thank You for letting me live this story and for giving me the chance to share it with others.

# INTRODUCTION
## MOUNT MORIAH

For years, one particular Bible story moved my heart. The story of Abram, a man who left everything behind to follow God. A man who climbed Mount Moriah with his son Isaac, willing to sacrifice the very gift God had promised him. Abram must have been afraid. But he knew God well enough to trust Him.

I wanted to know God like that.

Yet I had no idea saying yes to God would lead me as a young wife to India to be an "undercover" missionary in a place politically hostile to the gospel and often socially unaware of its existence. I had no way to know I would birth two babies in the Himalayan mountains and watch a high caste Hindu woman be "reborn" a Jesus follower. I had no way of knowing God would use my meek voice by the power of the Holy Spirit to cast out demons, speak peace into chaos, and bring the name of Jesus where it was unknown.

My husband Joshua and I launched to India as missionaries in 2010, just four years after we got married. We lived among high caste Hindu people for seven years, squeezing our English thoughts into the Hindi language and our Western ways into Eastern ones. We ate with our hands and accompanied our worship music on a harmonium. We listened more than we spoke, prayed more than we preached, and sought to be genuine friends of the people on Christ's behalf.

God brought me to my personal Mount Moriah many times during our service in India. He asked me to give up everything. Though I didn't feel I had the strength, I said yes. My willingness put me in the center of miracles and deliverances. It made space for God to replace my secret doubts with a lasting faith.

This book tells that story. The story of what God can do through someone, not because *she* is mighty but because *He* is.

Perhaps God is asking you to trust Him in one small thing. Or maybe He's calling you to do something daring and different. Whatever it is, friend, let me give you one piece of advice. Look your fear in the eye and say no. Then look up and say yes to God. He has an amazing, beautiful plan for you and for each person who will follow Him wherever He leads.

# 1

## PROMPTED

H*e's crying. Go to him.* The thought was clear, annunciated. I opened my eyes, heavy from deep sleep, and listened. The cries of our landlord's young grandson filtered down from their home on the floor above ours.

*It's Neenoo. You must go to him.* Was this God speaking to me? But why would God ask me to do something so crazy?

Pulling on my glasses, I glanced at my husband, Joshua. He still slept. I stumbled out of our room to the stairs that connected our home with our landlord's. A lock on either side of the door stayed latched unless Joshua was away. Then Mrs. Pandit unlocked her side in case I needed something in the night. The Pandits used an outside entrance.

*Go upstairs.*

Instead, I sat on the stairs. *I can't do it, God!*

*Go.*

*I know we've been working on me doing things I'm scared to do. But I can't just barge into someone's house in the middle of the night.* Despite the seriousness of the moment, I chuckled at the thought. Parvata friends had entered my home at many inconvenient times in our five years in India. Knocking was unusual in that close-knit Hindu community. Even so, I suspected visiting in the middle of the night would be considered socially awkward even for the Parvata.

*Their kids cry all the time, and so do ours. What if I'm hearing You wrong? What if they feel offended? Besides, their side of the door is locked.*

Little Neenoo continued to cry. My heart pounded in time with God's voice: *Go. Go. Go.*

*But God, I'm afraid of what they will think!*

*Didn't you tell me this afternoon that you are willing to die for Me? Isn't this easier than dying?*

"Okay," I said aloud. Crawling up the steep steps, I opened the lock on our side. The door swung open an inch. *Strange,* I thought. *Their side isn't locked.* Taking a deep breath, I walked through the door, then continued on to the only room that showed a light and peeked inside.

In the center of the room stood a *tandoor,* the Hindi word for wood stove. The women of the family sat around the tandoor on colorful mats, staring down at Neenoo, who lay on the floor. He was still crying and had black smudges around his eyes. I recognized this as *kajal,* a cosmetic believed to protect from the evil eye.

Mrs. Pandit, Neenoo's grandmother, glanced up at me. She didn't seem surprised to see me.

"He woke you, too, huh?" she asked. Her black hair frizzed out from under a red headscarf. The powdery *tilak* on her forehead, a sign of devotion to the gods, was smudged.

"Um . . . no," I said. "God did."

Mrs. Pandit nodded as though this was normal. I sat on the closest mat and tried to make myself small.

*Pray for him.*

I bowed my head.

*Show you are praying.*

I folded my hands. Neenoo rolled over on his back and continued to cry.

*Go to him.*

I struggled for a moment as everyone's gaze focused on me. But I had to continue, if only to find out God's purpose in prompting me to come. Standing, I walked to the mat nearest Neenoo and sat down again. He rolled towards me, still wailing.

Now Mr. Pandit arrived. He glanced at me, then took a seat on a mat next to his daughter-in-law, Neenoo's mother.

Mr. Pandit sat the same way he walked. Like someone important. My heartbeat pounded in my ears. A professional spiritualist, Mr. Pandit was the closest person to a witch doctor I knew, though he looked nothing like the stereotype. Even now, in the middle of the night, he wore a wool suit coat over a long, white tunic.

Ever since Mr. Pandit and his family had moved in upstairs, people had been coming to see him non-stop. Sometimes I heard him at night working with a client for whom he would tell the future or curse an enemy. Beside him, I felt small and immature, like a child playing at religion.

*God, do this through me,* I prayed. *I am nothing!*

*Lay your hand on the child.*

I reached out my hand and rubbed Neenoo's back. He looked up at me, eyes wide.

*Pray out loud.*

I felt my stomach tighten, and all the hairs on my arms stood on end. *Just open your mouth,* I told myself. *Take the first step.*

"God in Heaven," I prayed, the Hindi words coming easily. "I ask in Jesus' name that if anyone has put a curse or the evil eye on this child, it will be broken by the power of Jesus' name. I pray that Jesus' blood will cover Neenoo and prevent any harm from coming to him. I pray You will give him peace and rest. Send Your Holy Spirit into this house to grant this family sleep. In Jesus' name I pray, amen."

I opened my eyes and looked down at Neenoo. His eyes fluttered, then shut. With a sigh, he fell asleep. After a long moment, Mrs. Pandit broke the silence. "Christians believe in the evil eye?"

"We believe that humans have an enemy," I said. "Satan wants to kill, steal, and destroy. But when Jesus went to the cross, He took all curses and the evil eye upon Himself. He let evil and sin kill Him. But when He rose from the dead, He showed that He has power over everything—curses, magic powers, sin, and even death."

"Huh," Mrs. Pandit grunted as though I'd said something strange. I felt strange, too. I'd never thought of the gospel like that. We all sat for a long time, watching Neenoo sleep.

"Goodnight," I said at last and left.

Back downstairs in our bedroom, I found Joshua sitting cross-legged on our bed.

"What's going on?" he asked. "I woke up and saw you'd gone upstairs. I've been praying for you."

When I told Joshua what had happened, we rejoiced. Maybe this was the breakthrough with the Parvata we'd been praying for. Maybe this was the very seed that would cause this spiritual desert to blossom, as God had promised through the prophet Isaiah:

> For as the rain and the snow come down from heaven,
> And do not return there without watering the earth
> And making it produce and sprout,
> And providing seed to the sower and bread to the eater;
> So will My word be which goes out of My mouth;
> It will not return to Me empty,
> Without accomplishing what I desire,
> And without succeeding in the purpose for which I sent it.

ISAIAH 55:10-11

We claimed the Bible promise yet again, then crawled under our woolen blankets. All was quiet. No smell of incense drifted down from upstairs. No puja bell clanged. Not a drumbeat punctuated the stillness. No beggars cried out for alms at the door. No migrant children clambered over the fence to play. No visitors sat waiting for chai. This was a rare moment of peace, a moment to think.

As I lie there waiting for sleep to come, my mind wandered over the past ten years of my life. I could never have known a decade earlier that God would place me in the center of a fight over people's souls. Yet here I was.

*Keep leading,* Lord, I prayed. *Only You can change people's hearts. I know from experience. After all, You changed mine.*

# 2

## JOSHUA

It was in the choir room at a Christian university that I first noticed Joshua's smile. It was the kind of smile that verged on a laugh, catchable like a yawn. A freshman like myself, Joshua had clean-cut blonde hair and wore a plain T-shirt and jeans. He bounced when he walked and walked fast like he knew where he was going.

As it turned out, he had no idea where he was going. But then neither of us could have guessed we'd one day marry and serve as undercover missionaries in a country known for its persecution of Christians. On that first day, all I knew was that Joshua had a great smile. And a guitar case.

After eating together in the cafeteria, we brought our guitars to the lobby of my dormitory. Soon a random girl walking past us stopped in her tracks. "Awww!"

Surprised, I side-whispered to Joshua, "Do you know her?"

"No. You?"

"Nope." The girl awwwed again, then pointed to us. "Somebody should take a picture so they can show their grandkids!"

A blush crept up my neck. As the girl left, Joshua and I glanced at each other and laughed. What a thing to say about two people who had just met!

Despite that little distraction, Joshua and I spent the next several hours talking. He'd grown up a Christian but had focused most of his goal-oriented mind on becoming a famous rock guitarist.

"So what changed?" I asked. "You don't exactly look like a member of a heavy metal band."

"My dad got me a new Bible for my fifteenth birthday," Joshua said. "I decided to read one chapter a day. It was a slow process, but God completely changed my desires."

He went on to share how God had redirected the course of his life. It happened one day as he sang at a church with his high school choir. They'd performed a choral piece based on a prayer of St. Francis of Assisi: "Make Me an Instrument of Thy Peace."

"For it is in dying that we are born to eternal life." As the choir sang those lyrics, the Holy Spirit grabbed onto Joshua. The words seared into him. He was unable to sing until the final line of the last song when he belted out: "My soul is a witness for my Lord!" After the service, he went behind the church and wept, wondering if God was telling him he would die a martyr. Following him to the parking lot, his mom suggested maybe God was calling him to "die to himself" and join the ministry rather than to die a literal death.

"That's why I'm studying theology," Joshua finished.

"That's amazing," I responded.

"What about you? What's your story?"

"Well . . . " I tucked my bobbed brown hair behind my ear and wished I had a more normal-sounding life story to tell. But it was no use pretending.

"I grew up a Christian too. But my family went through a lot of crises when I was growing up. My mom struggled with depression, and sometimes we thought she might not make it. She's doing better, now. But my parents are in the middle of a divorce, and my mom is converting to orthodox Judaism. She doesn't believe Jesus is the Messiah. That's been pretty disorienting, so I'm doing a lot of searching as to what I believe and why."

I felt exposed sharing all this. Joshua leaned forward, his blue eyes intent. I smiled to show I was okay. "When I was growing up, it was sometimes hard to believe God loved me or was paying any attention. That's why I started writing music. My songs are like my prayers."

"You write music?" Joshua's face lit up with interest. "Can I have your autograph?"

"Ha, ha."

"Seriously, it might be worth something someday!"

"Only if you write me a letter in Greek and teach me to read it."

"Deal."

Joshua and I soon started dating. During classes, I daydreamed about being a pastor's wife. I planned to hold Joshua's arm and walk out of the church with him after sermons like I'd seen our pastor and his wife do.

Around this time, a youth pastor friend of ours started a campus co-ed prayer group, which included me, Joshua, and a handful of others who gathered every evening to pray. Inspired by a sermon, we started specifically asking for the Holy Spirit's anointing. As Christians, we believed the Holy Spirit was always with us, prompting our hearts to seek God and encouraging us in times of distress. But one day after we'd been praying about it for several weeks, the Holy Spirit came in a different way.

I'd learned that the word "holy" means "set apart." Holiness is something different, something separate. That's the only way I can describe the atmosphere in the chapel that night. It felt different. There was a quietness, a safety you could feel.

"Guys, I need to confess," one young man interrupted our prayers. He said he'd been ignoring God's voice calling him to be a spiritual warrior instead of going along with the crowd. The rest of us surrounded him, laid hands on his shoulders, and prayed for him. After him, a former witch who was once again dabbling in magic broke down crying. She asked God to forgive her and close the door she'd opened to Satan.

As several others confessed sin, I felt my heart pressed by the Holy Spirit to be honest with myself, and everyone else. "My mom doesn't believe in Jesus. And… I'm not sure if I do either."

When I heard myself admit those words aloud, sobs rose from my chest. I hid my face in my hands. Then I felt hands on my shoulders and heard prayers and tears for me. I heard Joshua praying, too.

*Oh, God,* I thought. *Even if I have to lose Joshua, even if I have to lose everything to know the truth, I have to know. Is Jesus Your Son? Is He the Messiah or not?*

---

SCARCELY HAD I admitted my doubt than our choir began practicing to perform Handel's *Messiah* at Christmas time. Since we had only a few weeks to learn the demanding oratorio, we practiced the usual five days a week plus extra multiple-hour rehearsals in the evenings and on weekends. As we labored over *For Unto us a Child is Born* with its head-spinning runs, I realized we were singing verses straight out of the Bible.

Many of the songs in Handel's *Messiah* take their lyrics directly from Old Testament Messianic prophecies. I used to go back to my room after every practice to look up these verses-turned-lyrics in my Bible.

We performed just before Christmas, and it was after our performance that I decided to share what I'd found with my mom. I opened my Bible to Isaiah 53, took a deep, shaky breath, and dialed my mom. When she answered, I read aloud the words I'd sung every day for many weeks:

> Surely he hath borne our griefs, and carried our sorrows: yet we did esteem him stricken, smitten of God, and afflicted. But he was wounded for our transgressions, he was bruised for our iniquities: the chastisement of our peace was upon him; and with his stripes we are healed. All we like sheep have gone astray; we have turned every one to his own way; and the Lord hath laid on him the iniquity of us all.
>
> (ISAIAH 53:4-6, KJV)

"I know, honey," Mom responded. "I've read it."
"But don't you feel anything?"
"No."
"But why?"
"God is one. He said to have no other gods before Him."
"But Jesus is God. He is God in the flesh, come to earth. He was sent by God and promised by God hundreds of years before—"

Mom interrupted me. "Honey, I know you believe that. But I don't. Not anymore."

My mother's doubts entered my heart like a sword. What if she was right?

# 3

---

# MESSIAH

On Valentine's Day, Joshua bought me a new Bible with my name embossed in the corner. I nearly wore out the binding from reading and filled the pages with underlining and notes. I had to know if Jesus fulfilled the Old Testament prophecies about the Messiah.

Sometimes at night, I imagined facing God in the judgment. If I continued to follow Jesus, but He turned out to be nothing more than an idol, I would be condemned. But if Jesus was God's plan to bring salvation to the world, how could I stand without Him?

That year, the song *"Give Me Jesus"* was popular on our university campus as both a solo and congregational praise song. Every time I heard it, I would put my head in my hands and pray, *If Jesus is Your Son, Father God, then give me Jesus. Take away these doubts. But if it's all a lie, don't let me stop searching until I know the truth.*

---

THOUGH A FRESHMAN LIKE MYSELF, my roommate Trisha was mistakenly assigned a fourth-level religion class that quarter. The class was on the Pentateuch, aka the first five books of the Bible. One evening, Trisha ran into our room, out of breath with excitement. "I knew I took this class for a reason. It's for you!"

"What's for me?" I asked.

"Sit down." Taking my Bible from beside my bed, Trisha opened it to Genesis 15 and set it on my lap. "Read."

I had read the entire Bible, many sections more than once, but this was one chapter on which I'd spent little time. In Genesis 15, Abraham cuts a series of animals in half, placing the halves on either side of a path. As Trisha explained, this was how contracts were made in ancient times. Instead of signing a document, the two parties agreeing to the contract would walk between halves of severed animals.

"It was basically like saying, 'If I don't hold up my end of the bargain, may I become like these dead animals.'"

"Okay," I responded. "And how is this for me?"

"Because Abraham never got to walk through the pieces. God caused him to fall asleep, and He walked through Himself. Twice!" Trisha waited for me to understand. When I did, I stood so quickly I had to catch my Bible.

"In other words," I said, "if Abraham didn't hold up his end of the bargain, God would be the one to die. Humanity didn't keep its contract with God, so Jesus came to die in our place on the cross!"

"Exactly!"

I felt all the hairs on my arms stand on end. Could it be true that Jesus's sacrifice was foretold as early as the first book of the Bible?

---

JOSHUA WOULD LATER SAY he'd wondered whether a theology major should date someone who wasn't sure about her faith. But the all-consuming nature of my search and Joshua's own faith in God helped him wait. In the meantime, he bought me books on the divinity of Christ, listened to me debate with myself, and kept praying.

In late spring, a soloist performed "Give Me Jesus" for our weekly chapel service. As he sang, I put my head in my hands and pored over my doubts and beliefs for the hundredth time. *God, show me the truth!*

I believed there was a God. To me, science and nature each presented compelling evidence of God's existence. As for God's identity, growing up a Seventh-day Adventist Christian and attending an Adventist university meant I'd studied bible prophecy extensively, especially Old Testament prophecy. For me, prophecy sealed the deal on the Creator's identity. God had predicted hundreds of years in advance the rising and falling of nations. He was a God with a plan.

But was Jesus a part of that plan? The students singing His praises all around me in chapel that day believed He was *the* plan, *the* point of the entire Old Testament. But I couldn't just believe something because everyone else did. I had to be sure.

I mentally listed the points for and against Jesus as Messiah. Even as I did so, disturbing thoughts about the judgment flashed into my mind. I knew I needed a savior and longed to accept Jesus. I even felt it would be reasonable to do so. But my doubts would not let go. I felt as though my brain were underwater, slogging through ideas and philosophies that chased each other around in circles.

*God, show me! I can't know the truth without Your help.* Just then, I remembered something I had underlined in my new Bible:

> *Can a woman forget her nursing child and have no compassion on the son*
> *of her womb? Even these may forget, but I will not forget you. Behold,*

*I have inscribed you on the palms of My hands; your walls are
continually before Me.*

(ISAIAH 49:14-16)

For the first time, I realized the frenzied nature of my search might be related
to spiritual warfare. My questions weren't wrong. The quest for truth was a good
thing. It was the oppressive darkness that came over me every time I tried to
make a decision. Surely the God of the Bible was not the source of this
condemning confusion.

No, despite all my insecurities and flaws, God Himself had compassion for
me. He had provided all the proof I needed to decide. And He knew what I was
up against, why it was so hard. He knew I longed for my mother to accept Him
and felt almost paralyzed against choosing Him myself if she didn't believe. He
knew me.

He had written my name on His palms.

In His blood.

On the cross.

---

THAT MOMENT in chapel changed everything. Although I still had questions, I
knew answers would come. I had found Jesus, the One who wrote my name on
His palms. I could finally accept God's love. Though I was a person prone to
doubt and fear, I believed His perfect love would one day cast out my fear.

Joshua and I continued dating and grew closer as we shared our love for our
Redeemer. Then one day during our sophomore year, a woman from a Bible
translation society spoke at chapel. Marilyn Laszlo had translated the Bible into a
tribal language in Papua New Guinea. She shared a blood-curdling account of
contracting trichinosis, languishing with culture shock, and searching for a word
for "pen" in a place without a written language.

*I could never do that!* I thought to myself as she finished. Just then I felt a rustle
next to me. Joshua stood and clapped—the only person that day to give Marilyn
a standing ovation. That afternoon, Joshua told me he believed God was calling
him to be a missionary.

Going to my dorm room, I ground my forehead into the carpet and asked
God if He was sure He knew what He was doing. *Are you sure? I mean, faith is one
of Joshua's spiritual gifts. He would make a great missionary. But if You're calling him to
do that, why did you bring us together? Haven't you noticed? I would not make a good
missionary!*

I heard no response from God. I considered breaking up with Joshua. The
thought twisted my stomach in knots because he was fast becoming my best
friend. But I couldn't pretend I felt called to missions. I didn't feel strong, brave,
and full of faith. I didn't think I'd make it five minutes on the mission field. Yet
there was no way I would ask Joshua to give up his calling.

*Okay, God, if You want me to be a missionary, you'll have to change my heart.* Opening my eyes, I looked up at the white ceiling and added aloud, "Good luck!"

———————

ONE MONTH LATER, I signed up to serve as a short-term student missionary. Our university participated in a program that sent hundreds of volunteers overseas each year to work in schools and orphanages. Joshua had signed up as well, but our postings were several thousand miles apart. I figured if our relationship and God's calling survived the experience, it would be a sign we were meant to be together and called to cross-cultural ministry.

Joshua would serve in a region of the Philippines where the people spoke a dialect called Ilocano. One evening several months before we would part for our student missions year, he told me, "I really want to learn the Ilocano language while I'm in the Philippines."

"Maybe we should pray about that," I suggested. "Maybe God could show you He's really calling you to be a missionary by helping you learn Ilocano."

Joshua nodded. "Okay, let's pray."

As we held hands and prayed, I heard myself say these words: "Lord God, if You want Joshua to be a missionary for more than just a year, help him learn Ilocano."

Two nights later, Joshua had a dream. In it, he saw Lewis, a man we'd just met a few weeks before. Joshua heard a voice say, "Lewis speaks Ilokano." Then he woke up.

We'd thought Lewis was Hawaiian since he said he grew up there. But we soon learned he was Filipino and had grown up speaking Ilocano! Over the next several months, Joshua studied with Lewis. As a result, he spoke Ilocano before he even left for his year abroad.

At this clear answer to my prayer for a sign from God, a mix of peace and electric fear settled into my bones. Joshua and I were headed somewhere, to a place we did not know. I would not refuse to follow God's plan, for I believed His plans were good. Yet I trembled. The path to the Promised Land was not easy for Abram and Sarai.

# 4

CALLED

The day I returned after teaching for a year in Micronesia was a happy one. Joshua met me at the airport carrying a giant balloon shaped like a sheep. He'd written, "I Love Ewe" on the side. By fall, we were engaged.

Back on campus, I took a course on the major prophets in the Bible. During class one afternoon, we watched a film about Jeremiah. In one scene, Jeremiah sees his people with God's eyes. Their idolatry and oppression of the poor. The way they trust in gods they have not known. As the Holy Spirit rushes into Jeremiah, he prophesies, weeping over the children of Israel on God's behalf.

Something pressed deep between my ribs as I watched. After class, I hurried to the dorm, hand over my abdomen. Striding past my room, I entered a closet with the words Prayer Room on the outside. There I crumpled to the floor and sobbed, compassion washing over me in waves as I thought of the millions who trust in idols of wood or stone as the psalmist described:

> *They have hands, but they cannot feel; they have feet, but they cannot walk; they cannot make a sound with their throat. Those who make them will become like them, everyone who trusts in them.*

PSALM 115:7-8

Imagining people in such spiritual darkness that like idols they couldn't hear, see, or speak, I cried out, *Help them, God!*

*Who will be My hands so I may help them?* The thought swept into my mind like a wind. In all my moments of darkness and spiritual questioning, I'd had hope. How could I keep that hope to myself?

"I'll go," I cried aloud. "Just show me what to do."

SEVERAL WEEKS LATER, Joshua showed me a copy of a magazine he'd first read in the Philippines, published by a mission organization that sends missionaries to "the unreached."

"What does that mean?" I asked Joshua. "Does that mean non-Christians?"

"It says here that the 'unreached' are people groups with no access to gospel truth because there is no viable Christian presence among them," Joshua replied.

"In other words, people who either haven't heard the gospel or haven't understood it."

"Exactly. And this organization has a unique way of doing things that's interesting to me."

"Oh?"

"They believe in incarnational ministry." Joshua pointed to a picture of a missionary wearing a purple headscarf. "That means fewer programs and compounds and more personal connection. Missionaries learn the language and culture of the people, bond with them, then share Jesus in a relevant way. Sometimes they start schools or do service projects, but only after they understand what people need."

I read the caption under the photo. "'Friendship evangelism.' That sounds interesting."

What would it be like to know and love a people group for the sake of Christ? What would it be like to tell the gospel story to someone who had never heard it? I wondered whether I could handle the stress of cross-cultural missions, whether I could empty myself like Christ and live like someone else. But God had led me so far. And if anyone knew my strengths and weaknesses, it was Him.

THAT SPRING, after three years of dating, Joshua and I married. For our recessional march leaving the church, a friend played the missions hymn *Joy By and By*. From then on, whenever I read the story of Abram and Sarai, my heart stirred with twin dreams wrestling for dominance. I longed to follow God wherever He led, to let Him grow me into a woman of great faith. But I also wanted a normal life.

Joshua and I graduated from college, got jobs, and moved into our first rental home. But even as we moved in, we were planning to leave. We lived on rice and beans, sat on used furniture, and didn't use the air-conditioner so we could pay off our student loans and be free to travel as soon as possible.

We would leave the creek full of singing frogs in the backyard. We would leave Joshua's job at a small church and my music teaching position at the nearby school. We would sell Joshua's motorcycle and our bed, and the last time we drove away, I would not turn around to see the cherry tree that could have made the perfect treehouse someday.

For God was leading us somewhere else—to a place we did not know.

"HMM." Joshua pulled a slab of papers from a manila envelope. "Psychological evaluations. Interesting that they included this as part of the missionary application process. Is that like saying we're crazy to do this?"

"Definitely," I said. "Check out this question: 'Do you like people, or do you like people to like you?' I don't know!" I pretended to choke and fall over on the couch. Joshua laughed.

*I probably like people to like me,* I thought. *What kind of missionary needs people to like them?*

"Hmm," Joshua said after reading more questions. "Do I enjoy hurting small animals?"

"I think the right answer is no."

"Yeah. But does anyone actually say yes to this? Wouldn't most people know they should say no?"

We joked and laughed about the questions. After three years of dating and two of marriage, we still managed awkwardness and stress with laughter.

We found out our psych evaluation was the same one given to potential air traffic controllers and others who held people's lives in their hands, who must stay calm in life-or-death situations. This seemed like a hint that being a missionary requires incredible inner strength. I wasn't sure I had that.

*God, are You sure?*

IN THE SPRING OF 2009, we joined several other potential missionary families at our mission organization's headquarters for orientation. By the end of the week, we would either accept the call to long-term service or go home and say we'd almost been missionaries.

"There are plenty of wrong reasons to be a missionary," William, the head of the training department, told us. "Don't do it to have an adventure because after a month it's not! Don't do it because you want to be a Christian rock star or some kind of savior. Don't do it to escape your problems. Do it because God asked you to do it. Only that will keep you in the field when you want to come home."

William warned us the temptation to come home would sometimes be overpowering. He told us wonderful and terrifying stories of missionaries before us who had struggled and made mistakes and prayed. He told us to count the cost as though trying to talk us out of it.

"A service cycle is three years in-country, followed by a four-month furlough in the USA. You'll do as many service cycles as it takes to complete a given project. A project is completed when a church community—whether they meet in a home or a physical church—is formed and equipped to bring the gospel to nearby communities."

William paused. He stepped closer to the group and lowered his voice. "There is a reason the places we send missionaries are unreached. They are the toughest places in the world for people to know and follow Christ—and to be missionaries. While we ask for a ten-year commitment, this is about a task, not a timeline. We are looking for a commitment to bring the gospel where it is not known."

I tried to imagine myself as a missionary. Would I live on the forty-fourth floor of an apartment in a huge city? Or would I live in a hut and wash my clothes in a river? Could I do either for ten years? I thought of the women I would meet who might never have heard of Jesus.

"Are you called?" William paused again, making eye contact with each of us. A young mother, a baby on her lap, squeezed hands with her husband. A single man straightened. A couple from Norway swallowed. The clock sent its steady ticks into the silence.

"Go ask God. Then let us know. Are you in or out?"

---

JOSHUA and I fasted that day and spent hours praying and talking. The next morning, we told William we were in. But where was God calling us *to*?

"There are several well-established projects for which we think you are a good fit. You would be with experienced teammates. We also have a brand-new project, no partners, nothing. The Parvata Project in the mountains of India."

The administration's one concern was our age. Joshua and I were both 25 years old, the youngest missionaries to accept a call with the organization at the time. We were still newlyweds and would be completely alone if we went to India. There were no other missionaries from our denomination in the entire subcontinent, not even a firm project location—just a target area. The nearest Adventist church was four hours away by bus.

"As far as other denominations, there is a Christian hospital in Pahargaun," the target town," William told us. "Short-term foreign missionaries serve at the hospital occasionally. They're allowed to come for two months maximum on official missionary visas. There is a small church connected with that hospital. Other than that, we don't know of any other Christians in the area."

We hadn't considered India and knew almost nothing about it. To us, India meant rice and snakes and curry and tigers and *The Jungle Book*. Where was God calling us? How would we know?

"I want you to have the final say," Joshua told me that afternoon. "It could go either way for me. But I would never want you to feel like I dragged you off somewhere. I want you to be totally committed. To feel you had a say in it."

I swallowed hard, feeling both valued and terrified. "Let's go back to the office and see if we can talk to whoever researched the Parvata project. I want to know more."

A former missionary to India named Mark had done the research. He told us, "The Parvata people live in an area that's a stronghold of Hinduism. Most belong to the Brahmin caste, the highest, priestly caste."

"What does it mean that the Parvata project is 'closed access?'" Joshua asked.

"There are people who don't want missionaries in India. If you go, you must be careful. That means no Facebook posts with the 'M' word—as in, 'missionary.'"

"Is it dangerous?" I asked.

"The area where the Parvata project is located is relatively stable," Mark said. "But I'll be honest. That state is governed by a Hindu extremist party. And there has been violence against Christians in other areas. When my family and I lived in India, a missionary and his children were killed in Orissa. So please, if you choose to go to India, be careful."

---

THAT EVENING, Joshua and I watched a video about India. The whole thing was warm-toned. Red and pink saris hung over women's shoulders as they carried baskets on their heads. Shops were lined with brown burlap sacks heaped with every shade of brown lentil. The flesh of a firewalker shone bronze in the light of orange and yellow flames.

Then there was a snapshot of masses of people, all going somewhere. Joshua was into charts and he'd been crunching numbers. Only one percent of one percent of the Parvata people were Christian. What was the likelihood that most of them even knew a believer? They couldn't believe because they'd never heard because no one had yet been sent.

The scene changed. There was the firewalker again, eyes rolled back in his head. Suddenly, the same overwhelming compassion I'd felt for idolators while watching the movie about Jeremiah the prophet washed over me. At that moment, I knew God was calling us to India. When I told Joshua, he agreed.

---

AFTER ACCEPTING the Parvata project call, we had a strategy meeting with several of the home office staff, including William and Mark.

"You'll spend at least a year fundraising," William said. "Then attend three months of training."

Mark walked to a giant map on the wall, where eighty little flags indicated the various missionaries our organization had stationed around the world. He pointed to the location of the Parvata project. There was no flag. "Your goal at launch is Pahargaun. It's a small tourist town in the Himalayas. Once you get your bearings, you'll prayerfully search for the right project location."

"Of course, we'll train and support you as much as possible," William added. "But as the first ones there, you'll have to decide how you want to do things. You will become the experts on the Parvata."

I liked the sound of that. We'd have the freedom to be creative. We'd plow new ground, witness a movement for Jesus from its beginning.

"As far as the language goes, we have software to get you started learning Hindi," William went on. "But people won't hear what you have to say if you haven't listened. So we recommend learning the language through relationships."

"Then there's your visa," Mark said. "Most visas to India allow you to stay for only six months at a time. That's not sustainable in the long term, so you'll need to switch to a business visa as soon as possible. And keep in mind the Indian authorities will Google your names. Since you are officially entering as business entrepreneurs, not missionaries, be sure to tell your supporting churches not to post your real names online."

I nodded, but my head was spinning with information overload. Joshua spoke up. "What about ministry? We get set up. Learn language. Set up a business. Then what?"

"Then you'll begin more formal evangelism," William responded. "What that looks like will depend on the people. During your first term, you'll complete a cultural research project on the Parvata. After that, we'll do another session of training to coach you in designing a relevant evangelism strategy."

Joshua was literally on the edge of his seat. I knew he'd buckle himself into a plane in five minutes if he could. Me? I felt like I was about to jump off the edge of something.

Blindfolded.

# 5

## PREPARATION

Joshua and I prayed for our parents, knowing our decision wouldn't be easy for them. We tried to decide how to break the news.

"How about, 'Hi, Mom. Your future grandchildren will be raised in India many thousands of miles away from you,'" I suggested.

"Let's keep praying," Joshua said.

Since Joshua's parents had witnessed his call to ministry in high school, I figured they would be supportive. They were. My own parents had always been very concerned that I not die nor stand close to anything that could potentially cause death—such as tall jungle gyms.

*God, comfort my parents! Help them see You are leading!* I prayed. Then I picked up the phone, called my dad, and told him we were moving to India.

For a moment, he was quiet. I held my breath until he spoke. "A missionary visited our church yesterday. He shared all these amazing miracles God did. I believe God arranged that visit just to assure me He is leading you and going to take care of you."

After advising me not to get myself killed or maimed, my dad assured me of his support. I treasured this conversation like a personal memo from God—Miracle Number One of our mission. Now it was time to tell my mom we would follow a Savior she didn't believe in, to a place she'd never been, to tell people she didn't know something she didn't believe. Was this how Abram felt?

When I made our announcement, the line went quiet. Hoping she was still there, I asked into the silence, "Are you okay, Mom?"

"You need the freedom to follow your dreams, Abigail," she responded. "Go."

OUR NEXT STEP WAS FUNDRAISING. We spoke at churches and met with small groups and individuals in their homes. Before we began, I told Joshua, "Maybe you could take the asking-people-for-money part. When I was growing up, we didn't ask for anything but dinner."

"We both have to do it, Abby." Joshua often used my nickname when encouraging me to get outside my comfort zone and always said it with a tender voice.

Despite my terror, I understood our mission: to build a team of people who would pray for us, encourage us when we felt alone, and invest financially in our mission to the unreached. But asking for money felt like jumping off a high dive.

I prefer the low dive. Or the side of the pool. Or the stairs.

As we shared our ministry plans, we discovered so many of God's people living unnoticed lives of heroism. They fed us spaghetti or casserole. We told them about the Parvata people. They told us about their challenges. Lost jobs and lost sons. Dreams and diagnoses. The wars they waged in prayer that few knew about. Some cried to learn that the Parvata people needed Jesus when they had leaned on Him throughout their lives.

One elderly couple sat us down on their sofa. The husband clamped down on his dentures to keep them in, then leaned forward from his rocking chair and said, "We love you guys. We love you like our kids. We're going to support you out there. And I want you to remember something. If God calls you to die, don't be afraid to do it. If He asks you to give your life, don't hold it back from Him. Don't be afraid to be a martyr."

Could his comment be a sign? Would we die in India?

———

MEANWHILE, we researched the Parvata people online and read stacks of assigned books and articles on missions. One article, *Bonding and the Missionary Task*, by E. Thomas and Elizabeth S. Brewster, recommended that new missionaries:

- Be willing to live with a local family.
- Limit personal belongings to under fifty lb.
- Use only public transportation.
- Carry out language learning in the context of relationships.

This was how we would do missions. We would incarnate like Christ, living among the Parvata just as they lived. Then when we finally told them about Jesus, they would understand.

We made plans to sell or store all our belongings. We bought puffy orange sleeping bags rated for 10°F for the cold Himalayan nights and backpacking backpacks. We would bring only what we could carry.

As we read, preached, and planned, we still both worked full time. The long hours caused stress, and we began to bicker, which affected me a bit—kind of like the way the A-bomb affected Bikini Atoll. Once I even slammed the car door shut and walked the rest of the way down our gravel driveway. I don't even remember why we were mad at each other, but it felt important at the time.

*Oh, God, forgive me!* I prayed into my pillow. *I can't even be a nice wife, let alone reach the unreached. You've got to do something—and fast. It's only six months until we launch!*

Since both of us were musicians, we fought the bickering with music. One Sabbath, we wrote an instrumental song for our two guitars. We called it *Hope Deferred*, after Proverbs 13:12: "Hope deferred makes the heart sick, but desire fulfilled is a tree of life."

Many evenings, we would sit in our living room with our guitars and play *Hope Deferred* over and over and over. It seemed to express a longing that words could not, a desire for the Parvata to know Jesus.

---

MY DAD ARRANGED for us to visit his friend Raj. Raj had grown up a Hindu in India.

"So, you want to work with the high caste?" Raj asked. "That will be very difficult."

He turned the page to a picture of Durga, a multi-armed goddess with blood on her tongue. She held a head in one hand and a knife in another. A man lay on the floor in front of her. She had one foot on his chest.

"This is Durga, right?" I asked.

"Yes," he said. "The other gods actually created Durga to kill demons. But she went on a rampage, killing everything in sight. This was the only way to stop her."

"This?" Joshua asked.

"Her shame. She was ashamed at placing her foot on her husband. That's why she stopped."

"I see," Joshua said.

Raj chuckled. He could tell we didn't see. "The feet are considered dirty in India, so a wife putting her foot on her husband is taboo. It is shameful. Shame and honor are important concepts in Indian culture."

"Can you tell us more?" I asked. "About what it's like to be a Hindu? About how you came to Christ?"

"I became curious about Christianity after reading a book of poetry by a Hindu," Raj explained. "The author was inspired by the Psalms. I read the Psalms after that. David knew and loved his Creator in a deep, personal way. That's how my journey began."

Raj smiled again. "But if you want to know more about Hindu gods, you'd need to ask someone like my mom. In my experience, Indian women tend to be more religious than men. By the way, how long do you plan to stay there?"

"Our organization suggests ten years," Joshua said. "But we like to say we're committed to a task, not a timeline."

"We want to give our lives to this," I added. "We'll be there as long as it takes to reach them."

AFTER A YEAR AND A HALF, our fundraising was complete. The church where Joshua had been working threw us a goodbye picnic at a park. There were kids in shorts and jumpers running around in the sun, adults talking and laughing in groups. I looked around and tried to suppress my desire to stay.

Susan, an older friend and mentor of mine, walked over to where I stood near a willow tree. "How are you feeling about going?"

"Nervous and excited."

"I'm nervous and excited for you! What are you most nervous about?"

"Our future children. I hope I'll be a good missionary mom and that our kids will be happy."

"Don't worry. Jesus will take care of that." Susan had this way of talking about Jesus like she knew Him personally, like He sometimes stopped by her house for casserole and some pie. Like He'd asked her to say hi if she saw me.

"You're right." I tried to emulate the warmth of her smile.

"I'll be tempted to worry about you, but Jesus will take care of everything," she said again. "You know, when my son left for college, I felt so burdened and anxious. I knelt on my bed and thought about him so far away. I couldn't do anything to protect him. I prayed, 'Please, God, take care of him, because I can't!' Suddenly, in my mind, I saw the entire globe. I saw a zing of light shoot from our city to his."

I could see it in my mind, too. "That's amazing."

"It was, Abigail. God showed me that when I pray, my prayers aren't just bouncing off the ceiling. He hears me and does something with my prayers. When I pray, God dispatches angels."

"I've never thought about that before," I responded. "That we can be angel dispatchers."

"Well, girly, instead of worrying about you, I'm going to pray. I'll be sending angels to you while you're out there in India."

"Thank you so much." I hugged Susan and mentally added her to a list of women I wanted to be like. The women on my list had various personalities. Some were quiet, some talkative. Some wore dramatic clothing and jewelry, some jeans, T-shirts, and a simple wedding band, like me. Some were mothers, and some were not.

But they all loved Jesus like they knew Him. Like they'd been places with Him, relied on Him, and found Him real and dependable. I wanted "peace that passes understanding," like I'd read about in Philippians 4:7. Or as I liked to call it, "the peace that makes no sense."

"Maybe we could be prayer partners from afar. I admire your relationship with Jesus so much."

Susan laughed. "You know, my relationship with Jesus has so little to do with me and so much to do with Him. Let's do pray for each other. In fact, let's pray right now."

So we did. Susan prayed for me, a beautiful and insightful prayer, and I tried to put myself in her place to pray for her needs, too. As Joshua and I walked home, we were quiet. I was thinking about angel dispatchers.

---

ON OUR LAST MORNING, I sat on the living room floor and looked around our empty house. Outside our white-framed windows, the sky was heavy and gray.

"Walter from church and his wife are here to get the bed," Joshua announced, poking his head in the door. My heart lurched, but I smiled and walked outside.

"We do so appreciate this, Mrs. Follows," Walter's wife drawled. "Been sleepin' on a thing that sags down to the floor. Walter's back can't take it no more."

"I'm so glad you'll be able to use it."

I smiled until it hurt as Joshua and Walter loaded the mattress into the back of a pickup. Then I went back inside the house. I listened as the truck drove down the gravel driveway, taking my mattress with it. My bed. Tears pricked my eyes, then slid down my face in warm streams.

"What's wrong?" Joshua asked, walking inside.

"Nothing. I just miss our bed."

It was the only new thing we'd ever bought together. Again, my desires fought within me. I wanted to go places with Jesus. I wanted Him to bless the world through me. And I also wanted to run down the driveway, drag my mattress home, and wake up in the morning to a normal life.

I had no idea what awaited us in India. Would we be called to die? Would anyone come to Christ because we went? I felt my insufficiency and my smallness. And now I felt my vulnerability, too, for this was the day our homelessness began.

We would have somewhere to sleep, of course. We had camping pads, and we'd attend three months of training, then stay with family until we left. Surely we would find places to stay in India. But this was the moment it got really, really real. Life as I knew it was ending, and something else completely unknown was about to begin.

# 6

## FIRST IMPRESSIONS

*North India. Five months later.* We flew into Delhi, the closest affordable airport to Pahargaun, and stepped out into a sepia world. The morning mist was golden. The buildings our taxi raced past were also tinted sepia, giving everything an old-photograph look. Later that day, I learned this was due to apocalyptic levels of pollution in the air. But at the time it looked like a vintage postcard.

We spent two weeks with our denominational leadership at their headquarters. They greeted us, fed us the spiciest but best food I'd ever eaten, and graciously taught us how to eat with our hands, though they said city people generally preferred spoons. They also urged us not to get ourselves drugged or kidnapped. Everyone from the union president's wife to the secretary to the IT guys taught us new words in Hindi. These we wrote in small, yellow notebooks.

After securing an Indian Punjabi suit for me—billowing pantaloons with a long tunic shirt and long, draping scarf—we lugged our packs onto a bus with wooden seats and began our twenty-hour journey north to Pahargaun. We spent most of the trip in a jet-lagged delirium, but in the early morning, I woke up.

Just ahead of me on the other side of the bus, a Parvata woman sat with her feet on her bag, knees up. She wore a long, hand-knitted sweater over a Punjabi suit, golden rings on her flip-flopped feet, and a scarf knotted on her head. I wanted to know her name, her dreams, her worries. But I could not know her. I had only nine pages of Hindi in my notebook.

When our bus stopped, I followed a flock of colorful, chatting women to an outhouse. Inside, I wrestled with my Punjabi suit and chiffon scarf while the "mystery woman" from the bus guarded the door. How did Indian women keep their clothes out of the squat pot?

Mission accomplished, I emerged. I practiced my words on the mystery woman, and she said a lot of things I didn't understand. We laughed together as we boarded the bus again.

"Look, Abigail," Joshua said. "I think we're in Chotashaher. That means just a couple of hours until Pahargaun."

Chotashaher was a large town, the southern limit of our mission target area. Here I got my first glimpse of the Parvata people. Nearly everyone wore something made of wool, either knitted or woven. Women strolled with babies or hay tied to their backs. Men sauntered after cattle, letting their cows get distracted by bits of grass here and there. No one seemed in a hurry.

Before we arrived in Pahargaun, the mystery woman stood. She lifted her bag and turned to smile. Then she was gone. What was her name? I had something she didn't with no way to give it to her, no way to make her understand. I prayed God would follow her up the dirt path and bless her.

Our pink-turbaned driver, a white smile under his black mustache, asked us to drink chai with him and his conductor. I thought of what we'd heard in Delhi about drugging and poisoning foreigners and urged Joshua not to agree. He didn't. But by the end of the day, I'd learned that offers for tea are a normal part of life in India, and not always the sign of an imminent kidnapping.

PAHARGAUN IS a small tourist town hidden in the folds of the Himalayan foothills. Today the sky was ice blue, and the mountains north of us wore a dusting of snow. We had booked something called a "homestay" online, hoping to live with a family and experience Parvata life. Joshua stopped to check his map, then strode up the steep path. I skipped to keep up with him.

Then we saw it. A quaint painted sign: "Harvest Homestay." A Parvata woman greeted us in English and took us down a long hall to our room, a cell-like concrete cube. It was chilly but clean. The smell of cut hay drifted in the door. The woman showed us the shared toilets and showers. Just then, a group of European tourists passed us heading to their rooms. They reeked of marijuana.

"It's like a hotel," Joshua whispered. "There's even a restaurant for meals."

"I thought it was a homestay," I said through smiling teeth. The woman smiled back. Then she left us.

"Strange," Joshua said. "Maybe 'homestay' is how you say 'bed-and-breakfast' around here."

Joshua and I said a prayer, heaped our two backpacks on the floor and locked our room. Then the adventure began.

MAYBE WE WERE STILL JET-LAGGED, but walking around Pahargaun for the first time felt full of meaning and symbolism. Every encounter felt like a divine appointment. There was the Yak Man. He listened to our Hindi babbling and let me take a picture with his giant yak, which chewed beneath a nose-length set of bangs. And the woman selling homemade socks. She had gentle brown eyes and thoughts, feelings, and words I couldn't yet understand. I had to settle for nouns and the occasional verb. I wrote everything I could in my notebook, though most words blended together.

Other than shopkeepers and the Yak Man, most of the people we saw were tourists. Pahargaun crawled with tattoo-encrusted, dreadlocked, prayer-beaded young adults as well as a few bent-over old men who'd probably been there a while.

The shops seemed to cater to a specific kind of tourist. There were tattoo parlors. Shops selling Buddhist prayer bowls. Markets lined with giant paintings of Bob Marley's face or black-and-white elephants or mandalas. Exotic musical instrument shops with broken sitars. Innumerable holes-in-the-wall selling "pizza and snakes."

"Hey man," a male voice whispered. When I turned around, a man with slick hair was standing close to Joshua. "I got hashish. You want some?"

"Nah," Joshua said.

"Magic mushroom? I've got—"

"We don't do drugs," I said. The man disappeared into the crowd.

"There's another section of town at the base of this hill." Joshua looked at a map he'd picked up that morning at the homestay. "That's where the mission hospital is and a few temples. Maybe it will feel more local."

"Let's find out."

THE LANDSCAPE of shops changed as we walked down the hill from bongs and prayer beads to fabric, medicine, and bread. Here we found local people. Men strolled, the older ones in neat trousers, button-ups, and wool vests, the younger in tight jeans, T-shirts, and leather jackets. Workers carried things here and there, wrapped in warm, sooty fabric. Older women wore the woolen *patu* dress, a blanket that is folded, pleated, and tied in the middle with string. Younger women wore wool Punjabi suits with scarves that flowed over their collar bones and hung behind, sometimes catching the wind.

A man in a jewelry shop gave us pages of words to write. I wanted food, but it seemed more essential to speak than to eat. Soon, a blue twilight wrapped our Himalayan pocket in cool mist.

"Let's go home," Joshua said. "We'll eat there."

Tucking my hands into my sleeves to keep warm, I thought of how Joshua and I had taken to calling wherever we were currently staying "home." That night, I pulled my sleeping bag up to my chin. The colors, sounds, and smells of the past week all swirled in my mind.

*God,* I prayed. *How will we learn language and culture in this hotel?* I was asleep before I said amen. Several hours later, however, the sound of someone vomiting jolted me awake.

"Guess he tried the magic mushroom," I observed aloud, assuming Joshua was awake.

"Must have been a good party," he agreed.

We listened for a few moments as the expensive contents of a night of drinking and drugging were vomited into our shared toilet.

"We'll look for another place tomorrow," Joshua said.

"Please."

The next morning, we trekked back down the hill to a tourism office Joshua had seen the day before.

"We want to live with a family," he told the man at the front desk. "We want to stay in a local home and take our meals with them. Is there anything like that between here and Chotashaher?"

"Yes," the man said. "Actually, the government gives loans to families wanting to open homestays. Here's a list." He handed Joshua a stack of stapled papers. There were hundreds of names and numbers on the list.

Joshua made a few phone calls, trying to decipher their Hindi and his map. He wrote the names of three places on his hand, and we walked to the bus stand.

"We need to pray," Joshua said. "I didn't understand much over the phone. And we have no way of knowing which places are real homestays and which are run like bed-and-breakfasts."

"God knows where He wants us."

Clasping hands, we prayed, asking God to put us in the home of someone willing to know Him. Then we lugged our backpacks onto a public bus and made our way into the unknown.

# 7

---

# ROSE

We passed several villages and saw cows, cars, auto-rickshaws, and kids playing cricket in the street. The bus lurched to a stop, and someone got off.

"This is the first village on my list: Kushigaun," Joshua said. "Let's go."

The buildings lining the road wore cheerful coats of turquoise, purple, and yellow paint. A wild rose had crawled beyond the confines of its yard and now lie draped over the edge of a cement wall. We prayed again. Then I motioned to a side road. "Why don't we try this way?"

"Okay," Joshua said. We started up the steep path. Soon, a three-story cement house came into view. Sunflowers and pansies grew in the courtyard. Above, a sign read, "Devi Homestay."

"I think this is one of the places I called," Joshua said. "I can't believe we walked right to it."

We entered the courtyard, feeling tall, awkward, and touristy with our backpacks. A young woman peeked at us from behind a half-open door. Joshua called out, "Namaste."

The woman emerged, buttoning a stretched-out sweater over her pregnant belly. She smiled, a straight, white smile, as she adjusted a green headscarf. Black ringlets peeked out the back of the scarf. A red necklace lay across her neck.

"Maybe you called before?" she asked in English.

"Yes, I called this morning," Joshua said.

"Come. I will show you the room." The woman took us upstairs and opened a wooden door. Light streamed in two windows and lit up a fuzzy, red blanket on a bed. "Some college students live in our other two rooms. They aren't loud."

"We don't party," Joshua said.

"And we don't drink or do drugs," I added.

"What's your name?" the woman asked me.

"Abigail. What's yours?"

"Rose." Rose explained that she and her husband lived with her husband's parents and brother. I knew from some of our prior reading that most Parvata homes were multi-generational with new wives joining their husband's households. The homestay really belonged to Rose's father-in-law, but she did the cooking and cleaning.

While Joshua called her father-in-law, Rose and I chatted. She'd been married for about a year and was expecting their first child in two months.

"I can tell you more later," she whispered, gesturing with her large, brown eyes at my husband. With a laugh, she added, "Normally our guests take their meals in their rooms. But if you stay, you could take your meals with us. We could be friends!"

I felt instantly drawn to Rose. I wanted to know her, to speak her heart language. Maybe God had brought us to her and her family for a reason. Joshua looked at me. I nodded.

"We'll take the room," Joshua said.

That evening, we gathered on colorful floor mats around a wood stove Rose called a tandoor. It had to be stoked constantly as it wasn't big enough to hold much wood. The family turned on the TV, and we watched funny, caricatured Indian sitcoms, laughing even though we understood nothing. The room was warm and smelled of pine and cumin. I sighed. This felt like my childhood home on better days, laughing, talking, and waiting for food. Maybe I could do this after all. I just had to figure out what they were saying.

---

OVER THE NEXT SEVERAL WEEKS, I witnessed the grueling workload of an Indian daughter-in-law. Cook three meals a day. Wash all the dishes. Sweep the carpets with a stiff broom after every meal. Wash the laundry of the entire family in cold water. Fold the clothes. Nurse the sick. Give massages. Clean the toilets. Do the mopping by hand. Rose explained that she didn't have as much work to do as most women since her family didn't own a cow.

"This is our 'cow,'" she chuckled, gesturing toward the three rooms of the homestay. "Otherwise, I'd milk twice a day and cut grass too."

"You're like Cinderella," I said. Rose smiled and nodded. "Wait, Rose. Do you know who that is?"

"No." We both laughed.

Even with the incredible volume of housework, there was a lull around two p.m. Neighbors sat in their courtyards on plastic lawn chairs, letting the intense sunshine warm them. This was the time for visiting, knitting, drinking chai, gossiping, and doing nothing.

Rose tried to teach me to knit but wasn't successful. Her mother-in-law Shanty taught me a song instead. Rose translated it for me: "Beautiful country, our country! It sparkles like the stars." I learned the song, accidentally making myself a showpiece for Rose's family, who asked me to sing it whenever visitors came.

In the early mornings, Joshua and I would reference a book we'd received at training titled *LAMP: Language Acquisition Made Practical*. It gave practical steps for how to learn a language socially. The first step after finding a language helper was to record the helper saying an introductory text. The text was then memorized and said to at least thirty people.

Rose helped me record my first Hindi sentences: "Hello, my name is Abigail. I want to learn Hindi. This is all I can say. Goodbye." Getting the recording from friendly, giggly Rose was easy. We sat together on my bed for an hour, talking, recording, and practicing.

"I have to go now," she said. "Time to work again."

I walked her out. She grabbed a flowery-pink bucket, filled it with cold water from a hose, and plunged her husband's brother's clothing into the water. I knew they were his because I'd seen him throw the clothing in the pile earlier that afternoon. Rose pulled out a pair of pants and slapped them on the cement, then dragged a gritty laundry bar across the fabric. Forming the pants into a lump, she beat the lump with a stick.

I turned. There were wrinkles on the bed where we'd sat. I smoothed them. The metal voice recorder lay on the bed. A pair of white earbuds trailed to the floor. I hesitated. Maybe I'd do some laundry. I washed a shirt in the bathroom sink and hung it on the railing outside. I lingered to watch a cow saunter up the road. Then I turned back to our room. There sat the recorder on the bed, untouched. I smoothed the bed again.

*I'm avoiding this,* I observed. It wasn't that I didn't want to learn Hindi. But listening would remind me I had to say my text to thirty people the next day. And that terrified me.

I could avoid the voice recorder, but I couldn't avoid Joshua. He'd been out talking to people already that day. I heard him whistling as he walked up the stairs.

"How's it going?" he asked. "Got your text?"

"Yep! We had a great time."

"Awesome! Ready to say it?"

"I don't know. I think I might need more time."

"Well, have you been listening to it?"

"Um . . . " No point in lying. "Sort of. Once. You know, we checked it together to see if it sounded right."

Joshua looked at his watch. I glanced at some smudges on our window. "Come on, Abby. You've got to do it. This is why we're here."

What he meant was, "We're here to get outside our comfort zone, bond with this entire village, learn their language, and offer them the gift of salvation!" But I already knew that.

"Yeah, I'm going to do it. But, you know, the ladies all wash their clothes in the afternoon, so I did, too."

"You could listen while you work."

"I didn't want to get electrocuted."

"You've got to listen to your text. That's why we're here!"

I felt my lips purse. I organized the headphone cord for a while before sliding the earbuds into my ears. Then I took a deep breath and pressed play.

A garbled string of syllables flowed into my ears. I couldn't even hear where one word ended, and another began. I had to replay three seconds' worth of text over fifty times. I was tired of the text and hadn't even learned it yet.

After two hours, I could say it. But my nerves were frayed. Would it always be this hard?

## 8

# DINNER WITH A DEVTA

I f I could just stay with Rose, drink chai, wash clothes, and learn to knit, I could be happy. Outside, everything mattered too much. Every interaction felt crucial like it could make or break a person's salvation. I needed time to think, plan, and analyze. My eyes burned with fatigue. I rubbed them.

"You can do it, Abby," Joshua said. "Come on. Let's go!"

Joshua's extroversion was so cute, so fun, so... annoying. I wished I were more like him: energetic, outgoing, ready to save the world. I felt more like a clam. A clam being pried out of its shell into the light where mistakes can be made, where shriveling up and dying is a real possibility.

WE SET off down Link Road, so named because it links the main road to itself when it loops around a corner. A woman in a closet-sized shop wove *patu* dresses out of black, white, gray, and red-dyed sheep's wool. She had a friendly, lipsticked smile and knew a handful of English words. I said my text to her. She praised me.

Further up the road stood several shops owned by women. We couldn't remember people's names and were realizing through observation that everyone older than us was called brother, sister, aunty, or uncle. So over the coming weeks, we gave them our own private names.

There was the Momo Lady. She made *momos*, small, white, cabbage-filled dumplings similar to a pot-sticker. Energetic, she wore her straight hair in a ponytail that bounced when she pounded the momo dough. She listened to my text, then babbled unintelligibly at me for about fifteen minutes. I nodded a lot while trying not to stare at a long, thick scar across her neck.

As we passed the Momo Lady's shop, a boy with a clean-shaven head marched towards us, surrounded by others his age. A thin ponytail extended out the back of his shaved head. Was this the style for preteen boys in India?

"Hello!" He smiled and stuck out his hand, looking pleased with himself, well aware of his watching friends. I took it, and we shook. "Hello."

Past the Momo Lady was the Short Shopkeeper who sold ladies' things: hair dye, henna, nail polish, cheesy picture frames with photos of white people in them, string, "flesh-toned" socks the color of a peach crayon. Today she was getting dandruff out of a customer's hair using her nails.

Next was the Nice Shopkeeper. Someone later told me she was a witch. Whether she dabbled in magic or not, I don't know, but she had laugh lines around her eyes. Rows of yarn, hand- and machine-spun, lined the shelves of her shop, which was smaller than some closets in the United States. She spoke slowly. I liked her.

We tried to say our phrases to a restaurant owner. I'd recently added, "Can I come and talk with you a little each day?" to my repertoire.

The owner heaved a crate of pop bottles onto a counter. "No, too busy. I don't have time!"

This shouldn't have bothered me. But it did. I wanted to cry, give up, go home, and not care. But the feeling soon passed. Day after day, we plodded through conversation after conversation. Each night when Joshua and I prayed together, I asked God to give me the gift of tongues.

---

I LOOKED FORWARD to the respite of Sabbath each week. From sundown Friday to sundown Saturday, Joshua and I took a break from the mental strain of language learning to hang out with God. On Saturday mornings, Joshua and I would take crackers, bananas, and boiled eggs and go to the river for a picnic.

Two bridges spanned the river in our village, a sturdy bridge for cars and a rickety one for cows. We would cross the cow bridge and walk along the riverbank or down a ravine and find a boulder to sit on. There we'd eat our lunch and have our own two-person worship service, singing hymns and praying for the Parvata.

---

"WILL you have dinner with us and our friends?" Rose asked one afternoon in November. We had been in India for a month. "On Thursday evening at their house."

"We'd love to. Where is it?"

"Not far. We'll take the bus. So you'll come?"

"Of course!"

A few days later, I put on a new Punjabi suit, buttoned a thick sweater, and topped it off with a wool shawl. The evenings were chilly now, and most people wore sweaters, vests, and shawls even in the sunshine. I smiled at myself in the mirror. Although I had short hair instead of a long braid, I felt I looked very Indian.

An hour later, Joshua and I emerged from a bus with Rose and her mother-in-law. Rose wore a dark green Punjabi suit stretched tight over her belly, her curly hair half up, and lipstick. Four ladies passed us, dressed in crisp suits, sweaters, and lipstick. They walked up a steep path. Men wearing caps joined them. My gaze followed them. Up the hill, a house swarmed with people.

"Are we going there?" I asked Joshua.

"No idea," Joshua said.

Rose linked arms with me, and we walked up the path together. Soon we entered a courtyard where people sat on the cement in long rows, eating rice off plates on the ground. Just beyond the courtyard stretched a big, yellow tent, and in the tent stood a crowd.

"Uh, oh," I said. "This is not dinner."

"It looks like it might be dinner with an idol!"

In the midst of the crowd stood two men carrying two thick, wooden poles over their shoulders. Atop the poles sat a small wooden box. It looked something like I imagined the biblical Ark of the Covenant looked. Except this box was covered in faces cast in silver with their eyes closed.

The box began to sway back and forth. We walked to the edge of the courtyard to see, joining thirty or forty other people.

The box rocked harder. Nobody moved the box. The men who bore it crossed their arms and didn't touch the poles. Drumming vibrated the air and the ground so that I could feel it deep in my lungs, pounding in my ears, and buzzing in my feet.

*God*, I prayed silently. *Please be with me. Protect us!*

*Greater is He who is in you than he that is in the world.* The verse from 1 John 4:4 popped into my head, and I focused my thoughts on it. I strained to discern any unconfessed sin. I wanted nothing between my soul and my Savior. Something about this situation scared me.

The box swayed, then tipped toward an old man who stood nearby. Everything stopped. The drumming. The talking. The swaying of the box. Everything stood perfectly still—except the man. It was as though all the energy in the assembly entered his body. The man shook and convulsed. He shouted.

*He's possessed*, I thought. My stomach twisted.

I glanced around. The people watched the man with rapt attention. After several minutes of shaking and shouting, the man froze and bowed his head. At that very moment, the box thrust away from him wildly as though something invisible had exited the man and entered the box. Everyone bowed their heads and crossed themselves as though they'd heard the voice of a god. I found Rose and asked what the box was.

"It's a *devta*," she explained. "A village demi-god. They are holy beings that help us solve problems. They even predict the future. Technically, the box isn't the devta. That is his vehicle. The devta is in the box. The devta is what entered the man."

Suddenly, I remembered we were here to eat dinner. How could we do that? I tried to explain that we could eat nothing offered to an idol.

Rose frowned. "No, no! We're not eating *prasad*. That's other food." Grabbing my hand, she dragged me toward the feast. "Come. Eat with us."

"What is *prasad*?" I asked. The drums were beating again, and people were lining up to eat. I glanced at Joshua. What was the right thing to do? We pressed Rose, trying to find out the purpose of the ceremony.

"They're just happy," Rose said. "They want to feed everyone. It's not *prasad*."

"What is *prasad*?" I asked again.

"Food offered to idols," Rose said. "Come. Let's eat!"

In the end, we ate. But the food felt like rocks in my stomach. We didn't want to offend our hosts lest they get the idea that Christians were unfriendly and too proud to join them. But we feared to offend God lest we take ourselves outside His protection. Especially after seeing the possessed man. We needed wisdom, and we needed to understand the culture.

I knew this was one reason our organization asked its missionaries to complete an in-depth cultural study. Surely a Parvata Christian would have to wrestle with the same question of whether to participate or not. We'd planned to begin our study once we knew more Hindi. But from that day forward, we asked questions constantly. Whether we could understand the answer or not.

# 9

# THE HIMALAYA SONG

A friend in Delhi had given us the phone number of her sister in Chotashaher. The sisters had grown up Christians, but the one in Chotashaher had married a Hindu. We found her in a labyrinth of closely spaced apartments.

"Namaste," she said. "Come in!"

As her extended family crowded around, I observed the woman. She wore a red *bindi* dot between her eyes and a powdery, red line I'd heard called a *sindoor* in the part of her hair, drawn to guarantee a long life to her husband. A Christian in Delhi had told me that believers sometimes wore the decorative bindi but not the sindoor. Was this woman still a Christian?

We ate a delicious meal. Then the family brought us up on the roof. We played with the kids, chasing them around the laundry that hung from ropes strung across the rooftop courtyard. Then we sat. The Christian woman's sister-in-law spoke English. She spent the next hour describing some of the wonders of India. India had made many important contributions to mathematics and science and boasted an old, rich culture.

"Why are you here?" she asked suddenly, staring at me hard. "What do you want to do? Do you want to help people?"

"We like helping people," I said. "No matter where we are."

"Maybe you could start a school. People would be glad for you to start a school. Just don't go thinking you can make us into Christians. We don't want or need your religion!" She wasn't angry but lively and firm. She seemed like a spokeswoman for Mother India. And her official statement was, "We don't want what you have."

I glanced at our hostess, who smoothed the front of her tunic and didn't make eye contact. I smiled, nodded, and said something soothing, but inside I worried.

Did we look so much like missionaries? Were people's hearts so closed before we had even said a word?

"You see that up there?" Mother India's spokeswoman pointed to a far-off peak. The sun glinted here and there, maybe off the snow or rock face. "That glint is the eye of my god."

After visiting that family, I felt burdened. We'd seen so much in just a month and a half. We'd met many more than our thirty-person language learning quota, many of whom were kind and generous with their time. They were gifting us with their language. How would we give them a chance to know Jesus? How could we bypass their prejudice and assumptions? How could we disarm them for just a moment? Forcing someone to follow Christ is against the religion of the true Christian. But telling? Telling is the essence of the Christian identity.

Ten years of mission service seemed like a drop in the bucket of need. Joshua agreed. Maybe we would stay in India forever.

———

ROSE ARRANGED for a favorite teacher to give us a tour of her former school. I pictured her there in two braids. She'd married her husband after his betrothed— her cousin—eloped with another man. Rose was only seventeen.

"Please," her aunt and uncle had begged. "Marry him and save us from the shame." She'd agreed, so one day she wore pigtails to school, the next she was the wife of a man she didn't know.

We observed the kindergarteners sitting cross-legged at low desks, perfectly still and unmoving, reciting after their teacher. It was three o'clock, and they would be in school for another two hours. One boy slept, his cheek squashed against the wooden desk.

We ate together in the cafeteria. As Joshua chatted with Rose's teacher, I took a moment to think about all we'd seen and heard in the past few weeks. It all seemed to swell inside my chest, ready to explode. I grabbed a napkin from the table and a pen from Joshua's coat pocket. I couldn't write fast enough.

Our room was dark when we returned "home" that night. I picked up my guitar. When Joshua returned from showering, I played the song I'd just written, singing in a whisper lest the English-speaking college students next door hear.

"I like it. But the chorus needs work." Joshua took the paper and a pencil and wrote a new chorus. I took it back.

"Yeah. That's good!" I changed the new chorus to match each of the verses while Joshua turned my simple chords into beautiful ones. As we recorded the song, images raced through my mind. The Momo Lady. The boy with the shaved head. Rose. The possessed man. The woman who had seen the eye of her god in the glint of the sun off the snow.

*Oh, God!* I prayed in my heart. *Reach these people. Somehow, use us to reach these people.*

———

Testify (The Himalaya Song)
*by Abigail and Joshua Follows*

*O Himalayas, white with snowfall,*
*Sparkling like the stars above,*
*Singing sad songs for your children,*
*For what they see when they look up.*
*For in your peaks they see the eyes*
*Of a deity you've not known,*
*While the hand that carved your surface*
*Longs to break their hearts of stone.*

*Testify, towering mountains. Let your mighty arms point up*
*Past the temples on your ridges to the one who reigns above.*

*O crashing river, swelled from snow melt,*
*Rushing through this valley green,*
*Are you singing lamentations*
*For the lips that drink your streams?*
*For they bow to kiss a golden*
*And unseeing face enshrined,*
*While the One who gave you bounty*
*Longs to flood their dusty lives.*

*Testify, endless waters. Let your curving banks proclaim*
*That the Spirit longs to fill them who are empty and afraid.*

*O Child of God who knows my Jesus*
*And the blessings of His love,*
*Is your heart within you breaking*
*For the broken of the world?*
*For while they know of gods in thousands,*
*The one true God is still unknown.*
*Will you go bring Jesus to them?*
*Will you go because He calls?*

*So testify, you His people. Let the light within you shine*
*To pierce the darkness all around you with God's love, grace and might.*

*So testify, you His people. Let the living waters flow*
*To reach the thirsty ones, the dying who are waiting to know.*

*They are waiting to know.*

# 10

# NEVER SAY THANK YOU?

Joshua and I spoke with Mark about our language learning. He suggested a two-month break from our interpersonal model to attend a formal language school. "Sociolinguistic learning is great. But getting some grammar drilled into your heads wouldn't hurt. And changing up who you talk to is helpful, too."

That December, Joshua and I left Kushigaun with a plan to return after two months. Three buses, one train, and two taxis later, we found ourselves at the base of an old British hill station. Our taxi driver explained that vehicles weren't allowed past a certain elevation to cut back on pollution. So Joshua and I stashed our belongings in a hotel and began our ascent to the language school on foot.

Our calves burned as we walked past a Tibetan restaurant, playing boys covered in fine, white dust, painted cement dragons. A woman scolded her child, who toddled after a ball on the sidewalk. Brown monkeys crawled over the roads and trees, stealing from shops and customers. Larger monkeys with long, delicate limbs and downy, white fur swung into the forest as we passed.

"Some missionaries never own a car," Joshua commented. "They meet a lot of people that way. I'm not sure we should get a car. Public transportation works for local people."

"Makes sense. Buses go everywhere anyway. Except up this hill." I peeled off my jacket. Joshua was already holding his. "Maybe we should live close to the school so we don't have to climb this mountain every day."

"Maybe," Joshua said. "But listen."

I listened. It was quiet.

"We might intend to talk with people," Joshua said. "But if we don't have to, we won't."

"Agreed," I said. "After four hours of class, I'm probably not going to feel very social. We're going to have to make it so that we have to talk."

"Then let's live in the main area of town," Joshua said. We stopped and looked down the hill over a fluffy evergreen forest to the busy marketplace below. "We'll meet tons of people. Practice every day. What do you say?"

As tempting as it was to skip the on-foot commute, I had to agree with him. "You're right. We aren't here for a vacation. Let's live where we can work!"

---

JOSHUA and I spent the next several days getting oriented. We found a one-room apartment in the busiest area of town. That night, I awoke to the sound of Joshua vomiting. I brought him a glass of water. "Not feeling good?"

"I've been better." Joshua was awake and miserable the rest of the night. The next morning, I consulted a local doctor by cell-phone.

"The doctor thinks you have giardia," I informed my husband as he dry-heaved into a trash can. "He gave me the name of the meds you need. We don't need a prescription, so I can pick it up for you this morning."

I tucked Joshua into the side of the bed nearest the bathroom, then headed out. *Joshua's relying on me. There's no one else to buy medicine, pots and pans to cook dinner in, or plates to eat off. So my language skills will have to be enough. I can do this!*

---

LATER AS I haggled for a pressure cooker, I heard a creak above my head. A preteen boy struggled down a steep ladder, carrying a stack of boxes.

"Put them there, Chotu, and be careful," the shopkeeper ordered.

In the next shop, I bought raisins and saw another boy standing in front of a lit candle. He scooped up a handful of almonds, funneled them with his hand into a plastic bag, and used the candle flame to seal the bag. The result looked factory-sealed.

"Chotu," the shopkeeper said. "Do the walnuts next." *His name is Chotu also?*

I soon learned that every boy in every shop was Chotu, a non-name that means Shorty and refers to child servants.

---

WITH MEDICINE AND AN ELECTROLYTE DRINK, Joshua began to feel like a human being again. We settled into our apartment and started language classes. The experience was rather like drinking out of a fire hose. Between class and practicing with neighbors, Joshua and I walked and talked. I for one needed to process.

"Yesterday I visited the baker's daughter. When I tried to leave, they asked me to sit and stay longer. So I did. Then I tried to leave again. But they complained again, so I sat."

"They must enjoy your company."

"But they didn't really want me to sit. I could tell. They kept glancing at each other like they wanted me to leave but couldn't get me out. And I wanted to leave too, but they kept telling me to sit so I kept sitting. It felt like there was some kind of cultural code word I needed to get out."

"Ha! How did you escape?"

"Someone finally said, 'Don't you have to go feed your husband or something?' I said yes and left. I'm blushing just thinking about it."

Joshua laughed. That made me laugh. If embarrassment felt like death to me, laughing over my weakness with Joshua was resurrection.

---

ONE AFTERNOON, Joshua burst in the door and took my hand. "Come with me. The jeweler wants you to meet his wife!"

I had heard about the jeweler before. Joshua had met nearly everyone in the busy marketplace. The jeweler, whose shop was near our apartment building, was especially friendly. When we arrived, Mrs. Jas of Jas Family Jewelers was sitting by her husband with a wide, relaxed smile, a heavy shawl wrapped around her shoulders. Gold earrings swayed from her ears. They looked like tiny bird cages.

"What is your *shauk*?" she asked me.

I blinked. She laughed, and I laughed, and soon we were all laughing, which is what you do when you don't understand. I discovered that *shauk* meant interest or hobby. I pantomimed playing guitar. She smiled. "Come home with me."

I followed Mrs. Jas—who I was already calling Aunty—to her house. There I met her teenage daughter and college-aged son Sai. He was the only one in the family who spoke English. Soon, Aunty brought chai.

"*Dhaynavad*," I said.

"No," Sai said. "Don't say thank you."

I smiled and sipped the piping-hot tea. Sai talked for well over an hour about Indian culture and customs. He told me that cow urine is pure and the recipe for a popular hand-soap is based on its chemical composition. He told stories. He compared India and what he'd heard about America. He said flings and one-night stands were common among his age group, though taboo in his culture.

Soon, Aunty and her younger daughter emerged from the kitchen with food. When I left, she urged, "Come every day. Really, I mean it. Every day."

---

THIS IS what it's like to learn a language. First, it's blurry. Like losing your glasses. You can't hear the spaces between the words. You soon learn people will stop talking if you look too confused, so you nod and laugh when everyone else laughs, but you still have no idea what is going on.

Then you notice things that are repeated a lot but useless, words like "the" and "and." Then a noun you know jumps out at you—bread. Maybe the person is talking about bread. Or maybe it's a word that rhymes with bread. You have no idea.

Then one day, someone says, "Do you like chicken?" and you understand it. It's just like putting on glasses. The words materialize in your mind. You see a roasted chicken, and you taste it. You aren't translating the words in your head. They have meaning in themselves. You celebrate, hoping that one day everything will have meaning and you'll be fluent.

In the meantime, you make many, many mistakes. Like the time I accidentally called myself a hooker (Sai corrected me!). Or the time Joshua asked a woman who had invited us for dinner to make every Indian dish he'd heard of because the word "and" in Hindi sounds like the word "or" in English. As in we'd like curry and dahl and *palak panir* and... and... and. We had a huge meal that evening and couldn't even explain it had been a mistake.

On bad days, you wonder if you'll ever learn. On good days, you laugh until you cry, and then you sigh because you know humans must crawl before they can run.

---

ONE AFTERNOON AFTER CLASS, I visited Mrs. Jas. She gasped as she did every time I came. She reached out to pull me into her house as though I were a birthday present. She brought chai, and I took the cup with a smile. "Dhanyavad!"

Her son Sai's hands shot into the air. "Stop saying that! It's bad!"

"How can thank you be bad?" I asked, puzzled.

"It's a formality."

"A formality?"

"Family doesn't say thank you."

"My family does."

"Your culture is bad!"

Adrenaline seared my veins. My face felt warm as I tried to respond politely. "I don't talk that way about your culture!"

"Our culture is better." Sai's unsmiling face made clear he wasn't joking. I took a deep breath. I had to stay calm. There was something crucial here, something cultural. What was it?

"Okay. Tell me more. Why is saying thank you bad?"

Sai rolled his eyes at me. "It's a formality, Abigail."

"What does that mean?"

"Look," he said. "If my mom gives me a glass of water, I don't say thank you. If I did, she would be offended. She would say, 'What am I, a waitress?'"

"So, you thank a waitress but not your own mother?"

"Exactly! It's a useless formality."

"You keep saying that. But when I say please or thank you, it's not a formality. I mean it!"

"Well, stop it. For us, it's like saying you don't want to be part of our family. It's distancing yourself from us like we don't know each other."

"But that's not what I mean! I mean I appreciate your mom's effort to make me feel comfortable."

"But isn't it a mother's duty to bring water to her child?"

"I guess so. But nobody has to do anything. If someone in America gives me water, I always say thank you because they didn't have to do it. They chose to do it, and I appreciate that. You know?"

Sai shook his head. "No, Abigail. It's not like that here. Mom has to bring you water. It's her duty. She's fulfilling her duty."

His words swirled together in my mind, blurry. I frowned at a spot on the wall. Suddenly, everything snapped into focus. I looked at Sai. "Wait. People in India *want* to be obligated to each other?"

"Yes!" He exploded off the couch. "That's it! The more people we are obligated to, the better!"

"You actually want to owe people."

"And we want people to owe us. It's good to be obligated, to have a duty. When we fulfill our duty, we know we've done well. 'Thank you' is for people who work in hotels or strangers or kings. Or it's reserved for when you've done something incredible. Something self-sacrificial beyond your duty. Dhanyavad is too strong a word for a cup of water, Abigail."

"I see," I said. "Well, I'll try to stop."

From that day forward, instead of saying thank you, I would smile or say something pleasant. I noticed the satisfaction of my hostess, who smiled as though I really did belong to her. Eventually, I would learn that the concept of duty is so important in the Hindu culture that the word for duty is the same as that for religion: *dharm*.

SOMETIME LATER, I caught the flu. I was fevering miserably in front of an electric heater when Sai came. Joshua let him in. I squinted up at them both.

"Mom says you need to come home," he stated.

I raised an eyebrow. This was the last thing I expected or wanted. "But I'm sick."

"Exactly."

In the Jas home, Sai's mother tucked me into about a hundred fluffy blankets, felt my head, and fussed. "It's not good to be alone when you're sick. It's too sad."

Taking a spoon from behind her back, she held it up to my mouth. "Eat!"

Would my politeness stand the test of the goo on the spoon? I looked frantically from one face to another. The whole family plus Joshua looked down at me on the couch.

"You'll hate it," her daughter said.

*If I'm going to be a part of Indian culture, I have to be flexible,* I told myself. I opened my mouth and squeezed my eyes shut. Everyone laughed. Mrs. Jas slid the spoon into my mouth. "Swallow!"

I sucked the liquid off the spoon. "Mmm! Ginger and honey!"

Everyone laughed. Mrs. Jas smiled. "See? You'll be better in no time."

Later, I would think of that day and feel a pang of sympathy for Indians who move to the United States of Mind Your Own Business. To an Indian, being alone is just too sad.

## 11

# THE GOD WHO SEES

Shortly after Christmas, Joshua and I discovered we'd be parents. I felt dizzy with joy. We were going to hike the Himalayas as a family. Our baby would learn to walk on the streets of India and lisp in Hindi and English. Our child would have such a happy and interesting childhood. Of course, life didn't promise to be perfect, but together we could laugh away the little traumas and disappointments. I would be kind and fun and firm. I would be a good mother. We would collect happy memories like children gather leaves in the fall.

The advice came early from strangers and friends alike. Don't eat cucumbers or almonds. Don't travel. Don't walk. Walk every day. Take bed rest. Keep working. Don't look at anything scary or ugly during pregnancy. Do thus-and-such to ensure you have a boy.

I reacted with grateful smiles on the outside and slight irritation on the inside. In America, you don't tell a mom what to do. Everyone knows that mothers know instinctually how to mother. They research, too, so that any instincts not clinically proven can be replaced with a recommendation by the American Academy of Pediatrics. It's our own special flavor of face-saving.

In India, telling each other what to do is like reciting a catechism. It's how people pass down values. How they remind their collective consciousness of what they believe to be true. I tried to ignore the clashing of our cultures. To press into my role as a learner.

"Okay," I said a lot.

"Yes, that's how it is!" they said a lot.

OUR TIME at language school flew by. It was February and time to return to Kushigaun. When we said goodbye to the Jas family, Sai's mother pressed a shimmering sea-green sari into my hands. "Wear this! Don't give it away."

"You are the only Christian who has ever eaten with our family," Sai said.

I had no idea whether we would see the Jas family again. I hoped the wordless gospel of a shared meal would be enough. *Lord, save them*, I prayed. *Reward them for the many cups of water they have given me.*

On our last day in the hill station, it rained a soft, gray rain. We brought blankets, pots, and other things we couldn't travel with to a row of slum houses we'd seen just outside town. The gifts were received into the darkness behind black plastic doors.

Once again, it was just us and two backpacks.

---

JOSHUA THOUGHT we should take public transportation back to Kushigaun rather than a private bus or taxi. This meant changing buses twice and spending over twenty-four hours traveling. I reluctantly agreed.

For a while, the road was flat and straight. Joshua and I talked. I wanted to find a house, but he thought we should stay with Rose's family again. "We've seen Parvata families renting just one room. Even with kids."

"Well, I want a home eventually," I said, trying not to panic. "But we can stay with Rose a little longer."

I knew Joshua's thoughts were focused with laser-like intensity on our task. He wasn't anti-taxi, anti-home, or anti-owning-a-car. It was all about reaching people. Living with the Parvata and riding the bus with the Parvata would connect us with the Parvata.

I told him we needed balance. But deep inside I felt guilty for not placing an entire people group's salvation above my desire for comfort. I put my hand on my still-flat belly. Would I have to choose between what was best for the baby and what was best for the mission?

The second bus was crowded, so Joshua stood. We heaved over the uneven road. I squeezed myself into half a seat, avoiding the sweaty man on my left. Then began the swerving. We were entering the mountains. I closed my eyes and tried to detach from the nausea. Occasionally, I was jerked back into reality to utilize the open window.

Night descended. We still had many hours to go. How would I make it? If only there were a way to reach our angel dispatchers. To ask someone to pray.

But maybe there was a way. *God, I can't even pray right now. Will You ask someone to pray for me?*

---

WE MOVED BACK into Rose's homestay, this time to a room that opened onto a concrete balcony. The snowline gradually descended on us, muffling everything with white. It was very cold, and the village electricity was not reliable in the winter. Rather than brave pregnancy-offending smells in Rose's house, I spent most days in my big orange sleeping bag.

One day, hoping to be inspired by the view, I peeked out of my bag. Cold flooded in. Outside our window, the landscape was a frozen ocean of gray and white. I stared at it, wondering why it didn't look more beautiful to me, wondering if a person's eyeball could freeze in their head.

Joshua came in what seemed like hours later. "Have you been in there all day?"

The question was half cheerful, half condemning. Instead of answering, I cried. Again. Joshua went on, "Why don't you come for dinner with Rose's family? You've hardly seen her new baby."

"I can't!" I wailed. "The smell of their food makes me sick."

"It might help to be with people."

I squinted up at Joshua. Should I tell him that, although I had a faint memory of having enjoyed the smell of fried onions in the past, I now considered them poisonous? "You have to go by yourself."

"Okay." He sighed.

I knew what that sigh meant. It meant this was why we were here. It meant that people's eternal salvation rested on my choice to get outside my comfort zone. What he didn't know was that a comfort zone and a hormone force field are two very different things.

As Joshua left, the color drained from my world. Dizziness and sleep washed over me. I dreamt of a giant frozen food aisle. Except it was in a nearby alleyway because dreams are like that.

"This has been here the whole time?" I asked, sweeping food into a cart like on one of those old game shows.

"You don't understand," someone said. "The entire store is yours!"

Just before I could devour a plate heaped with crunchy tater tots, I woke up.

*Now I'm crying over TV dinners. Perfect!* I recognized the feeling. This was depression, and it was trapping me in fog. I had to claw my way out. What scared me was that I felt too tired to try. *God, help me! I'm drowning!*

---

*THE POWER HAD BEEN out for days* when I peeked out of my sleeping bag sometime later. Instead of the gray hillside, I saw Rose's mother-in-law Shanty outside on the balcony, staring at me through the window. Her grin turned into a laugh when she saw me sit up. *I must have looked like a giant orange slug in my sleeping bag.*

"*Tunda hai!* It is cold!" she said, letting herself in. "Everything okay?"

"Yes. Except for my stomach." I pointed to the middle of the sleeping bag. Shanty nodded, still laughing. It was contagious. A chuckle caught in my throat. Suddenly, it *was* funny. I mean, when I thought of my mother being thousands of miles away or of how Mary must have felt when she birthed baby Jesus in a stall, it felt tragic. But right now, it was funny.

A week later, power was restored to the village. The electricity was still intermittent, but I appreciated the occasional five minutes with our space heater. I charged our computer and checked my e-mail. There was a note from an angel dispatcher—Kimberly.

"Hey," she wrote. "Let's try to Skype soon. I want to tell you something."

"I'd love that," I wrote back. "Joshua just bought a thumb drive that lets us get internet on our computer. It's not fast, but it's also not dependent on electricity."

We set up Skype. After several echoey, robotic failures, we got a good connection.

"I have to tell you," Kimberly said excitedly. "I had a dream about you last week. It was so vivid I've been praying extra for you ever since."

"Oh? What was your dream?"

"I saw you walking along a path by a river. There was a huge, dark forest on one side. You were pregnant. I could tell you were really upset and needed help. Then I woke up. I thought maybe God wanted me to pray for you. So I have been ever since."

Goosebumps swept over me as I thought of the river and trees that bordered Kushigaun. I thought of my pregnancy and my prayer on the bus. "Kimberly, God sent you that dream! I *am* pregnant, and I've been struggling."

That night in our sleeping bags, Joshua told me the parent of one of my former music students had called. He'd felt impressed to pull his car over to the side of the road because I was going to have a baby and his family needed to pray for me. He wasn't surprised to learn we were expecting.

"You're kidding!" I exclaimed "I got an e-mail from the missionaries in Benin too. They said they woke up in the middle of the night feeling impressed to pray for me."

"That's pretty cool," Joshua said.

"Yeah. By the way, thanks for the crackers you brought me earlier."

"No problem. Aren't you supposed to ask for pickles and ice cream or something?"

"A banana and seaweed chips sounds good."

"You are so pregnant."

I lay awake for some time, watching my breath swirl gray above me in the dim light. I remembered my prayer on the bus. I had asked God to ask someone to pray for me. He had asked three people.

I remembered then the Biblical story of Hagar. God knew all about Hagar. Her unhappy "marriage" to Abraham. Her pregnancy. The struggles she'd had with Sarah. God had seen her faults and needs and had met her in the desert. She must have felt like I did now, staring up in awe, feeling noticed. That was why she'd named Him "The God Who Sees Me."

# 12

# A PLACE OF OUR OWN

Our organization employed several supervisors to provide support, advice, and accountability for field missionaries. Our supervisor was Bill, a thoughtful, red-headed fan of puns who'd been a missionary in Papua New Guinea for nineteen years. Hoping to encourage their newest, youngest missionaries, our organization arranged for Bill to visit us. He flew all the way from the United States to Delhi, then took the long bus ride to Kushigaun.

After Bill arrived, he huddled with us in front of our space heater. Between dry heaves, I tried to act like nothing was wrong. He assured me, "Just in case you're feeling down, don't panic. It will get better."

The three of us went for walks along the road. Bill fussed over me. He made corny word jokes. He pointed to the mountains that rose out of the snow. "This is seriously the most beautiful place I have ever been."

I looked up, surprised I hadn't noticed. *It must be beautiful. Why don't I see it?*

Sometime later, Bill suggested, "You may want to find a way to cook some food." He searched the ceiling for the right words to use in this delicate situation. "And maybe some plates and cutlery."

I glanced at Joshua. He rubbed the back of his neck. "I tried to get a gas cylinder from Rose's father-in-law. But he's been saying 'one more week' for the past month."

"Could you get an induction cooker?" Bill asked.

"Maybe. But the power is sketchy. Another issue is we don't want to look rich. We want to be relatable."

"People watch when we walk down the street," I explained. "They comment on everything we own and ask what everything costs. But it would be nice to cook some ramen. Not that the crackers and bananas aren't good."

"I see how you both feel," Bill said, still eyeing the ceiling. "But you need to get set up to live. It will make you more effective at everything else."

Bill kept talking with Joshua about how our supporters would want us to spend the money to own a knife. Then he suggested we all take the bus to Pahargaun. If we couldn't buy cooking gas, we'd have to get creative.

---

IN PAHARGAUN, I walked behind Joshua and Bill, gagging at the smells assaulting me from gutters and grills. Bill bought us a knife, and we found a kerosene stove. He asked, "Have you been to the hospital yet?"

We'd both been to the hospital many times for various scary abdominal disturbances. Bill asked if we'd seen the delivery ward. We said no. He wanted to be with us when we did, so we went to the hospital and asked to see Labor and Delivery. A nurse in a white coat led us to a nearly bare room.

I stepped in. A pair of stirrups hung over a skeletal bed. I tried to pep talk myself. *It's a little bare-bones, but maybe it could work.*

I learned that men were not allowed to accompany their laboring wives, a policy meant to protect the privacy of other laboring women. I also learned that the OB/GYN doctor served thousands of women and was planning a vacation at the time of my due date.

"It'll only be nurses here," the doctor told us. "I recommend you find somewhere else."

Somewhere else? The closest "somewhere else" was two hours south of us in Chotashaher! As we left, the sensation of my assumptions bursting into oblivion left me reeling. I cried.

Bill looked at me like a father whose child is greatly disappointed. "That's why I wanted you to look."

Bill and Joshua spent the evening attempting to light the stove, which sent out fumes, smoke, and the occasional fireball.

"This isn't gonna work," I yelled, sheltering in the tiled bathroom we shared with other guests. This was ridiculous! We had to move somewhere with a real stove, refrigerator, and a washing machine. There would soon be cloth diapers to wash. We were going to be parents. We needed privacy and space.

Yet I knew most young families in our village not living with in-laws rented single rooms. Wouldn't we look rich if we purchased everything needed to set up a home? In our minds, looking rich meant being inaccessible to the people.

*God, please!* I prayed. *If You want us to stay here, I'm willing. But I really want a home of our own. Help us find the right place!*

---

JOSHUA AND BILL went house hunting. One house looked promising, a cozy cottage tucked into the side of the hill. But it was more than we could afford.

"It's not extravagant," Bill said. "If you guys like this, I can help you fundraise for the extra money. Your supporters would want you to get settled."

Joshua shook his head. "Look at it! It's so far from people."

I looked around. Joshua was right. The house was a fifteen-minute walk from the village. While being isolated sounded beautiful at that moment, we weren't living in India to be isolated.

"Well, I'm due to fly back to the States in a few days," Bill said. "I'd feel better leaving if you had a place of your own. Let's keep looking."

We did. Some places were too expensive. Others were too isolated.

"We need to pray," I said one afternoon two days before Bill was scheduled to leave. I bit my lip to keep it from quivering.

"Okay. Let's pray," Joshua said. His bounciness had been reduced to a low dribble. It wasn't like he wanted us to be miserable.

We knelt, and I poured out my tears before God. "Lord, lead us to a place where they will want to know You."

"Lord, lead us somewhere we can be used by You," Joshua prayed.

"Show your missionaries what to do and give them peace," Bill prayed.

That evening, there was a celebration in the village. Though Joshua and Bill begged me to go with them, I needed time to process. I lay on our bed, occasionally rotating to allow the heater to cook the other side of me. And I prayed.

Sometime later, Joshua bounded in the door. "Abby, you've got to see this!"

"See what?"

"An apartment! You'll never believe it, but this kid just ran up to us and said, 'Do you want to rent my house?' I think this is the one!"

I hurried outside to find a boy blowing on his hands. He wore a thick beanie and scarf coiled several times around his neck. He stuck his hand out to shake mine. "*Kya aap pehechhante hain mujhe?*"

"What?" I asked, trying to make sense of the garbled syllables.

"I'm Ajay," he said in simpler Hindi. "Follow me!"

Ajay marched down a narrow cement path, head high and smile gigantic. We followed him to an iron gate. Beyond was a large courtyard. To the right of the courtyard stood a tall, traditional Parvata home, with a cowshed beneath and living quarters on top. Diagonal across the courtyard was a raised, one-story cement building containing two apartments, each with two doors to the outside. One of the apartments blazed with cheerful yellow light.

A middle-aged, plump woman emerged from the traditional Parvata house, adjusting her knitted headscarf. "Namaste. I'm Ajay's mother. Come in!"

Family members appeared from every corner, all talking at once. The boy took off his hat, and I noticed his head was shaved with a thin ponytail sticking out the back. I suddenly realized he was the same smiling boy who'd shaken our hands when we first came to Kushigaun. Now I understood his question: "Do you recognize me?"

Ajay's large family whisked us up some cement steps, across a veranda, and into the brightly lit rental. As Joshua made small talk, I smiled and nodded. And I peeked. The room we stood in had several low couches. Off this room was a bathroom with a washing machine. *This is amazing! A furnished apartment! With a washing machine!*

We filtered into a kitchen where a red refrigerator cheered a corner. Off the kitchen was another room with a bed and two metal lockers.

After looking at the apartment, we were taken to the main house and seated on a bed. The family sat around us, chattering and laughing. Joshua asked about Ajay's ponytail. He explained that his grandfather had died just a few months prior. The men in the family had shaved their heads in grief, but a Brahmin should never shave all his hair.

"The hair is like a spiritual antenna," Ajay's father said.

A thin boy in a faded blue sweatshirt and jeans almost came in the door but stopped when he saw us. He smiled but looked at the ground.

"That's Chotu," someone said. Chotu—a child servant. This Chotu had a thin, mottled face. I wondered what his real name was.

"You should have seen him before we took him in," Ajay's mother said. "He was so skinny. He would drink a whole glass of milk every night. Now look at him!" She grinned. "He's so fat! So healthy and handsome!"

The boy scuffed his toe on the ground and tried not to grin. Then he disappeared. Soon a teen girl arrived, carrying a platter with steaming hot cups of chai tea. I took a deep breath and forced myself to take a sip.

"Oh! This is good." Surprised, I took another sip. Warm milk, sugar, clove, and cinnamon swirled in my mouth. "This is just what I wanted."

I patted my belly and smiled at Ajay's mom. "It's hard to eat these days."

She became more animated. "Good news! You have good news!" In other words, you're going to have a baby. "You must leave that little room and come live with us. Well? Do you want the place?"

I thought of the fridge, red as Laura Ingalls Wilder's red-checked tablecloth. "Yes."

Ajay's father asked when we'd like to move in. Joshua glanced at me. "Tomorrow."

I nodded my agreement. The family all looked at one another just for a moment. Then Ajay's father said, "It will be ready."

*Thank You, Lord, I prayed, for helping us find this home that is so close to people. Please use us to reach Ajay's family!*

# 13

## MOVING IN WITH BRAHMINS

The next morning when Bill returned from hauling our pink wash tub to the new house, his forehead was scrunched. Joshua followed him but didn't make eye contact with me. They each picked up a backpack and strode out the door with their heads down. I swept the carpet and tried to ignore a sinking feeling in my stomach. What was wrong?

"Namaste." Rose's mother-in-law Shanty walked in but didn't sit. "We treated you like our family. But now everything will change."

I tried to explain that we needed space. That we hadn't intended to live with them forever. That we needed a home. But Shanty wouldn't listen. Something about this move, something cultural I couldn't yet see, was deeply significant to her. I tried to reassure her.

"It's only a few yards away," I said. "We'll visit. And you're welcome to come any time. Maybe I can even cook you dinner! After all, you've cooked for us many times, and—"

"We're not family anymore," Shanty said and walked out.

*Maybe it's the money. She's losing our rent. Please, Lord, don't let this ruin our chance to witness to Shanty and her family!*

It was my turn to leave. I hugged a smiling Rose, who whispered into my hair that she understood.

---

THE APARTMENT BUILDING looked smaller in the daytime. Two adult cows and a calf stood in in the courtyard, chewing their cud.

When I first walked in the door of our new home, I wondered if I had entered the wrong building. It was dim. The living room was bare except for a bed. I glanced into the bathroom. No washing machine. I looked around the corner into the kitchen. No fridge. A two-burner stove sat in the place of the four-burner. The adjacent bedroom contained a small, dusty couch and two chairs.

Ajay's mom peeked into the room, smiling. "We were up all night moving everything out."

I smiled back to hide my shock. *Someone in the family must have been living in this apartment. They'd moved out so we could move in!*

"Tell my children if you need anything. Remember, our door is just a couple yards from yours." She pointed to the main house. It stood so close to the apartment building that it blocked most of the light. So that's why it was so dim! "I would help you myself, but I have to cut grass!"

I stifled a wave of tears that tingled in the back of my nose. Bill and Joshua gathered around me. Looking up at a collection of eight-armed goddess pictures that lined the wall, I tried to joke. "At least they left their idols."

Bill chuckled. Joshua spoke up apologetically. "Bill has to go, Abby. His bus to Delhi leaves in an hour."

"No problem," I said.

"Are you going to be okay?" Bill asked.

"Let's pray," I said.

We stood there and prayed, all three of us swiping at tears. Then they left, and I was alone.

*God, how am I going to do this?* I looked around. First, I would remove the idols and pray for this home to be a dwelling place of holy angels. Then I would scrub the kitchen. At least I had a kitchen. And privacy.

Our new landlord seemed a bit confused that we hadn't wanted to keep the idols. After returning them, I got to work scrubbing the kitchen. Just then, Ajay arrived with his older sister Lovelina, the teenaged girl I'd seen the evening before. "Can we help you?"

"Thank you so much," I said. "But no, I'm fine."

"Oh, please!" Lovelina begged. "We want to help you."

"Well, okay." I forced myself to smile. I wanted nothing more than to be alone. I needed time to think. But something rang out loud and clear in my heart. *Welcome these children. They'll be in your home a lot.*

I gave Lovelina a scrubber. She began to scour the counter. Ajay loitered in the doorway. I smiled at him. "I don't have much work to do. You can go play if you like."

He retreated to the bedroom, chewing a wobbly lower lip. My heart softened. I held up a rag. "Want to help mop?"

He sprang off the bed. "Yes!"

The two kids helped me all afternoon, long after I wanted them to leave. But when we finished, the kitchen sparkled. I only had to wipe out the drawers and everything would be ready. When they left to help their grandmother care for the cows, I allowed myself a sigh, then retrieved our knife and opened a drawer. A pungent smell wafted into my nostrils.

I began opening all the kitchen drawers and cabinets. Black mold covered every interior. I backed out of the kitchen and sat on the bed. The mattress was uneven. *God, You cannot possibly want us to stay here! Isn't there something in the Old Testament about mold in a building being unclean?*

I suddenly saw Joseph in a dingy, moldy dungeon. That prison had been part of God's plan. And Daniel. Stolen from his country, forced to march on foot over scorching sand, tempted by a brainwashing and indoctrinating school system. All part of God's plan. And Jesus. Nowhere to lay His head. God's plan.

*But I'm not Jesus! I'm not even Joseph or Daniel! I'm not strong enough.*

No cosmic answer came to my mind. My feelings threatened to crush me. I wanted more than this for my baby. I wanted a clean, white bathroom with a bathtub. I wanted the good mattress back that Joshua and I had bought together as newlyweds. God was silent, but I thought I felt His presence as though He sat with me on the edge of that uneven bed, listening.

*I don't know why You brought us here,* I prayed. *But I believe You did. Maybe there is someone here You want us to reach.*

I remembered again the challenge I'd given God when I hadn't wanted to be a missionary at all. I would have to pray the same thing now.

*Okay, God. I'll stay. But only if You change my heart!*

---

JOSHUA and I bleached the cabinets but kept them shut, stacking our few kitchen utensils on one clean shelf. Ajay's mom was Mrs. Opee, though she asked me to call her Didi, which meant big sister. She told the funniest stories we'd ever heard, making herself and us laugh so hard we'd have to catch our breath. She was a good cook, tidy—and a hypochondriac.

"Do my eyes look small to you?" she asked one day, squinting to accentuate the smallness of her eyes. Her eyes did look small like pictures of hypothyroid patients I'd seen in a simple medical book our organization had given us. One afternoon, Mrs. Opee brought me a thick medical file to peruse.

"It looks like your body doesn't make enough thyroid hormone," I said after looking up her medications on my laptop.

"That's what the doctor said. Will the medicine fix it?"

"No. You have to continue taking it."

"The doctor said that too." From then on, Mrs. Opee referred to me as Dr. Abigail and daily rehearsed to me all her medical complaints: aching knees, a late period, thinning hair, insomnia, excessive sleepiness, poor appetite, nervous tension. I gave her massages and hot foot baths, which were all I could offer besides looking up medications online.

"I'm always worrying about everybody else," she would say as I ground the tips of my fingers into her shoulders. "I just can't handle it when someone is hurting. Do I look sick to you?"

The cows in our courtyard, though well-maintained, drew flies. One afternoon, Joshua killed more than a hundred. Mrs. Opee shook her head. "I could never do that. I can't kill anything. What if I came back as a fly, and somebody smashed me? It feels like a sin."

We gave our food scraps to Mrs. Opee every afternoon, and she fed them to the cows. Later, we learned her cows were vegetarians. Vegetarians in India do not eat eggs. When Mrs. Opee found out she'd fed her cow eggs from our kitchen scraps, she gave herself a mark on her forehead bowing before the idol for forgiveness.

Cows are considered holy in India. In fact, Ajay informed us we had three mothers: Earth Mother, Cow Mother, and Durga Mother, the same multi-armed goddess who was created by the other gods to go on a killing rampage.

MEANWHILE, Joshua spent time with the man of the house, Mr. Opee, who was a Brahmin priest. Twice a day, Mr. Opee wrapped his lower half in an orange dhoti to worship an idol in the backyard. The idol was made of hardened ghee, aka clarified butter, with little metal eyes poked into it. Mr. Opee said it was an evil devta that would harm people who offended it.

It especially disliked being around menstruating women, who weren't allowed in the house, anyway. Some slept outside. Others stayed in special rooms built just for the occasion. Mrs. Opee later assured me that so long as I stayed out of their house and away from the temple when I had my period, I wouldn't have to sleep outside.

Standing before the shrine, Mr. Opee would ring a bell, circle around, wave peacock feathers, touch certain parts of the temple, and offer incense on a metal plate by slowly moving it in a circle in front of the idol. This was *puja*: the Hindu form of worship.

Then he'd dip a finger in a little mound of colored powder from the plate and dab it on his forehead and on the foreheads of family members. He'd give some food from the plate to each person. They'd touch the food to their foreheads before tossing it into their mouths. Eating prasad, as it was called, was accepting the blessing of the devta. It was food offered to idols.

Joshua asked Mr. Opee about idols. He said that Hindus don't worship idols. They worship the spirits that inhabit idols. "Think of an idol as a doorway from the unseen world to us. When we worship an idol, we invite the spirits into our world."

Joshua noted how visible Hinduism was. Every ceremony, every ritual was multi-sensory and public. There was always something to hear, taste, smell, touch, and look at. It was highly social too as the family and community participated in religious life together. In contrast, we noticed how internal our own religion was, something personal and private.

"We need to be Christians in a way they can see," Joshua said. So we began leaving our doors open when we had morning and evening worship and on Sabbath.

As we learned about Parvata culture, Lovelina and Ajay learned about ours, often joining us for "church." Lovelina once choked when I read about the father of the prodigal son killing the fatted calf for his party. Despite that setback, Lovelina and Ajay enjoyed our worship times and even learned several praise songs.

"Azad ho," Lovelina sang into my hairbrush. "By the blood of Christ, be freed."

---

OUR MOVE HAD DEFINITELY OPENED doors. We ate almost daily with one neighbor or another. By the middle of my second trimester, I could usually hold down food until we returned from a visit. I hoped the delay between eating and throwing up helped some nutrients get to the baby, but my arms and face had become very thin.

Joshua got to know a neighbor called Bablu, a trekking guide who had the dark, muscular look of someone who climbed around in the sun all day. We were at his house one evening when Bablu commented, "You know, we couldn't invite you over when you lived at the homestay."

"Oh? Why is that?" Joshua asked.

"They are low-caste. Our religion forbids eating with low-caste people. But don't worry, your landlords are Brahmin. Since your people don't have a caste, it matters only who you live with. So we can eat with you."

So that's what Rose's mother-in-law had meant when she said we weren't family anymore! Bablu's mother pulled her lips back in a grimace. She had slate-gray hair woven into a braid, fine wrinkles all over her face and neck, and sunken cheeks due to a lack of teeth. "The low caste are dirty. And promiscuous. We avoid them for a reason."

---

I SOON REALIZED no one knocked in our new community. People would just poke their heads in and say something. In fact, Mrs. Opee once walked in on me post-shower. She just turned around and kept talking while I dove into a Punjabi suit.

The snow melted halfway up the hillside. Then began an incessant drumming and the drawn-out howl of a horn. For several days everyone washed blankets, swept corners, and washed food storage containers. Ajay told us the devta was coming.

The devta was the same entity that had convulsed the man at the dinner party, the same kind of spirit in Mr. Opee's tiny backyard temple. One of these spirits claimed each village in the valley. They were as much a part of daily life and government as the elected village *pradhan*, or chief.

The Kushigaun devta's box was carried straight to our front yard. I watched Mrs. Opee, dressed in her wedding *patu* and wearing a giant golden nose ring that hooked back to her ear, worship the devta. The smiling silver faces with their closed eyes sat motionless, seeming to accept the sprinkling of flowers and red powder. Smoke rose from a censor held by one of the *gurs*, persons chosen by the devta to serve as mediums.

Gurs were highly respected. It was their duty to perform uncomfortable rituals to induce trances, which enabled the spirits to use them like puppets.

We'd seen gurs walk circles in the snow with bare feet, beating their bare chests with chains for hours until they became possessed. But devta could enter civilians too. The first man we'd seen possessed had just been an ordinary guy.

That evening, I felt strong enough to accompany Joshua and Ajay on a walk. Joshua bought me a brown paper sack of fried pakoras. They smelled like French fries and tasted delicious. But within two hours, food poisoning hit.

I lay on the bed, gripping a large bowl. The heaving was uncontrollable. Fearing for the baby, I asked Joshua to pray. As he prayed, I hugged the bowl and closed my eyes. For a moment, I wished I were in my childhood home on my bed with my mother holding my hair back. What if my baby died? What if I died?

Reality morphed. I was suddenly at the foot of the cross of Jesus. I was holding the cross, holding it hard, because it had roots that stretched deep into the ground. Its arms were like shade above my head. The cross was solid, keeping me from flying off the face of the earth and into oblivion.

*Staying here is my cross,* I remembered and tried to breathe. *Staying right here is holding onto Jesus, and He's got me.*

# 14

## TEAM CONFLICT

I survived. We bought a refrigerator and washing machine and slowly gathered other essentials. Shopping in India is not usually self-service. People shop knowing what they want and where to buy it. We learned that underwear and candle wicks are sold in the same store as eggs, but socks and hand cream are sold in the shop that sells umbrellas and mascara. Shoppers don't browse but ask the shopkeeper for items.

Yog was our favorite shopkeeper in the Kushigaun *bazaar*. Thin with a deep, gravelly voice and equally gravelly chuckle, he was a thoughtful person, always talking about spiritual matters. He said he cared about the river, the trees, and clean air because God made it all, and that made it all holy.

Despite being the size of a walk-in closet, Yog's shop had just about everything. We privately called it Yog-mart. Yog had several unmarried sisters who took turns manning the shop too. They'd taken a liking to Joshua and me and always noted aloud whether I was looking fatter or thinner than the last time they'd seen me. I learned this was akin to asking about my health.

"You're looking thin. Have you been sick again?" they'd comment. Or "You're looking nice and fat. Feeling better now?"

Yog and his sisters joined a growing list of people who visited frequently. I tried to be a good Indian hostess. I learned to make chai and always kept something sweet and something salty on hand to serve. I was starting to enjoy pretending to be an extrovert. Except when I didn't.

There were two doors into our home. One opened into the room with the bed. The other opened into the room with the dusty couch. We left both doors unlocked. Usually. When I felt too tired for the jolt of another unexpected visitor, I'd sneak out one door and snap a combination lock on it. This made it appear we'd left. Then I'd run back inside and lock the remaining door. If we locked both doors from the inside, a neighbor would just knock and knock until I answered.

Only after locking myself in could I totally relax. I knew they were being kind. As with the Jas family, so here too being alone was bad. It seemed even introverts in India preferred a crowded solitude.

One day, feeling my brain would burst with new words, I decided to rest. I peeked out my window. Nobody! I went out as quietly as I could, slid shut the outside lock on the main door, and eased the combination lock closed. Then I ran for cover.

"Ahh," I sighed to myself, locking the other door from the inside. "Peace."

I'd been asleep for half an hour when Joshua came home. I heard him fiddling with the combination lock. He came in and stood looking at me with his arms folded. "Why do you do that?"

"Do what?"

"Lock the door like that."

"I needed alone time."

Joshua sighed, paced, and ran his hand through his hair. I suddenly felt guilty. I was keeping out people who needed Jesus. I could see Joshua's frustration in his body language, and it surged into me like an electric shock. Yet surely a pregnant woman should be allowed to take a nap without being disturbed. I pushed back.

"I need rest, Joshua. I'm growing a baby."

"Rest is what night is for."

"It's normal for a pregnant woman to need extra rest."

"Did you visit anyone today?"

"I'm not feeling up to it right now."

Joshua sighed again.

"Did I mention I'm growing a baby?"

"You really have an opportunity here," Joshua said. "You can visit people. You can be in their homes. I don't know why you wouldn't take advantage of that."

"Because I'm tired."

"But this is why we're here!"

"But when you tell me what to do, I don't want to do it anymore."

We argued. My irritation grew. Then I looked at Joshua, really looked at him. He looked like something had crushed the spring in his step.

"Is something wrong?" I asked.

Joshua knelt next to the bed and rested his forehead on our wool blanket. Then he looked at me. "I'm sorry for pressuring you, Abby. It's just, you have access to the ladies. They want to talk to you. I'm having a hard time connecting with the men. I visit the shops every day. I sit and talk to them for hours. I play sports with them. But there's this wall up. We've been here for months, and I haven't truly connected with anyone. There's no sincere friendship, let alone spiritual interest."

"Joshua, that must be so discouraging." I touched his arm. It was thin from frequent bouts with giardia. "Do you want to pray about it?"

"Yes," he said.

We prayed that God would open a door for Joshua and give me the energy to keep connecting with people. As soon as we said amen, I thought of Yog, planting trees to save the world in his spare time. "Joshua, what about Yog? I thought you'd been having a lot of spiritual conversations with him."

"I'd forgotten about Yog. You're right. He's a thoughtful person."

"Maybe you should invest your time in Yog," I said.

"Maybe I will!" Joshua stood and strode out the door. I suddenly understood that it was driving my husband crazy to have all that energy, work ethic, and a clear call from God but have nothing to do.

*God, I know You want to bless the world through Joshua! Help me support him. And use me, too!*

---

WE OFTEN BAKED cookies to share with visitors or to deliver to hosts. The smell of them baking (or burning) worked like a bat signal to summon Ajay. Once as I pulled a batch of chocolate chip cookies out of the oven, I heard the screen door slam.

"Namaste!" Ajay sniffed his way into the kitchen.

"Namaste," I replied. "Here for a cookie?"

"Hand it over."

I gave him a cookie, laughing at how abrupt Hindi can sound. Ajay's demand for a cookie was one way of making himself my real little brother. He didn't say thank you.

We sat on the couch. Ajay chowed down his cookie while I sewed the finishing touches on a cloth diaper. I felt so domestic with all the extra sewing and baking I was doing. I'd be such a calm, capable new mother. Maybe I'd even start remembering to set the oven timer!

I glanced outside. Chotu in his blue sweatshirt was shoveling manure. He stood up and stretched his back and neck. I got to my feet. "Be right back."

Going to the window, I called out to Chotu. He walked up to the open screen door but stopped outside, staring at his feet. "Namaste, *Bhabi*."

*Bhabi* means "my older brother's wife." An increasing number of people were calling me Bhabi these days. Despite Joshua's concern about connecting, nearly everyone in the village referenced him as *Bhai*, or brother.

"Want to come in and have cookies with Ajay?" I asked. "You two can eat while I finish my project."

"Not now. I have work." Chotu paused. "But you could give me a cookie."

I brought him a handful. He took them with the briefest of eye contact. "Dhanyavad."

---

DESPITE MY DESIRE for alone time, I did go visiting. I visited the Momo Lady and the Nice Shopkeeper and the Short Shopkeeper. Joshua and I went on walks.

Every time someone said *betho,* or sit, we sat. We drank gallons of chai. I visited Rose, even though her high caste neighbor lady watched me.

The neighbor could see Rose's front door from her own yard. She'd stand hunched over with her elbows up like a vulture and focus her good eye on me as I walked up the stairs.

"You'll be in trouble if you eat with me, you know." Rose giggled like the prejudice was lame instead of hurtful and stifling.

"I don't care," I said. "I don't believe in caste."

"Well, come in the kitchen, anyway," she whispered. "We'll eat where nobody sees."

Taking my hand, she dragged me inside. She made chapattis. We sat eating and talking on the floor underneath the window. The two of us just fit into the space. Rose's eyes sparkled, and I willed myself to absorb her language, listening for what she found insulting, what brought her joy, comparing it to what others were saying.

I learned a lot from Rose, my low-caste friend. I also learned a lot from Bablu's family, who hadn't wanted to eat with us when we lived with Rose because they were high caste. Bablu was away a lot, leading treks in the mountains. The women in the family held down the fort and welcomed me as one of their own.

There was Bablu's proud mother Ama with gray hair and a cackling laugh. Then there was Bimla, Bablu's thin, pale wife with dark, expressive eyebrows, and their three-year-old daughter, who looked just like her mother in miniature. Bablu's twenty-something sister Tripti lived at home, too. A sturdy, curvy girl, she had lighter eyes, almost green. When she wasn't doing housework or plowing up a field by hand, she tutored neighbor children.

Then there was Bablu's grandmother Nani. Hard-of-hearing, she always sat in a corner with a blanket over her legs. The others often teased her, finding it hilarious that she couldn't hear their jokes. Once she asked Joshua how the mango business was going. Somehow, she'd gotten the idea he sold mangoes. As the others laughed, it seemed as though Nani watched through soundproof glass, but she gave no response.

Tripti said Nani liked me. I would sit next to her and hold her hand, wishing I could hear all about her life and tell her all about Jesus. I wished I could tell everyone. There were many words I still needed to learn, so much about their culture I didn't understand. But I was learning. Maybe this was why we were placed at the Opee's house. How else would I ever have met any of them?

---

JOSHUA HAD his own divine appointment. Every morning before work, Yog and his youngest sister walked to the riverbank to do yoga. One day they invited Joshua to come along on their pilgrimage. He began accompanying them each morning. They would worship the sun while Joshua prayed and read his Bible. On the way back, they would discuss spiritual matters.

We prayed for Yog and his sisters daily. We prayed the Holy Spirit would grow their love of nature into a love of the One True God. And we prayed that God would use Joshua to plant gospel seeds in Yog's heart.

———————

ALTHOUGH WE SPENT as much time as possible in Kushigaun, Joshua and I occasionally visited the Pahargaun mission hospital church. Most in attendance were Christians from other parts of India who served at the hospital, some for months, some for years. There were no Parvata people with their distinctive wool clothing.

One Sunday, we met a couple from the United States. They were church-planters like us and had been in India for several years. They knew of only a handful of Parvata Christians living within a two-hour radius of the hospital and no ethnically Parvata pastors.

"We have a pastor at this church, and there are a few others in Chotashaher," they said. "There's a church there too, but most Christians groups meet in homes."

"We'd love to hear more about what you're doing here," Joshua said.

"We'd love to talk more," the missionaries said. "But we're packing our things. We have a furlough coming up and have to catch a bus to Delhi in the morning. Hopefully, we can connect when we get back!"

Unfortunately, we later learned that these missionaries and several foreign doctors at the hospital had to leave India permanently. Some couldn't get their visas renewed while others were asked by the government to leave. We'd heard tensions were high in various parts of India between Hindus and Christians. While we hadn't seen this attitude in our region, we didn't want anyone feeling we'd forced our religion on them. Both to safeguard our ability to stay and to respect their right to choose.

Yet we also knew the Bible urges Christians to preach the Word with boldness. How could we be both bold and sensitive? How could we share Jesus without getting kicked out of India?

———————

I'VE FORGOTTEN NOW what prompted the argument. It may have been because I said I wanted to go home. That often started it.

"Why do keep saying that?" Joshua demanded.

"Because that's how I feel."

"But we can't leave."

"Just because I say I wish we could go doesn't mean I actually want to go," I said. "I'm committed. I wouldn't leave Rose or Bimla or Mrs. Opee just like you wouldn't leave Yog or Ajay or Mr. Opee. But living here is like having no walls. I open the door, and someone's face is there. I'm committed, but that doesn't mean it isn't hard. Don't you see that?"

"Then why do you keep saying you want to leave? I thought we were doing everything in our power to stay. How can you say that if you're truly committed?"

"Because I'm trying to be honest. I'm homesick! Joshua, we agree. We live here now. We talk about living here forever. Unless they kick us out, we're staying."

Why wasn't this working anymore? I had always shared my feelings with Joshua. He was always so level-headed. He was my coprocessor. Why were we crashing?

Joshua washed dishes in the kitchen with a vengeance. I sat on the bed and cried. I hated this. This was everything I didn't want. Everything I had worked so hard to avoid. I didn't want a home full of bickering. I didn't want to burden Joshua or be clingy. I didn't want to distract him from the mission God had given him. The thought repulsed me.

Joshua returned and knelt on the bed. His eyes were red.

"Are you okay?" I asked.

"No," he said.

"It's funny." I wiped my eyes with my sleeves. "I know our denomination doesn't put a ton of emphasis on hell. But I was just thinking, whenever or wherever hell is, I'm probably going there."

"That's odd," Joshua responded. "I was just thinking the same thing about myself."

I felt strange then. Suspicious. Wasn't it odd we'd thought the same thing at the same time in different rooms? It was as though we had both been listening to the same radio.

# 15

# THE PEOPLE WHO WALK IN DARKNESS

Ten minutes after we thought we were going to hell for arguing, Joshua and I were on our knees, begging God's forgiveness, protection, and help against spiritual attack. We asked God to clothe us with His armor as described in Ephesians chapter six, including the helmet of salvation.

Then we opened our laptop and e-mailed our regional supervisor Bill. He reminded us we'd soon have a break, a retreat our organization held every two years in Thailand. "Let's talk there. In the meantime, I'll be praying for you."

It was hard to believe we'd already been in India for almost six months. Our current tourist visa stipulated we get out of India every six months and stay out at least two. By the time we flew to Thailand, Joshua and I weren't an emergency anymore. We were just a young couple who cried their eyes out while everybody else sang hymns because they hadn't heard a Christian song in their native tongue since leaving their home country.

We spent some time talking with our regional supervisor. Bill advised us to "give each other grace"—a beautiful way to say "cut each other some slack"—and promised to keep praying for us.

During the retreat, an offering was collected and given to the newest recruits, which in this case was us. "To bless your people," we were told.

Joshua and I walked under palm trees, letting the warm air thaw us. How would we find a way to use that money? Pastors in India are sometimes accused of bribing people to become Christians. Giving money might be misunderstood. The penalty could be losing our visas or jail time or worse.

"We'll have to let God show us how to use the money," Joshua said.

While there, I grilled other missionary moms about birth and child-rearing. They gave me books, including one detailing a medication-free, relaxation-based approach to labor and delivery.

"Okay," Joshua would say. "Relax your eyebrows. Let your jaw fall open. Um, relax your kneecaps. Relax your eyelashes."

Stifling a laugh, I reminded him, "This is going to be the real thing, eventually. Try to cooperate!" Then I got back into the Position, lying on my side. I breathed. I imagined pain, then ignored it. *Breathe. Breathe. Breathe.*

As we practiced, I thought of what I'd learned about the emotional stages of labor. First, labor begins. Mom-to-be is excited, nervous. She is interactive and may even smile. Labor is usually "easy." In the second stage, Mom goes internal: she is less responsive, maybe even confused, as she searches inside herself for the strength to do the work of labor. At stage three, Mom realizes that she really, really can't do this. And right when she thinks she can't do it, she does: A baby is placed in her arms.

AFTER THAILAND, we flew to Nepal, hoping to continue practicing Hindi among the Nepali people. We stayed near a Christian hospital, where we got to know several older missionary families. These families took us under their wings and answered the zillion questions we had about missions and practical living in Southeast Asia.

By this time, I'd had prenatal checkups in three different countries. Joshua's bout with giardiasis had now lasted approximately ninety percent of our overseas experience. Yet despite all the sickness and dislocation, we wanted to have our baby in India. Going back to the United States for the birth would take us away from Kushigaun for too long. What if we forgot all the Hindi we had learned?

And what about the people? Maybe there was someone out there "waiting to know." Maybe we'd meet them in the coming months. Or maybe giving birth in India would connect me with Indian women. Help me really understand them.

So we went home to India.

I KNEW the arguing and sickness were normal parts of cultural and bacterial adjustment. But after Joshua and I both thought we were going to hell over an argument, we paid more attention to the spiritual battles around us.

One such battle took place in a church. We wanted to visit the closest church of our denomination, so we took a four-hour bus ride to another Himalayan valley. The bus stopped before the main village, so we hitched a ride with some construction workers on the back of a truck. They drove us to the bottom of a steep hill and pointed up.

Church in India isn't pipe organs and red pews. It is women sitting knee-to-knee, their heads draped in chiffon scarves because you cover your head when you come near divinity. It is men keeping time with a hand drum. It is a pile of sandals outside the door because you take off your shoes when you walk on holy ground.

In bringing the gospel to India, our goal was never to make Indians into Westerners. Our goal was to bring Christ into their culture. To restore the beautiful. To transform the painful. Our goal was redemption. In them and in ourselves.

This particular church was situated on the side of the hill. We had to walk up a dirt road to get to it. The church was one simple, white-painted room with rows of wooden benches and two windows that looked out over the hill. We smoothed our clothes, wrinkled from the journey, and took our seats. A dozen ladies, their heads draped in sheer, multicolored scarves, sat around us. They clapped to keep time with the music, and someone played an accordion-like *harmonium*.

After the sermon, Joshua and I stood outside near a baptismal tank growing moss in the courtyard. A few members were still in the church.

Suddenly, we heard a high-pitched scream. Other voices joined the screaming one, shouting: "Get out! Get out of her in the name of Jesus!"

Joshua and I peeked inside. The pastor held a Bible over the head of a shrieking, writhing woman. The pastor's wife and several others sat behind her, their heads covered, yelling at the spirit to leave.

After a few minutes, the screaming subsided. The pastor escorted us to his house. "My wife will continue praying with her. Please come home."

The deliverance complete, the pastor's wife served us plates heaped with rice and a tart, juicy bean sauce. Joshua and I sat on the floor, said a prayer, and waited for the pastor to be served.

"I won't be eating with you," he said. "My family and I fast on Sabbath."

"Oh?" Joshua asked. "Why is that?"

"Villagers often bring their possessed relatives to church. Jesus said some spirits do not leave without prayer and fasting, so we want to be prepared."

"You mean what happened today is normal?" I asked.

"Well, if you call that normal," the pastor said, grinning. Then he sobered. "Unfortunately, possession is a common problem here."

"We've seen a few possessions, too," I said. "But most of them involved the devta. Is this different?"

"Christians know it isn't different. But to the local people, it's completely different. The devtas are considered good. The spirits who harass people are considered bad."

"Our landlord said something similar," Joshua said. "They want the devta to come, but not 'the evil spirit.'"

"You can ask my wife all about it. She was a Hindu once from this very village."

"Your wife was a Hindu?" Joshua asked. "How did she come to Christ?"

"I was a young man, a brand-new preacher when I was sent to this village. There were no Christians anywhere. I preached my heart out, but only a handful of people accepted. Even though I didn't have many results, I truly loved the people. So I decided to stay. One of the original ladies to accept Christ later became my wife."

"That's so beautiful," I said.

As if on cue, the pastor's wife came in, carrying more food. She had a round, soft face and a pleasant smile. She spooned more rice onto Joshua's plate.

"Eat!" she commanded. "You're too thin!"

"Dear, they are asking how you came to Christ."

"There is no power like God's power," she said, straightening. "You saw Satan in there bothering that lady. The moment the poor thing came in, I sensed she was in chains. But God can make Satan leave. He sets people free."

"My wife has come a long way in her walk with God." The pastor smiled at his wife. "She does more deliverance ministry than I do these days."

"Do the people stay after they are delivered?" Joshua asked. "I mean, do they decide to follow Jesus?"

"Some do," the pastor said. "One thing I tell them before we begin, however. If Christ sets a person free from demons, they must stay close to Him. If the Lord casts out a demon and the person goes right back and bows to an idol and worships in a Hindu temple—I've seen it time and again—they end up worse off than before."

"Like in Jesus's parable," I said. "Jesus said that if you cast a demon out of its 'house' without filling the emptiness, later it would try to come back, bringing others with it."

"Exactly," the pastor said. "We must fill the empty house with God's presence. Then the person is safe. Sometimes people stay close to Jesus and continue coming to church, but often they are summoned to some family ceremony. They bow to an idol, and the demon takes over."

"But why do the ladies yell?" I asked the pastor. "Couldn't they just tell the demon to get out in Jesus' name?"

The pastor leaned forward, examining my face. "Has someone ever broken into your house?"

"No," I admitted.

"Well, imagine someone is breaking into your house. They have no right to be there. Wouldn't you be angry? Wouldn't you yell at them to leave?"

"I suppose I would."

"You'd know what it's like if you had to tell a demon to get out," he said. "You'd be offended that they came in the first place."

We stayed that night in the pastor's house. Joshua and I prayed, then he slept. I lay awake listening to the crickets and the wind and thinking.

Mr. Opee had told Joshua that idols are not gods but the "doorway" of the gods. I thought of 1 Corinthians 10:20, where Paul says that eating food offered to idols is like "partaking of the table of demons." For the first time, I connected that verse with the Bible passage that had originally inspired me to become a missionary, Psalm 115:7-8, where the psalmist says that those who worship idols are just like them.

It dawned on me that idolators are not just blind but blinded. They are not just mute but silenced. They are not only deaf but deceived.

*God, send Your Spirit to set these people free!* I prayed.

# 16

## MAKE ME WILLING

After our return, I relaxed my pride and let Joshua teach me Hindi words he'd learned. But I had my own words to share. Words women used like "hard worker" and "fry onions" and "poor thing."

Mrs. Opee visited every day. She taught me never to put shoes nor brooms upside-down for this has a bad meaning. She taught me not to hand a woman a needle. She said taking a needle out of someone's hand could cause a woman to bear a girl child. This was my first clue that girls in India are unwanted.

Mrs. Opee taught me that Parvata women sweep only in the morning, never the evening, and scolded me if our dishes were left until morning. She drove me crazy and inspired me so that I both loved her and wanted her to go away. I pressed into the discomfort of being told what to do, sensing this was how values were passed on among the Parvata. I was this mountain woman's apprentice.

Bablu's wife Bimla visited too. As I got to know Bablu's family, I noticed that Ama, Tripti, and Nani pecked at Bimla, always finding fault with her. I noticed that the difficulty of being a daughter-in-law was the theme of many a Parvata folk song. But Bimla didn't complain, and though the women pecked, they were helpful, too. They often took Bablu and Bimla's daughter for walks so Bimla could rest.

One such day, Bimla talked with me about childbirth. "Are you scared?"

"Scared of the pain?" I smiled, noticing again how thin Bimla was, almost spindly. But her high cheekbones and thick eyebrows made her beautiful. "A little. What was it like?"

"I just kept pushing on my stomach with my hands and yelling at the baby to get out."

By now I knew pressing on the abdomen to "help" the baby come out faster was common for both Indian women and their midwives. I knew there were other dangerous rituals. Packing the womb with cow manure. Expelling all the colostrum before breastfeeding the baby.

"Anyway," Bimla went on. "You'll find out soon enough what it's like to have a baby. Poor thing!"

I remembered then with a jolt that we still hadn't found a place to actually *have* the baby. Joshua and I took a bus to Chotashaher to search for a suitable hospital. The first was beautiful. An electric bug zapper glowed in the foyer. A woman mopped with a rag on the end of a stick. Better than I had seen in months.

The waiting room for the OB/GYN was empty. We walked into the doctor's office. She smiled, but I didn't like her smile somehow. I dismissed my feelings at first.

"I would like to give birth naturally, if possible," I told her. "What is your policy on medication during labor?"

"We will not give you any pain-saving drugs. You will just have to bear the pain." Her voice sounded almost threatening, and I felt one of my eyebrows raise.

"Okay. Well, I want my husband with me. Can you accommodate?"

She leaned back in her chair and chuckled. "Why do you ask so many questions? You've never even had a baby. You don't know. I'm the doctor, and I know. Just leave everything to me."

We left her office and crossed town. I wanted to check the government hospital. Walking into the large building, I assured Joshua, "It can't be that bad."

The squeak of our shoes and swish of my coat echoed up the stairwell. We walked around the corner, and there it was. I held my breath. Despite it being noon, the only light in the hallway was a bare bulb. There were cots on the floor and lining the hallway. Women lay on the cots. Some moaned. I felt frightened for them. Would they have their babies on the floor? When I asked, I was told they'd be transferred when ready to be delivered.

"I thought it would be like that," Joshua said. "Want to go?"

"Yeah." There was one more hospital to check, a three-story building with the usual rebar and unfinished cement on the back but a beautiful blue glass front. We were shown to the delivery room. The walls were splattered with something. *Could be water stains*, I comforted myself.

Over the stains hung a poster of a cute white baby. One delivery bed, barely padded, sat next to an uneven metal table that held the doctor's tools. I swallowed and followed the doctor upstairs. There was a nursery, a bilirubin light, an oxygen hood. The obstetrician seemed kind and capable, and everyone answered my questions politely. *This will have to do!*

We made arrangements. Joshua put his arm around me as we walked out of the hospital. Then he bought me an ice cream and booked us a taxi home.

As we rode the two hours home from Chotashaher that day, I closed my eyes and went completely internal, wondering about the purpose of pain in childbirth. I had a hard time thinking it was just to be mean that God gave this pain to womankind. *After all, even God's curses were blessings. He gave Adam work to do, so Adam could put his energy into something positive. But what about pain in childbirth?*

*What does it mean, Lord? I prayed. And what will it be like for me? Am I really doing the right thing by having our baby in India?*

I missed my mother. She wouldn't be here to see my first child born, to share this moment with me. I wondered if God noticed my sacrifice. It was small compared to His. But He praised the woman who gave only two coins. Did He notice that I gave the little I had? And would it make any tangible difference for the Parvata people?

I put on my headphones and stared out the window. I felt a sisterhood with Mary, who had changed all her plans for God even when she had no idea what God was doing. Mary, who had to travel to Bethlehem while great with child. Mary, who had her baby in a dirty stable without her mother there to tell her it would be okay. She may not have understood why, but she was willing. Willing to obey God, willing bear the Light of the World "to the people who walk in darkness."

*Make me willing, God,* I prayed.

# 17

## AYUSHI

**B**imla continued to visit, but her visits changed. We would chat for a few minutes. I would offer tea. She would use her cell-phone, speaking rapidly. Then she'd leave almost immediately after her phone call.

One day, Bimla didn't bother with tea. She brushed past me into my kitchen. I could hear her on the phone saying in a pleading, trembling voice, "Please. We're being bad. I want to stop now. This is wrong. I want out."

When she hung up, I peeked my head in the kitchen and told Bimla I was praying for her. She glanced up from her text messages, said thanks, and left.

I suspected Bimla needed help. I knew from Sai, our friend from language school days, that women were sometimes blackmailed after having an affair. I prayed for Bimla and for myself too. If Bimla was calling a boyfriend in my kitchen every day, it could hurt the reputation that gave me access to people's homes and hearts.

Just one week later, Bablu called Joshua to ask us to go on a walk with him. The night was dark and still. We met Bablu on the road and strolled together.

"You can't trust anybody here. Nobody." Running his hands through his hair, Bablu stopped and faced us. "She's gone! She ran off!"

I stopped breathing for a moment. Bimla was gone? But why? Then I thought of Bimla and Bablu's daughter. "What about the baby?"

Though she was a toddler, everyone called her the baby, anyway. Bablu shook his head. "She left her with me. I think she ran off with a guy."

"Bablu, this is a lot for you to process," Joshua said. "If there's anything we can do—"

"Yeah. Do one thing for me."

"What is it?" I asked.

"Don't trust me."

"What do you mean?" Joshua asked.

"You two are different. You are loyal. You are good people. Me? I don't trust the village. I don't trust my family. I don't even trust myself. We're liars, all of us, and cheaters."

We tried to reassure Bablu, but all I remember is how very dark and quiet it was that night and the way Bablu would stop walking and start again. Bimla tried to come back to Bablu a couple of weeks later. But he put her in a taxi and sent her away. He wasn't interested in reconciliation.

Five loaves of bread were enough in Jesus's hands. But I had done so little. I wasn't even sure I had planted a gospel seed in Bimla's life. She knew I was a Christian, and that I prayed for her. But that was it. Now she was gone.

That night, Joshua and I prayed again that God would lead us to someone willing to follow Him.

---

A FEW DAYS LATER, we went to Yog's shop and loaded a rainbow of lentils and beans into Joshua's backpack before taking a shortcut home. Just as we entered Link Road, a screen door banged above my head. Joshua and I glanced up. A young Parvata woman leaned over her porch railing and waved. She wore a tunic over jeans, and thick, straightened hair cascaded over her shoulders. A hint of bronzer shimmered on her cheekbones.

"Hello!" she said in English. "How are you?"

We talked for a few minutes. I expected her to run out of words, but she didn't. She looked about Rose's age.

"Your English is great," I said. "Where did you learn?"

She smiled, trying not to show her teeth, which were slightly crooked but in the cutest way. "I work at an English-medium school. Want to come in? I'm Ayushi, by the way."

Joshua and I climbed the stairs and followed the girl into her house. As Ayushi disappeared into another room to prepare tea, I looked around. A drawing of a tiger hung on a painted yellow wall next to a couple of children's toys on hooks. I leaned over and looked into the next room. There were no pictures of Hindu gods anywhere.

"Tea is served!" Ayushi backed into the room carrying a tray tinkling with cups. Sitting next to me, she told us that she worked as a teacher's aide at a local Christian children's home.

"A Christian children's home?" I asked. "I had no idea there was anything like that in this area!"

"It's run by Christians from eastern India," Ayushi said. "Though not all the teachers are Christian, of course. That's just not possible in this area where there are so few."

"Is it like an orphanage?" I asked.

"It's a boarding school where children from very far away can come to school. Some of those far-off villages have no education system. So they come to learn, and they learn about Jesus, too. Say, are you Christians?"

"Yes, we are."

"That's so nice. How wonderful."

"Are you a Christian?" I asked.

"I'm interested," she said. My heart jolted me into complete attention.

"Oh?"

"My uncle is a Christian, and I like the way he treats his wife." I couldn't believe it. Of a handful of Parvata Christians in the area, God had led us to the village where one of them lived!

The screen door squeaked, and Ayushi's family filed in. There were namastes and hellos all around. Ayushi's sister Leena was quiet, her voice so soft and thin I couldn't hear her greeting. Ayushi's father and brother Arjun shook hands with Joshua. Arjun didn't say much, but his father asked us all the usual questions. Why we were in India. Whether we liked it. Whether we'd had chai. If we would stay for dinner.

Ayushi's mother was also quiet. It seemed everyone was trying to make us comfortable, agreeing with everything we said. Ayushi was different, more outspoken than her family. Yet she fussed over us and obeyed her parents' instructions.

Ayushi's mother pointed to my belly. "When will we hear the good news?"

"Any day now," I said. "My due date is next week."

---

SOME OF OUR angel dispatchers sent us a baby shower in a box. There was a handmade blanket, tiny outfits, hats booties, washcloths, and swaddling clothes. I touched the folded mound of gifts, pastel-colored and soft. Our church family could not be with me. But they had sent their love in that box.

I washed the clothes in our new washing machine and hung them outside on a line to dry. Mrs. Opee warned me to be careful.

"I'm not worried," I answered. "Your dog is watching over the place. And besides, we have plenty of clothes."

"It's not that." Lowering her voice, Mrs. Opee glanced from side to side. "Someone can curse your baby through those clothes. I just know that's why Lovelina isn't close to me anymore."

I glanced down at the courtyard. Lovelina was watering the calf. Chotu must be in the woods with the mother cow. I knew it wasn't a curse that caused Lovelina to roll her eyes at her mother. It was the hypochondria. But Lovelina loved her mother. It was hard not to love Mrs. Opee for she could make you laugh until you couldn't breathe and then oxygen and life were sweeter afterward.

"Our God protects us from curses," I said. "I'm not worried."

Mrs. Opee went to help Lovelina, and I hung another white onesie over the line. A bell began to ring, and I glanced over at the temple. Mr. Opee bowed and rang, rang and bowed. Ajay watched, perched on a stool. Mr. Opee was waking up the family devta for his morning offering.

I smoothed my hand over my belly. Any moment now, the little one could make an appearance. It suddenly felt unreal that I was about to have a baby in India.

*Lord, I know this is a small sacrifice. But please, don't let it be in vain. Use us to plant gospel seeds in someone's heart even now!*

# 18

## THE BIRTH

That Sabbath, Joshua and I walked down to our river to a strip of sand near a thunderous waterfall. The cool mist wafted across the path. Closing my eyes, I let it tingle on my face. We played in the sand, prayed, and sang worship songs. "The Lord is My Light" was my favorite at the time. We ate cheese, bread, and bananas, then read from the Bible.

Back at home, Ajay and Lovelina came to share our "church." They knew most of our Hindi Christian songs by heart now. Worn out, I went to bed early. Sometime in the early morning, I opened my eyes. The baby squirmed for a few moments, presumably trying to stretch.

"Joshua?"

"Mmph."

"My water just broke."

"Mm, okay. Why don't you go back to sleep for a while? You need your rest."

"Yeah, okay," I said.

There was silence. Joshua would later say he hadn't really been awake yet when he answered. But he was now.

"I'm getting up," I said.

"Me too," he said.

We sprang out of bed. I showered and checked the hospital bag. Joshua boiled eggs and counted cash into piles on the kitchen floor. The power kept going out. We lit candles. I was having contractions. Although Mr. Opee was planning on driving us to the hospital in his car, we tried to be quiet as long as possible lest we be distracted from our calm preparations by Mrs. Opee, who could turn anything into a crisis.

Joshua made spaghetti. I walked around. I'd heard labor could take many hours. I called our families on the phone.

"How far apart are your contractions?" Joshua's mother, Mrs. Follows, asked.

"I don't know. I haven't timed them yet," I said. "Oh, here's one."

I leaned over and placed my forehead on the back of our couch. This one was strong. "Okay, it's gone!"

"Abigail, your contractions are only three minutes apart!" Mrs. Follows soon informed me. "You need to get in the car. Is your landlord ready to drive you?"

"Yeah. I mean, we're almost ready to wake him."

I could hear Mrs. Follows relaying what I'd said to Mr. Follows. He grabbed the phone. "Wake up your landlord, Abby!"

"Okay. I will. I'll call you back." Hanging up, I called my mom.

"Is it time?"

"Yeah."

"You're going to do so great. Just breathe."

A wave of longing to hold my mother's hand washed over me with the next contraction. No, I was strong. I could do this. I went to that place in my mind where I could focus completely on the seconds passing. The contractions were waves, and I was swimming in the ocean, going over the waves. They began gently, then increased in intensity until they hit a peak and subsided.

"How far apart are they?" Mom asked.

"About three minutes." I was timing them now. "Sixty seconds long."

"Get in the car!"

Everyone we called told us to get in the car. Didn't they know how long labor takes? It had taken my mother twenty-four hours to deliver me. It would be two hours by car to Chotashaher. That left twenty-two hours for laboring once we arrived. Plenty of time.

"I guess we're ready," I said to Joshua. Another contraction hit. I needed to focus on this one so I paused. "Better wake Mr. Opee."

Awakening Mr. Opee and his wife injected a special excitement into our morning. Mrs. Opee clucked and strutted around me, exclaiming, "You're in pain! You're in pain! Oh my goodness!"

She tried to come with us. I said I needed the whole back seat to lie down.

"See how worried I am for you! I just can't bear to see you in pain!" She talked faster and louder than ever all the way to the car. It was a blessing when the door shut and silence enveloped us.

I focused and Joshua timed. He would later remark that the closer we got to Chotashaher, the faster our landlord drove. Why was everyone in such a hurry? We checked into the hospital. It seemed a hundred nurses surrounded me. They were coming from everywhere, discussing me, the foreigner.

I answered their questions. They made me turn on my back to check the fetal heart rate. I remember only the backs of my eyelids, the waves of pain, and Joshua's voice like a lighthouse bringing me to the other side. "You're almost done with that one. Good job. Rest now. Relax your jaw."

The doctor arrived, looking bored and talking on a cell phone. I glanced up at the adorable baby poster on the wall, the same poster thousands of Indian women had focused on before me. The delivery bed was sparse and narrow, nothing more than a gurney with a hinge in the middle. I was afraid the baby would fall on the floor.

"Push!" The doctor frowning down at me. "You are doing a bad job. Push harder."

"Don't listen to him," Joshua said into my face. "You're doing awesome, and you're almost done."

"I'll do a C-section if the baby isn't born soon," the doctor said.

"Oh, good! Manoj, you're here," one of the nurses said to a young man who had just wandered in. He looked like an orderly. "Take out this trash."

Manoj lingered for a moment at the foot of the bed, holding the trash can, his mouth hanging open. A foreigner was giving birth right in front of him.

"You can do this, Abby," Joshua said. "You're the one doing this, nobody else. You're doing awesome, and the baby is almost here."

I focused past the doctor's voice, past the nurses, past the spattered yellow paint. I closed my eyes and locked onto Joshua's voice.

"It's a girl! You have a baby girl." The doctor placed a small, delicate baby on my belly. I reached out and touched her skin. Then I drew my finger back. She was so small it seemed I might break her.

My mother had told me I wouldn't care who was there, and I didn't. I did what I had to do. Have my baby. In India. She was born after six and a half hours of labor and weighed only five pounds.

I hemorrhaged. The doctor saved my life. The baby needed oxygen. The pediatrician provided it. Soon we were both stable.

"Oh, good," I said as they rolled me, flat on a gurney, to the OB ward. "At least we have a private room."

I looked above our door. There was a hole in the wall between our room and the nurse's station, so it wasn't soundproof, but there was visual privacy. Joshua chuckled.

"If I had saved fifty dollars by getting us one of those cubicles in the general ward, my mother would have killed me." Picking up our precious five-pound bundle, Joshua took a million pictures of her. He measured her big toe and her nose and her delicate wrist. I laughed. "I think they usually just report length and weight."

"Gotta record this," he said, e-mailing the information to his family. "For posterity."

"Can you go get me a pizza?" I asked. "A whole one just for me? I'm starved."

I stared at our daughter for hours. She was so small, so perfect. As I stared, I prayed that God would help us raise her to do what was right no matter what.

Later that afternoon, we made phone calls. Somebody asked me a question I would be asked many times in the years to come: What was it like to have a baby in India?

"God blessed us," I answered, thinking back over my few hours in an Indian delivery room. It hadn't been perfect. But I was alive, and my baby was alive, and what more could I ask for?

As I thought back, I realized something else. All my memories of the birth other than Joshua's words were in Hindi. During labor, I had both spoken and understood Hindi with no translation in my head. I just knew the meaning. It had happened. I was fluent!

# 19

---

# UNSOLICITED ADVICE

The word fluent comes from a Latin word that means flowing. I still had many words to learn. But from that point on, Hindi flowed for me, becoming faster and more natural with every conversation.

We came home from the hospital to absolute silence. We knew we would have only a few days of this. Until the umbilical stump falls off, a Hindu family with a new baby is considered unclean. Nobody visits.

"I told Mrs. Opee about the stump," Joshua said one morning.

"It's probably best," I answered. "They would have found out, eventually."

"Do you think we should have told them the day it actually fell off?"

"Nah. It's not like we waited an extra month. Just a few days." I smiled. Even Joshua wanted a little privacy now.

The screen door slammed. Joshua and I peeked out the door of our bedroom. Mrs. Opee was sprinkling liquid from a brass urn over the kitchen floor. She assured us quickly, "This isn't for you. It's for us! I mean, I know your religion doesn't do this. But if I don't do it, I can't visit you. That means no massages. No help with food. We can't clean your house for you."

I made a mental note to bleach the floors as I knew she'd sprinkled them with a mixture of cow urine and water from the polluted Ganga river. This was to purify our home after the birth of the baby. Before she left, she urged, "Make sure you don't eat fruit. You and the baby could get very sick."

"Oh, really?"

"Yes. By the way, what is her name?"

"Ashi," I said.

"Oh, you gave her an Indian name! And it is so fitting. It means 'blessing.'"

I was not prepared for how birth, death, and every other life event is so community-oriented in India. In the United States, we give each other space. Indians don't want space. They want people.

The Parvata assumed I wanted people, too. And their efforts to make me feel a part of their community *did* warm my heart. Grandma gave me massages. Mrs. Opee taught me how to bathe the baby the Parvata way. Mr. Opee advised me on the best breastfeeding position. He wasn't being rude. All our visitors, even children, told me how to breastfeed. I just smiled and nodded, whether the advice was useful or not. What I really needed was sleep!

---

LOOKING BACK, I don't know why we didn't just buy disposable diapers. Perhaps it was suppressed trauma from the first time Ajay showed us where to dump our trash. The thought of my child's swollen diaper floating on the bank of the river was too much for me.

But the cloth diapers I'd sewn turned out to be useless. Every two hours in the night, I fed the baby, then changed every item of clothing she wore plus her blankets. Change, feed, change. She was always freezing by the time we got her dry. She'd cry while Joshua warmed her on his chest and patted her.

Each morning I'd wash a mountain of laundry. Joshua would hang it out to dry, then bring it back in when it rained, then take it back out once it stopped raining. This routine did not leave a lot of time for sleep.

One night I sat in the darkness, feeding my miracle. Someone had said to enjoy every moment because it doesn't last long. So I was choosing to enjoy not sleeping for enough hours to give anyone a mental condition.

I heard a noise. I looked down at Joshua. He was banging on his chest with his hand. "Uh, Joshua? What are you doing?"

"I'm burping the baby."

"I *have* the baby."

"Oh."

Another time I dreamt Ashi was falling off the bed. I lunged to save her from certain death but woke with my arms around Joshua's waist.

"What are you doing, Abigail?"

"Saving the baby!"

"She's fine. She's on the other side of you."

"Oh."

---

ONE DAY, Joshua came home from visiting the village and found me standing by our closet. I was crying while folding and unfolding tiny pants. "What's wrong?"

"I just love her so much," I wailed.

"Aww, that's nice!" He went on into the kitchen.

I turned to the bundle on the bed, slid my hands underneath, and lifted. Slumped into my hands, limp and trusting, she weighed no more than a small melon. Her eyelashes fluttered, and her mouth puckered. A deep, primal love seized me. *If anyone or anything tries to hurt this child, I will kill them!*

At that moment, it occurred to me. What if I hurt her? She was small and fragile. But damage isn't always physical. What if I said or did something that traumatized my child? What if being a missionary kid damaged her physically, emotionally, or psychologically? What if I was not the perfect mother after all?

My thoughts made me want to lock us all in the house for the rest of our lives. There were so many things I could not control like kidnappers and the government and germs that cause terrible pain.

A special love for my own parents was born in my heart that day. They had loved me and done all they could to give me hope in an imperfect world.

---

I CONTINUED TO RECEIVE ADVICE, which I took personally. My cultural assumptions clashed with theirs. Mine insisted I should know how to parent. People shouldn't tell others what to do. I should have privacy right now. Theirs said we need to remind each other of the best way to do things. If we don't, it's because we don't give a rip about this person. Abigail would be lonely if we weren't in her house all the livelong day.

Once, I was so tired, hormonal, and suspicious that I convinced myself I was on the verge of an irrevocable mental breakdown. I wanted sleep, and I wanted it now. "Joshua, I don't want to go to sleep unless I can stay asleep. If someone wakes me up, I will literally go crazy."

"No problem," Joshua said. "I'll just tell any visitors you're sleeping."

"Good." Crawling into bed, I set my hand on Ashi's chest so that if SIDS (sudden infant death syndrome) tried to get her, I could fight it off. Just as my muscles began to loosen their death grip on my bones, I heard the screen door squeak.

"Abby is sleeping," Joshua whispered.

"No problem. She'll want to see me!" It was the crackly voice of Ama, Bablu's mother. I heard Joshua protest, but it was too late. She was in my room. I could hear her. I tried to look very, very asleep. I breathed deeply. I moved my eyes back and forth under my eyelids to fake REM.

"Namaste!" Bablu's mother shouted. She picked up Ashi. I jerked myself upright in time to see Ashi's head flopped back over the woman's bony fingers.

"You don't hold a baby that way!" I said, grabbing Ashi. "We support the head, okay?"

"You haven't bound your belly," Ama observed. "You must do that. If you don't, your belly will stick out forever."

"Hmm. Well, we don't do that in America, and our bellies are fine."

Joshua stood behind the woman, making a cutting motion on his throat, which I assumed was an indication that I be nice and not a suggestion regarding our guest. I forced myself to smile and say something soothing. Bablu's mom fidgeted. She gave some more advice. Then she left.

*God, I'm so sorry,* I prayed. *I do love Ama. I love all of them. Don't let my impatience hurt Your mission!*

Finally, blessedly, Joshua's parents arrived, bringing commercially produced cloth diapers and prenatal vitamins. After Ashi woke up at six a.m. each morning, they would play with her, take a zillion pictures of her, hold her, and tell her important things. And Joshua and I would sleep.

# 20

## THE DEDICATION

A new mother's duties among the Parvata are as follows. Nurse the baby. Receive massages. Be pestered by visitors. Don't shower for several weeks. Eat only a thick mush made of wheat covered in ghee. Needless to say, I didn't fulfill all my duties!

One of a new baby's family's duties is to perform a *puja* and feed the community, much like they do at a wedding. Everyone brings gifts of clothing and money, often inserting the wadded-up bills in the fist of the newest community member, who dons a black dot on his or her face as protection against the evil eye.

What would Parvata Christians do for their babies one day? Ganga water was out. Puja was out. The Parvata birth party provided spiritual protection and a chance for the community to celebrate and support a growing family. Could we do anything to fulfill those needs?

We announced we would have a baby dedication. Mrs. Opee ordered Chotu to sweep the cow manure from the courtyard. Then she scrubbed the cement on her hands and knees and rinsed it with buckets of water. Lovelina and others came to see the baby. They gave her baths and squeezed her nose to make it "beautiful."

"So what kind of nose isn't beautiful in your culture?" I asked Lovelina. "I mean, what would you *not* want Ashi's nose to look like?"

Lovelina thought for a while. "You know. A nose that's… well, like yours! If your parents had squeezed your nose, it would look much better."

I laughed aloud. Later I would hear you could tell a Brahmin by the shape of her nose. Later that same day, Lovelina got a phone call. She picked it up and spoke rapidly, perhaps thinking I wouldn't understand. "I'll call you back. I'm with my foreigners right now."

I laughed again, and she looked surprised that I understood. Then she laughed, too.

We may have been Lovelina's foreigners, but Ashi was everyone's baby, and they called her Indian even though she didn't have Indian citizenship, but American.

In quiet moments, Mr. and Mrs. Follows passed down their own knowledge about babies and children in a manner more comfortable for me. They'd tell stories of not knowing what they were doing at first. Of trying to get their own babies to sleep or burp or stop crying. Mrs. Follows had a way of accepting and celebrating who people were even when giving advice. She was one of the people on my list of women I admired.

One afternoon, Mr. Opee came over. He smiled, as usual, but I noticed he wrung his hat in his hands.

"Betho," I said.

He sat. "Who are you inviting to the party?"

We described the many people we knew. The guy with the big nose who is always drinking tea at the shop across from the Airtel store. The lady who never married and people-watches from her porch. The three Nepali workers who carry gas cylinders from ropes slung on their foreheads. Our backyard neighbors whose daughter's name meant sky.

Mr. Opee knew all their names and wrote them down on a piece of paper. He held up a finger for us to stop. He seemed to be counting. Then he clicked his tongue. "*Mushkil*! Very difficult!"

"What's wrong?" I asked. "Too many?"

"You've named high and low caste people."

"We want to invite everyone," Joshua said.

"We can't feed low-caste people on our property."

"What about chai?" I asked. "What if we give cookies and chai? I've noticed you give chai to workers, even low-caste ones."

Mr. Opee nodded. "That could work. If it's just snacks and you don't have people sit on the ground together."

"We could set up chairs," I suggested. "Then people can sit as far away from each other as they like."

"It's difficult," he said. "But if you don't feed them rice, it might work."

Activity ramped up in the days before the dedication. I made decorations. Lovelina, Mrs. Opee, and Ajay helped me clean. Joshua's parents cared for Ashi. Ashi slept, unaware of all the fuss over her.

Joshua seemed tired, but he was busy. He booked rental chairs and a sound system. He ordered snacks from the bakery. He interviewed people about Parvata party practices. By Indian standards, we had a small guest list and our party would be small too. But to us, it felt as complex as planning a wedding.

WE ASKED PASTOR THOMAS, an Indian pastor friend we'd met while traveling back through north India after Nepal, to officiate. He and his family arrived the morning of the dedication. We helped them settle in at Rose's homestay.

The tent people came and spread billowing pink fabric over our courtyard. Everyone was coming and going and asking for chai and water and cords to plug things into. Tripti came, her scarf slung over her shoulder and tied in a knot. She prepared tea in the kitchen.

Then it was time. Pastor Thomas is a singer and songwriter, and his wife is too. The sound system filled the village with their music. People put on their newest clothes and came bringing baby sweaters and money. Our Nepali worker friends came, wearing their dusty canvas, cotton, and denim and the characteristic Nepali hat. Their gifts were smiles.

Spotting Rose at the gate in her green suit with the polka-dots, I waved. Squaring her shoulders, she walked through the crowd to me, her arm linked with her mother-in-law's.

"I had to come," she whispered as she hugged me. Then she pressed a green and yellow sweater into my hands.

"I'm so glad you came," I said. "*Betho.*"

Rose straightened and took a deep breath. "We must go. I will come later."

"Okay." I watched Rose drag her mother-in-law back out of the circus of people. I wondered whether caste issues had kept them from staying.

Then it was time to dedicate Ashi to Jesus. She wore a white sweater dress edged in red and a matching cap with a red puffball on the end. The string lights of the tent shone down on her so that she glistened like a little white snowball in the sun. Lifting her, Pastor Thomas closed his eyes and prayed for her complete protection by God and for wisdom for her parents to raise her to love Him.

Then Lovelina and Tripti passed around plates heaped with snacks. Pastor Thomas played his harmonium. Everything smelled, tasted, sounded, and looked Indian. For a moment, I imagined this was the Christian dedication of a Parvata child. Would I ever see that day?

--------

PASTOR THOMAS and his family spent the following morning with us. Neighbors came to see him as they would visit a Hindu priest or a gur.

"I have pain in my side," one woman complained. "Doctors don't know why. I pray to the gods, but it doesn't go away. What should I do?"

Pastor Thomas prayed a long, generous prayer for the woman and every other visitor. My heart thrilled that even a few people were willing to pray to the God of Heaven for their needs. *Surely He must long to bear their griefs and carry their sorrows!*

We also sang together, our house filling with the upside-down trills of Indian worship music. We harmonized. Everyone smiled at each other.

Then Pastor Thomas and his family expressed they'd like to tour the higher mountains the next day. Joshua said he'd take them. Everyone dispersed to rest. Joshua slumped next to me on the couch and stared straight ahead.

*He must be tired to sit like that. Wait a minute!*

"Joshua, look at me," I commanded. "Are you feeling okay?"

Joshua turned his head towards me. "I'm tired. And my stomach has been bothering me."

I squinted at Joshua's face. "Stick out your tongue."

He did so.

"Joshua, you're yellow. You're jaundiced!"

21

# MEDICAL EVACUATION

$S$ ix hours, three hospitals, and two cat scans later, Joshua had a diagnosis—a hydatid cyst on his liver. Scrolling through a webpage, I discovered this was the egg sack of a specific tapeworm that can incubate in the sack for up to several years. The sack can burst, causing instant anaphylaxis. Or it can multiply, sending new cysts to nestle into the lungs or brain.

Instead of going up the mountain with the Thomas family, Joshua was immediately put on a heavy dose of anti-parasite medication and advised to schedule surgery as soon as possible. I joined him where he lay on the couch, a laptop on his chest.

"Let's go home," I said. "We were planning to get a business visa soon anyway, and we can only do that from the States."

"Maybe we should."

Looking at the laptop on his chest, I saw he was already booking tickets. Mr. and Mrs. Follows helped us prepare the house to be closed up. Pastor Thomas and his family prayed for us and left. We set a departure date for three days later.

Shortly after, I noticed a pustule on Ashi's arm. I put ointment and a Band-Aid on it. By evening, the bumps covered her body. I showed Mrs. Follows.

"Could be impetigo. But where would she get that?"

"Maybe someone at the party?" I frowned at Ashi's sores. "I'll look it up."

We put Ashi through a series of charcoal poultices and mild iodine baths. But nothing helped. What follows in my memory is a hurricane of images. Ayushi came to say goodbye, looking sad as though we weren't coming back. Rose brought a bag of oranges as a farewell gift.

Mr. and Mrs. Follows accompanied us on the drive out of the mountains and took their own flight home. We got an emergency passport for the baby but were told we needed a special stamp to take her out of the country. We arrived late in the day at the government office that offered the stamp. The guard wouldn't let us in.

"Please!" I begged, bouncing my sweating baby. "It's still one minute until closing time, and they are still processing visas. My husband is sick! He needs an operation." I felt my voice waver. Joshua sat on a bench with his head in his hands.

"Come back tomorrow," the guard barked.

I closed my eyes and prayed. Just then, a stocky Indian man in a suit and tie strode out of the office. Approaching me, he asked, "What's the matter, madam? Did something happen?"

"This man won't let me in," I said, pointing to the guard. "Our flight is tomorrow morning, and my husband is very ill."

The businessman walked over to the guard. "How can you keep her out? Look at her! You made her cry. She's a guest in our country. Let her in!"

"Please," I begged, swiping at my tears. "Let me in!"

The guard's jaw was clenched, but I saw a hint of shame in his eyes. The businessman stared up at him. "Are you going to let this dear woman in or not?"

"Go on," the guard whispered. He opened the door for me.

"Dhanyavad, sir," I whispered back to the guard. "Thank you, brother," I said to the businessman. *And thank You, God.*

---

A FEW WEEKS LATER, Joshua and I sat in a surgeon's consultation room. The surgeon was saying something, but I was busy imagining my husband unconscious on the desk between us. Abdomen slit open. Heart monitor beeping. Surgeon removing part of his liver. Would the cyst on his liver burst? I held baby Ashi, who gripped a lock of my hair in her fist. My heart felt like a stone dropped into water.

"If we remove the cyst, his liver could fail," the doctor said. "If we don't, he could die."

"Have you had a case like this before?" I asked.

The doctor shifted in his chair. "This condition isn't common in the United States. I've never seen it. My specialty is oncological surgery. Tumors. Cancers. I had to read up on this one. The procedure is quite involved."

I hoped he hadn't read about it on some random website as I had. Joshua and I looked at each other, then Joshua rose to his feet. "We'll think about it for a few days. I feel like we need to pray."

We prayed. We also took Ashi to a pediatrician for her sores, which hadn't gone away. Tests revealed no infection, neither internal nor in the sores themselves. Allergens were eliminated, both edible and topical. But nothing we tried helped.

What began as a red dot on Ashi's face grew into a tight network of pustules that almost covered her cheek. Soon I realized I sometimes frowned at that spot, willing it to disappear. I didn't want the image of me frowning at Ashi to be burned into her subconscious. So I only let myself do it while she slept.

We were staying with Joshua's parents. One evening, as I tried not to look at the pustules, someone knocked at their door. It was a couple from the Follows' church. They joined us in the living room, and we made small talk for a while.

"We know you've been praying," the wife said. "But sometimes things like this can be spiritual. An attack from the enemy. I mean, maybe it's not, but if it is . . ."

Leaning forward, the husband finished for her. "We came to pray for Joshua and the baby."

Joshua knelt on the carpet with Ashi on his lap. Joshua's parents, our new angel dispatchers, and I knelt around my husband and daughter. Joshua's brothers joined us via Skype. Placing our hands on Joshua and Ashi, we prayed that God would heal them.

But though I prayed, I wondered. Why was Satan allowed to harm us? Hadn't I told our Indian friends that God would protect our child?

A week later, Ashi's sores disappeared. They just faded away like the night gives way to the morning.

---

JOSHUA RESEARCHED how to get a business visa. We prayed for it, and so did our angel dispatchers. Meanwhile, Joshua took a handful of chemo pills every day. This would prevent anaphylaxis should the cyst burst, but the medication changed him. He was forgetful. We argued more.

"Are we here because we don't deserve to be missionaries?" Joshua asked.

We both felt that way. Like we'd failed. Like God had removed us from the mission field. Despite our efforts at perfection, we'd been selfish and hurt each other. Some days we'd wanted to leave. Cognitive dissonance plagued us. We examined our hearts, talking and praying about how to make it better.

One day we squabbled over something. Maybe the baby toys we'd been given. Joshua thought it was too much stuff, but I felt blessed. Suddenly, I realized how badly I wanted to win the argument.

*If you want to win, you can't win.* The thought was loud as though God had spoken. The realization seemed obvious yet revolutionary. Only one person can win. We could either both keep trying to win over each other or die to ourselves and win together as a unit. I knew I couldn't choose Joshua's actions. But I could choose mine. I cringed. It is hard to die to yourself when you are the only one.

I let my voice soften, and asked questions, though I felt vulnerable and squashable. As though one thought had entered both our minds, Joshua did the same. We didn't avoid the disagreement, and we didn't blow up. We talked and talked until we figured things out. We ended with prayer and a plan.

Everything was going to be okay.

---

JOSHUA'S PHONE RANG. I looked at the caller ID: It was Lars.

"Joshua, Lars is calling!"

Lars and Joshua had grown up together. For many months, we'd been telling Lars and his wife Kay they should apply to be our partners in India. As I listened to Joshua's side of the conversation, I thought back to the first time I had met Kay. Joshua and I were newlyweds fresh out of college, and Kay and Lars were recently engaged. They visited us for lunch one Sabbath afternoon.

It was hot outside. We decided to float down a nearby river on truck inner tubes. Lars and Joshua, each on separate inner tubes, finished their float without incident, swimming to shore right before running into a barbed-wire fence stretched across the river. But the inner tube Kay and I floated on deflated. I thought we'd end up dead or mutilated as the current dragged us toward the barbed wire fence.

Somehow, we made it to shore before being dashed upon the wire. As we climbed out of the water, Kay stood up, wrung out her curly hair, and said with a laugh, "That was a good memory!"

I smiled now as I thought about the incident. Not only was Kay a positive person but Lars and Joshua were always there for each other. Lars often called Joshua to ask how his relationship with God was going. I wanted people like Lars and Kay with us in India.

"I'll let her know." Joshua turned to me with a big smile.

"Do we have partners?" I asked hopefully.

"Yes! They applied and were accepted. Lars and Kay are coming to India!" It would take Lars and Kay some time to fundraise, and they'd attend three months of training as we had. But Lord willing, we'd soon have partners in Kushigaun.

Later, Lars called again to ask Joshua how he was feeling. "Why not try the Mayo Clinic in Minnesota? A friend of mine is a doctor there."

"I don't know," Joshua responded. "We're tired of second opinions. Honestly, I'm tempted to go for the surgery just to get it over with."

"It's different out there," Lars explained. "Each case has a team of doctors working together. Maybe there's something the others haven't thought of."

"You think it would be worth our time?"

"Absolutely. Want me to call my friend?"

"Okay. Yeah, that would be great."

Lars called his friend, and his friend arranged a place for us to stay near the Mayo Clinic. It was nearing Christmas when we arrived in Minnesota. The airport sparkled with lights, giant wreaths, and red sashes. Strapping Ashi into her baby backpack, we strolled downtown to see the Christmas lights. Ashi leaned her head back and stared wide-eyed at the twinkling lights and ice statues.

Joshua reached out and took my hand. I took a deep breath and sighed happily. I had no idea what was going to happen, but today we were both alive and together.

---

MAYO CLINIC IS JUST like heaven—if people in heaven have cancer, genetic mutations, and rare forms of eczema. Maybe the entrance to heaven is like the

Mayo Clinic. Maybe we'll all fly there and be shown into a golden palace full of plants and picture windows where everyone will care and listen and work together to heal what hurts. I imagined someone going in to see Jesus. Jesus healing their depression or diabetes. Jesus answering all their questions, like He had all the time in the world.

*If only my Parvata friends could meet doctors like this,* I thought. But my Parvata friends were part of an assembly line. Their doctors were so overworked they barely had time to sleep or eat.

One of our Mayo Clinic doctors was from India. She had experience with hydatid cysts, which were rampant in India's agricultural areas. She told us she could do the surgery laparoscopically with only a small incision. "I've done it many times. There are ways to ensure it's perfectly safe. However, surgery may not be strictly necessary."

"Wait!" I exclaimed. "I thought this thing was going to explode and kill Joshua at any moment. What do you mean, surgery isn't necessary?"

"I'm not convinced it is hydatid," she said. "It could be a simple cyst. Either way, your body is calcifying it. In other words, whatever it is, it's dying. I think if you monitor it for the next five years, you can safely avoid surgery."

"Can I get off these meds?" Joshua asked.

The doctor smiled. "Yes, you can stop the medication."

On our walk that afternoon, I noticed everything. The warmth of Joshua's hand in mine. The winter birds creating a breeze in the park with their wings. The way the air tingled as I gathered it deep into my lungs.

Just a week after Joshua stopped the medication, his mom and I were doing dishes in her kitchen. Joshua bounced in with a big grin and grabbed a banana off the counter. "This looks appealing!"

"Joshua's back!" Mrs. Follows and I chorused. We hugged each other and laughed.

---

JOSHUA CONTINUED TRYING to secure a business visa. He did paperwork, researched existing businesses, and made phone calls.

A friend we'd gone to college with now owned a business that arranged tours in exotic locations. Would he be interested in having Joshua lead a few tours each summer? He was interested and soon filled out the necessary paperwork to prove to the Indian government that Joshua had a legitimate business purpose in the country.

Six months after we'd returned to the United States, I found a thick packet in our mailbox. I couldn't wait for Joshua; I had to know. I tore into the package and held my breath. Among the contents was Joshua's passport, and there in the middle was an official Indian government sticker.

"Visa Type: Business," it read. "Duration: Ten Years."

# 22

## TEMPLE MONEY

F lights to Chotashaher were expensive and unreliable, so we usually traveled more than fifteen hours by bus to get home from the Delhi airport. This time, however, Joshua volunteered to take our stuff on an overnight bus so Ashi and I could fly.

My heart thrilled as I stared at the Parvata project site from above. The hills rose up in mounds of emerald and sea green. In the valleys, rivers shimmered like silver handwriting. Villages, reachable only by foot, spattered over the mountains. I prayed that one day Indian Christians would walk to those villages and tell their people about Jesus.

*If we don't get kicked out,* I thought. While we were stateside, a friend and his wife had fundraised to launch as missionaries to South India. They'd planned their upcoming mission service for months, scouting locations, praying. They weren't with our organization, but like us, they'd planned on long-term service.

A few days before their launch, the couple had posted about their mission on Facebook. Within two hours, they received multiple prison and death threats. They were forced to abandon their plans. They wouldn't be coming to India after all.

I looked down at Ashi, who slept on my lap. She'd grown chubbier and had just a hint of curly-blonde hair. I looked again at the Himalayan foothills.

*God, how are we to balance all this? If we get kicked out too early, we won't be able to tell anyone about You. But if we are too afraid to share, nobody will hear anyway. Show us how to be bold without getting kicked out. Show us who is interested. Make us wise as serpents and harmless as doves.*

Joshua met me in Chotashaher, and we traveled the remaining two hours by road to Kushigaun together. When we arrived at the Opee compound, their dog barked and jumped and sniffed Ashi. She made happy noises at the dog, and he ran around us a few times before lying down next to our luggage.

The sweet, tangy scent of milled pine hung in the air. Everyone gathered, smiling and talking. Then Mr. Opee took us to the backyard to see his building project.

"Wow," Joshua said, looking up. "It's... a temple."

"A beauty, isn't it?" Mr. Opee said.

"It's... very big," I said. The new temple was three times as tall as the old one. The walls were covered in carvings of Hindu gods and goddesses. A man sat on the ground next to the temple, using a chisel to carve a picture of Hanuman, the monkey-like god, into a slab of wood.

"It's almost complete," Mr. Opee said. "My friend here is just finishing up the door."

"Namaste," we greeted the man. I realized with a sinking feeling that idolatry is not just a social practice. It's not just religious. Idolatry is part of the economy, too. What would happen if the entire country of India turned to Christ? What work would the idol-carvers have? The priests?

The angels who appeared to the shepherds at Jesus's birth sang of peace on earth. But Jesus Himself said that He came not to bring peace but a sword. He came to give us peace in the midst of dying to ourselves and starting over. Following Christ destroys our pride and threatens our self-image and our livelihood. I knew it was worth the cost. But how could we tell that to the Parvata? Had we really given up anything of value for Jesus?

We entered our apartment. I'd forgotten its smell of uncured cement and mold. I opened the windows. That afternoon, Joshua and I bleached everything.

"You know," I said as I wiped down a wall, "Mr. Opee built that temple with our rent money."

"I know," Joshua said. We were interrupted by a new scent, minty and sweet and putrid. Marijuana.

"Smells like our neighbor is back," I said. An Italian man who enjoyed and trafficked in Indian cannabis rented the apartment next to ours.

"Mr. Opee said he never stays for long," Joshua reassured me.

---

ON OUR FIRST Sabbath back in Kushigaun, we walked to the bridge and looked out at the river that had inspired *The Himalaya Song*. What had been a massive, crashing flow of water was now thin and sluggish.

"What happened here?" I asked.

Joshua sighed. "Yog said they finished a hydroelectric power project further upstream. He tried to stop the project because he knew it would be bad for the environment. But the power company paid off everyone who supported his efforts. Everyone who owns land in our village got a cut. I guess this is what's left of the water."

"Look at all the trash," I said. From her baby carrier on my back, Ashi leaned out to look where I'd pointed. The riverbanks were covered in old shoes, broken cups, papers, diapers, and other trash.

"We already knew people throw their trash in the rivers," Joshua responded. "We just couldn't see it before."

But at least the mountains were still beautiful, golden and red and green in the spring sunshine. In a few short months, the snow would bring out their texture.

"I want to get out this summer," Joshua said one day. "Before the snow. Let's go camping."

So one weekend, we did. The foothills around Kushigaun are red-packed dirt studded with giant evergreens. We hiked through the trees, got temporarily lost, then bushwhacked our way through a swath of grass.

After a boulder field, we came to a clearing. A wisp of smoke rose from a fire. Next to the fire sat a multi-room tent made of yellow tarps and sticks. The camp had been set up by Grandma Opee and the boy-servant Chotu. They would stay in the clearing for several weeks to let the cows fatten on the mountain grasses.

Grandma looked surprised to see us but also pleased. We'd known they were there and had only stopped to say hi. But Grandma insisted we stay, so we bedded down on the soft, bare earth, tucking Ashi's legs into the arms of a down jacket and falling asleep to the white noise of cicadas.

In the morning, Grandma went to gather sticks for the fire. I eavesdropped on Joshua and Chotu. "Ajay said you're from Bihar. How did you end up here?"

"A woman came to our town. She promised a bunch of us kids we could eat apples and wouldn't have to go to school. I didn't like school." Chotu stirred sugar into a pot of steaming chai. "The woman said I'd work for three years, make some money for my family, and get to eat apples. So my parents let me go."

"You got your apples," Joshua observed.

"Now that I know how much work apples mean, I don't care if I ever eat another," Chotu said. "I've worked hard these three years and had my fill."

"So your time is almost up?"

"It's been up for a few months. My brothers came twice while you were away. It's expensive to come too, but Ajay's family wasn't ready to pay me yet."

I thought about the giant temple in our backyard. There couldn't be enough money left over to pay Chotu. Besides, why would the Opees want him to leave? There was grass to cut, milk to haul, and cows to water. Ajay and Lovelina were occupied with school and friends.

Chotu poured the creamy, brown chai into tin cups. Grandma was back, cooking breakfast over a fire. The steam from her aluminum pot dispersed into the air. Above our heads, evergreens pointed to the sky. I glanced back at Chotu, who still hadn't made eye contact.

*He's stuck,* I thought. *Having his money means they get to decide how long he keeps working for them.*

After breakfast, we left Grandma and Chotu to continue our hike. We met a shepherd, and he and his boisterous friends watched over our tent, protecting us that night as we camped between rows of wildflowers. When we awoke the next morning, the shepherds and their flocks were gone. After praying for the Parvata from thirteen thousand feet, we went home.

# 23

## HOW TO WANT SOMETHING YOU JUST DON'T

Ashi was crawling now, putting everything in her mouth. I once found her rolling something around on her tongue. Holding my hand under her chin, I commanded, "Spit it out for Mommy."

"Pthht!" she spat. Out came a fat, dead fly. I glanced out the window. Outside in the courtyard, I saw three cows and a goat. As if on cue, the goat let out a cry. He sounded just like a person pretending to be a goat.

It felt like this was a zoo and we were the animals on display. Our species was "foreigner," and we were constantly watched and commented on. My parenting, cooking, everything was up for discussion. I tried not to pressure Joshua about finding a new home, but it slipped out like steam from a pressure cooker.

"We should move."

"To where?"

"Somewhere that isn't three hundred and fifty square feet. Somewhere with windows that aren't blocked by buildings. Somewhere without an Italian drug-smuggling neighbor."

"I've been looking and haven't found anything that isn't way out of our price range."

"Let's ask God for a house."

"We can ask," Joshua said as though God might say no.

I called Mrs. Follows. She suggested, "Write down what you want in a house. Make your lists separately and compare notes. When you visit a place, pray first. Before you talk about it, pray again. God will guide you."

Joshua and I wrote our lists. I wanted two bedrooms—one for us, one for the baby—and a living room. I wanted an indoor toilet. I wrote bathtub on my list too, but with a star by it to remind God and myself that this was optional.

We saw a lot of places, most of them empty cement blocks. But one sounded perfect. We went to see it. The house still needed painting, but in my mind, I was already moving in. I imagined where I'd put our things. I mentally hung our curtains in the windows.

As we left, I said to Joshua, "I guess we should pray before we talk."

We did. Then I asked, "Anything?"

Joshua hesitated. "I think it would be okay with God if we moved into that house. But my impression is that if we trust Him and wait another year, He has a better plan. I feel there's more work for us to do in our current place."

"I thought the same thing." Even as I said the words, I felt my heart sink. That night back in our tiny apartment, I lay awake a long time, trying to pray, trying not to think about how logical it would be to move. The balcony to our apartment was high off the ground with no railing. Sometimes the courtyard streamed with cow urine. Where would Ashi play?

I longed to have room for a kitchen table. Room to host people. I longed to fill our home with laughter and friendship. I was tired of playing house. I wanted to be normal. Why did I care so much? If only I could take off my frustration like a too-tight sweater and throw it away. *God, how do I want something that I just don't?*

As though someone had flipped on a projector, an image appeared in my mind. It was Lovelina. She wore no makeup nor jewelry. No slick, black kajal lined her eyes. No black dot warded off the evil eye. She wore no bindi, and no iridescent eyeshadow sparkled on her lids. Yet her face shone. She wore a white robe, and all around her glowed a white light.

I saw her look up and laugh. Two hands placed a golden crown on her head. It was a question in a picture. *Is it worth it for her?*

*Yes, Lord,* I answered, crying tears of joy. *It's worth it for her!*

---

THE NEXT MORNING, I had a plan. We'd ask our landlords to remove their furniture. Then we'd line the larger room with floor mats. In the daytime, guests could sit around the perimeter of the room. At night, Joshua and I would drag the mats to the middle of the floor to make ourselves a bed. We'd keep our metal lockers against a wall and stash our blankets every morning just as Indians did.

We'd make the small room Ashi's bedroom. She could nap and play there undisturbed. There was more light in that room too, which meant less mold.

It worked. Joshua had a crib made. He bought a desk, and a couple of shelves, one for shoes and one for food. Yog saved his empty candy jars for us, and we filled these with our pantry staples: flour, pinto beans, red dahl, split peas, brown dahl, sugar, baking soda. They looked cute on the new shelf, all lined up with their matching red lids.

Shortly after, Ajay's grandmother stopped by. Heaving herself onto a floor mat, she called to Ashi. Ashi crawled over and plopped into her lap. There she sat, playing with the silver chain that kept Grandma's patu dress from falling off her shoulders. Grandma laughed and tickled Ashi under her chin. "You're happy with me, daughter."

Ashi grinned and patted the old, wrinkled hand. Grandma turned to Joshua. "You've done well for your family. When you came, you had nothing. But now look at you. Everyone has enough clothing. Your kitchen is set up so Abigail can cook. You have a little girl now. You've provided well for your family. I'm proud of you, son."

Joshua and I glanced at each other. For so long, we'd avoided purchasing anything lest we look rich and unapproachable. Now here was Grandma telling us that buying things didn't make us look unapproachable but responsible. Another confirmation that our home was as important as our field.

"God is good," Joshua said. "He provides."

"You've done well," Grandma repeated, nodding. "It is the will of the gods."

---

WE LOVED GOING ON WALKS, though it took some time to actually exit the village. There were hands to shake and grandmas to ask about. Everyone wanted to hold the baby. I smiled. Ashi babbled and grinned with her two teeth. Eventually, we'd be on our walk again and I could breathe. I loved the way people took the time to stop and chat, the way everyone felt connected. But being in India also reminded me I'd never want to be famous.

Sometimes on our walks, we saw shepherds leading hundreds of sheep and goats to greener pastures. Ashi and I laughed at the sheep, so innocent and curious, so easily distracted. They saw potential friends everywhere—dogs, people, passing cars.

One day, I looked up at the mountains and tried not to notice the blur of trash in my lower peripheral. As I did so, I noticed two men striding towards us on the road.

"Do you know them?" I asked Joshua.

"No. Looks like they're in a hurry, though."

The men soon reached us. "Who are you? Where are your passports? Where are you staying?"

"Who are you?" Joshua asked. "Why should we tell you who we are?"

"I'm the chief of police," one man said, puffing out his chest. "Where is your passport?"

"How do we know you are officers?" Joshua asked. "You're not even in uniform."

"We're undercover," the other man said, stepping closer. "Give us your passports."

"Prove you're with the police." Bouncing Ashi, I backed up a step. "We have to think about our safety."

"Here's my badge," the chief said.

Taking it, Joshua looked at me. "It's real."

"Of course it's real!" the man bellowed. "Now hand over your passports!"

"We don't carry them with us," Joshua said. "What if they were stolen?"

"It's the law to carry your passports with you everywhere you go! Where do you live? Why are you in India?"

We brought the men to our house and seated them in the living room.

"Chai?" I offered.

"No!" the chief replied.

*How rude*, I thought to myself.

"We'll take your husband to jail," one of them said.

"What did he do?" I asked.

"That's for us to discover!"

"We've broken no law."

"We'll see."

Ajay came into the apartment. I spoke to him, hoping the police heard me. "They're nothing but bullies. They should be ashamed!"

"Be quiet," one of the men shouted at Joshua. "We do the talking. We have the right to arrest you any time we want!"

Just when things were about to boil over, Mr. Opee arrived. He sauntered in the door and told everyone to relax. I could see he *recognized the* police officers. They sputtered out their complaint, sometimes yelling at Mr. Opee, who stayed calm and diplomatic.

Gradually, the conversation slowed, the voices sweetened. The police shook Joshua's hand, laughed, and told him to fill out a registration form. Then everyone left.

After this, any time the chief of police saw Joshua, he would shake his hand and pat him on the back. Once, he told a bystander he knew Joshua.

"He's with the CIA," he whispered with a nudge and a wink.

# 24

## WHAT IF?

Ayushi's family were the kind of people who apologized for a magazine on a table or a jacket on the back of a chair. But they were gracious with their space, always bringing out something for Ashi to play with. Ayushi's house became my second home.

This day, Ashi sat on the big bed that doubled as a couch, talking baby talk to a stuffed deer and hanging bangles on its horns. As Ayushi and I watched her, Ayushi spoke up. "I meant what I said before. That I want to be a Christian."

"That's wonderful," I said. "I know it's not an easy choice."

"No, it won't be easy. Especially if my family doesn't join me. They're supportive of my choice. My mom is even a little interested. But my dad has responsibilities to my grandparents." Ayushi took a deep breath and looked at me. "I want someone to give me Bible studies. I asked the teachers, but they haven't done it."

"I'd be honored to do Bible studies with you." This was the second time Ayushi had asked me. I'd hesitated as I hadn't wanted to overstep any bounds with her colleagues at the Christian school. But maybe they didn't have time for her request. "When do you want to start?"

"Next week."

---

MANY PARVATA FAMILIES made us their own, even assigning us relationships. I was many people's paternal or maternal aunt, sister, and especially bhabi, or older brother's wife. Soon our lives resembled one long, fun, slightly dysfunctional family reunion. It was rather like the movie *My Big Fat Greek Wedding* with all the love, laughter, and problems of a large, extroverted extended family. We were often introduced to visiting family members. Once, Mrs. Opee's brother came to visit. Ajay was beside himself.

"He's here! He's here! Shankar Uncle is here!" Ajay bounced on my exercise ball. "You'll love him!"

Before I could respond, Shankar pushed open our screen door. He was tall with a long face and sleepy-looking eyes. He shook hands with Joshua while watching me with a flirtatious smirk. I busied myself with Ashi.

After introductions, Shankar told me all about his various girlfriends. I tried to glue myself to Joshua's side lest he get the idea that I was a potential. Eventually, Ajay dragged Joshua into the kitchen to see something and Ashi crawled after them, leaving me standing in the middle of the living room with Shankar.

"I heard your sister mention your wedding," I tried to make small talk. "When's the big day?"

"Never."

"Oh?"

"I have a problem, see?" Shankar leaned down towards me and lowered his voice. "I'm sure you know about caste. Well, my true love is of a different caste. So we can never get married."

I took a step back from him. "How sad. Is there no way to make an exception?"

"None. Impossible."

"Then why are you dating her?"

"Because I love her!" Shankar smiled down at me, examining my face. A little too closely.

"Hmm," I said, backing up again. "Well, good luck."

"Of course, I'll have to get married eventually. Though I don't want to. I'm betrothed, actually."

"Interesting. What's she like?"

"I don't know. Our parents betrothed us when we were kids. She seems all right. Can't compare to my girlfriend."

I tried to hide my disgust. Shankar smirked as though enjoying my discomfort. "She keeps pressuring me to marry her already. I just want to forget that little obligation."

"Hmm. Well, you could let her marry someone who actually loves her. Might be nice to be married to someone who isn't always dreaming about someone else."

"I've thought about that." He shrugged. "Not a lot I can do. Anyway, I'm more into politics than relationships. I keep busy working to end corruption in India. It's a big problem, you know. Probably the biggest problem is that ordinary people don't recognize their contribution."

Now, this sounded interesting! But just then, Mrs. Opee walked in. Shankar greeted his sister, then left to talk with Joshua.

Mrs. Opee was always telling interesting stories about her family history. Today, prompted by the visit of her brother, she'd already told nine and a half of them. Now she held out her hand, as though cradling something.

"When Ajay was born, he could fit in my hand. He looked just like a little mouse. The nurse threw him in a garbage can, but an American doctor intervened. Dr. Sue said to wait and see. That saved my son's life. I'll never forget the first sound he made—just a squeak like a mouse. Dr. Sue is a Christian like you and Joshua."

Ajay emerged from the kitchen. He was twelve now and sported a peach-fuzz mustache on his upper lip.

"Now look how fat he is!" Mrs. Opee boasted. Ajay grinned.

"I think God saved you for a reason, Ajay," I said.

"It was to meet my big brother Joshua," he replied. "And you, Bhabi!"

"Yes. I think it was," I said.

I'd noticed Ajay's greatest interest in life—other than bicycles and trying to get us to let him use Facebook on our computer—was the spiritual life of his father. I saw how he watched his father perform the *puja* rituals, absorbing every movement. Each flick of a finger was meaningful in Hindu rituals.

Ajay was curious about our spiritual lives, too. Often as we waited for the pressure cooker to stop whistling, Ajay was there. Some weeks he ate with us every night. We had discussions on everything from caste to Christ. Sometimes he plopped down in the middle of our family circle as we sang Ashi to sleep.

"In a year, I won't eat with you anymore," Ajay told me once, his mouth full of rice. "I'll become a priest like my dad. Then I can only eat what my immediate family cooks."

"I will cry," I told him.

We learned that Ajay would one day have a string tied around his chest. This string, called *janeo*, would bind him to all the responsibilities of a Hindu priest. He would go away to school to learn the ritual prayers and songs. When he returned, he would not eat in our home anymore. He would not even accept water.

As I prayed for Ajay, crazy thoughts crept into my mind. What if Ajay was the next Abraham? What if God commanded him to leave his idol-worshipping family to testify of His love and grace in remote mountain villages?

What if Ajay was the next Gideon? What if God came to him in a dream and told him to tear down his father's temple?

What if Ajay, son of a Hindu priest, didn't get the string tied around his chest next year? What if instead, he became the first Parvata pastor?

# 25

## CHOTU'S GOODBYE

Chotu's brothers arrived, both adult men, one old enough to be his father. They stood with arms folded arguing with Mr. Opee and wouldn't accept an offer of chai.

"Come, Chotu," Joshua said. "Ajay says you've never been to Pahargaun. You have to see it before you go."

Joshua took Chotu and Ajay on the bus to Pahargaun. Chotu came back with two sets of new clothes, a backpack, and a picture of himself with a giant angora rabbit. The next day, Chotu returned to washing dishes, scrubbing floors, and milking cows. Meanwhile, his brothers pressured Mr. Opee about his promised earnings.

"Look how bad these people are, not paying their worker!" they said to us.

"Look how unreasonable they are," Mr. Opee told us. "They didn't even call first!"

"Maybe we should go on a walk," Joshua whispered to me. We walked up the hill, stopping to chat with a few people, and ate our lunch atop a giant boulder. The air was moist and clean after a recent rain. We talked about Joshua's trip to Pahargaun with the boys.

"Thanks for putting a little pressure on Mrs. Opee," Joshua said. "She would never have let him go otherwise."

"I guess I'm learning the rules to the 'shame game,'" I said. "All I had to do was ask if they'd ever taken him to Pahargaun, and she gave him permission."

"It worked like a charm," Joshua agreed. "Hey, did I tell you about the mob?"

"There was a mob?"

"They were beating up a couple of guys in Pahargaun. The two of them escaped just as we arrived."

"What happened?"

"I started telling Ajay and Chotu what Jesus said about turning the other cheek and being kind to your enemies. I guess the mob heard me because it got really quiet all of a sudden."

"Whoa! Were you scared? How did they react?"

"I was pretty surprised when they all started nodding. In fact, one guy said, 'Jesus was right. If we always retaliate, the fights will never end.'"

Just then, Joshua's phone rang. "It's Chotu."

I leaned in close to hear Chotu's voice. "I'm leaving and fast. Come quickly, *Bhaia*, my brother."

We ran down the hill, Ashi bouncing in Joshua's arms. When we arrived, Chotu did something he'd never done before. He followed us inside our house. His hands trembled.

"I've worked so hard for them. Three years! Now they're saying I didn't work hard enough. They're sending me away with no money!"

Chotu broke down in tears. Joshua drew him close for a hug. Then Chotu pulled away. "I have to hurry."

Taking his new backpack into our bathroom, Chotu changed out of his blue sweatshirt and dirty jeans into his new clothes. Anger welled up in me, burning my throat. Were we trying to share salvation with such pitiless people?

"Oh, God," Joshua prayed aloud. "How can we bless Chotu? And how can we bless this family without condoning their actions?"

We said amen and looked at one another. Then I exclaimed, "The offering!"

"I thought the same thing." Joshua dug the offering we'd received in Thailand out of a desk drawer and counted it. With a little extra from us, it totaled three hundred dollars, exactly the amount Opee's family owed Chotu. Joshua pressed the money into Chotu's hand.

Chotu shoved the bundle deep into his backpack. Then he straightened, searching Joshua's face. "You've helped me so much. Why?"

"Someone helped me once. He helped me so much that I can't pay him back. So I'm helping you."

"I will help someone for you too."

We emerged from the house. Opee's family crowded around. Mrs. Opee pleaded, "Don't go, Chotu. Just wait a few more months and we'll give you all the money we owe you. Besides, it's not like you were overworked here. We didn't give you too much work. Right, Abigail?"

Instead of answering, I found something interesting to examine on the ground. With a laugh, Mrs. Opee tried to make it all a joke. "We would have given you a going-away party. Why do you have to leave like this? But we can't force you."

Chotu blinked. Then he looked up, making full eye contact with Joshua and me. "Goodbye, Bhaia. Goodbye, Bhabi."

Bending over, he touched his hand to our feet and then to his heart. Recognizing the action, I swallowed. It seemed a caged bird was trying to escape my chest. *He's taking a blessing! He's making us his family.*

We all trudged to the bus stand. For the first time, I noticed how Mr. Opee, with his long, white tunic, short, black vest, and neatly pressed, embroidered cap, towered above Chotu. He laid a large hand on Chotu's back. "Come back soon. If you come back, we'll pay you all the money we owe you."

He pulled something from the pocket of his tunic. "But here, take a little something for your travels. Don't ask anyone for money. It doesn't look good."

As Mr. Opee went ahead to face Chotu's brothers, Joshua whispered to Chotu, "You don't have to come back if you don't want to."

"I'll come if you say," Chotu responded, chest out, chin up.

Joshua handed the boy a small, square memory card. "This is my cell-phone memory card. The whole Bible is on here. All the stories I told you. And the songs we sing on Sabbath. You can put it in your own phone to listen."

"I will listen to your stories," Chotu said.

———

"I TAUGHT HIM SO LOVINGLY!" Mrs. Opee mourned that night. "If he would have waited, we could have sent him away with extra money. But he wanted to go home. Now everyone feels bad. It's just terrible."

"If I were Chotu, I would miss my mother," I said. "I would want to go home."

"Yes. That's why I said he could go."

We talked long into the night about the situation as Mrs. Opee tried to save face with me. My indignation slowly melted into understanding. I thought of Mrs. Opee's health problems and the shame she must feel for not being able to send her servant away with extra money.

"I know how you must feel," I said, placing my hand on her arm. "That's why we helped. You're like family to us. So it was our debt too. We knew you wouldn't want him to go away empty-handed."

Mrs. Opee nodded. "You *are* family. Really. You've lived in the village for nearly two years now. You even had your baby here." She was not exaggerating. To the Opees, we were not neighbors. We were household members.

After this, a wave of other older brothers rode the colorful public buses into Kushigaun to rescue their indentured little brothers. When all the chotus left, I rejoiced as there would be no more sad, unwashed faces watching the "well-off" children trot off to school. But a gloom dampened the collective happiness.

The chotus had given the women a break. Now once again, the *bahus*, or daughters-in-law, had all the work to do. There were no more chotus to take cows to pasture, muck stalls, knead the dough for chapattis. From that time forward in the little village of Kushigaun, we saw only the freshly washed faces of children on their way to school in the mornings and the women prodding their cows with sticks as they took them into the jungle to graze.

# 26

## RAKHI

Ayushi and I studied the Bible together for several weeks, looking over some of the major Old Testament stories to give the gospel historical and spiritual context. One day, I asked her what had prompted her to learn more about Jesus.

"I watched *Passion of the Christ*." Ayushi sat with her legs crossed, facing me head-on. "They showed it at movie night at the school. Have you seen it?"

"No," I admitted. "I don't see many movies."

"Well, it really touched my heart. I kept asking myself what Hindu god would put himself through all that just for humans. I want to follow Jesus, and I'm glad we're doing Bible studies together."

Ayushi hesitated, then looked me straight in the eyes. "But there are laws. If I get baptized, I'll have to register with the government as a Christian. I won't be part of my caste anymore. I'll lose the affirmative action benefit."

"Oh?"

"There are government seats and even free education for—for people like us," Ayushi lowered her voice. "I'm sure you've already heard that we're low caste."

I nodded. "A few people have mentioned it."

"That's why I didn't come to Ashi's dedication. I'm so sorry. The one time I visited, they stared at me until I was ashamed."

"It's okay, Ayushi." I touched her knee. "I understand."

"Do they tell you not to come here?"

"Some people. Most say not to eat with you. But it's hard for us to relate to the way they think about caste."

"It's wrong," she said. "It's illegal to discriminate nowadays. It's illegal to ask what caste someone is. But they ask anyway. Caste is not even in the Hindu scriptures. They are just prideful."

"You mean Brahmins?"

"Brahmin, Thakur. All the high caste. It's not like we sweep the streets or pick up trash. My dad works in an office. I work in a school. Mom stays home. We're not 'dirty.' Yet we are treated like menstruating women, as untouchables."

"That must be frustrating," I said. "We've eaten in high and low-caste homes. To be totally honest, I don't see much of a difference. Both are concerned with cleanliness and ritual purity. Both are hospitable and friendly."

"We're people." Ayushi pulled up her sleeve and jabbed a finger towards her wrist. "Our blood is red."

"Yes," I agreed.

"But I have to follow Jesus even if I lose privileges." Ayushi paused, then went on, "There's one other thing that bothers me though."

"What's that?"

"Sometimes I see Christians who don't behave like Jesus."

"That's always confusing," I said, nodding. "You have to remember that not everyone who calls themselves Christian really knows Jesus."

"Then you think such people aren't true Christians?"

"We can't always tell who is walking with Jesus by their outward appearance or behavior. But what I've learned is that people who *do* walk with Jesus don't stay the same. As we obey, God transforms us to become more and more like His Son. Still, it doesn't happen all at once. God's grace covers us as we grow. If I had to be perfect tomorrow, I know I'd be discouraged and overwhelmed."

"I'm sure you're right," Ayushi sighed. "The teachers at the Christian school always tell me to look to God, not to others. I guess I have to keep my eyes on Him."

---

AJAY CONTINUED to spend hours in our home. He would put Ashi on his back and walk around on all fours. She'd laugh and kick her legs, grabbing hold of his hair to keep from falling off. He asked constant questions: "Why is there no caste system in other countries? Why do some Christians abstain from alcohol? Can I use your laptop?"

Ajay often listened to our conversations with his father. When an unmarried teen in the village had an abortion, Mr. Opee explained that Indian women are scorned and rejected for premarital sex, but not men. When I protested, Mr. Opee chuckled. "Boys will be boys!"

Then he stopped smiling. "I know it's not ideal or fair. But in our culture, we believe men have less self-control than women. They aren't as responsible for what they do."

I tried to keep my face from twisting in disgust. Despite Mr. Opee's dismissal, I knew he was respectful of women and loyal to his wife. But surely these low expectations affected the boys being raised with them.

I glanced at Ajay. His worldview had been in the middle of downloading, and Joshua and I had interrupted the process. Would Joshua's talks with Ajay about purity and respect for women be enough to shift his worldview?

Mr. Opee lowered his voice. "Now I know you're eager to comfort the neighbor girl. But you must not talk to her about her abortion. The only way for our village to protect her honor is to pretend we don't know. If we don't talk about it, she might be able to marry someone from another village."

"Okay," I said. "But I don't like it."

Mr. Opee nodded. "I know. But just trust me. It's better to pretend nothing happened."

---

LOVELINA CAME whenever she had neck pain or needed her hair done, and I'd give her massages or braid her hair. She often brought guests, and there'd be a pile of teen girls in our living room staring at texts on their new smartphones. I'd serve them popcorn and homemade pizza, and we'd talk. I learned many words and cultural lessons as well. It was time to document what we were learning and see if we had any knowledge gaps. So I began typing up all our cultural observations in a document.

One night, Lovelina came over with an armful of saris from her mother's trunk. Heaping the saris on the floor, she pulled a giant makeup kit out of her purse. "Let's dress up."

"Let me put Ashi to bed," I said. "And then we'll play."

That night, Lovelina and I played dress-up for hours. We tried on different saris. We did each other's hair and makeup. We took pictures of each other with my camera.

"Promise you'll come to my wedding," she said. "And that you'll do my henna."

"I promise. But when are you getting married?"

"A long time from now!" she said, laughing. "I want to finish college first. As much education as I can get!"

"Good for you. But don't you like anyone?"

"Maybe." Lovelina batted her eyelashes. "But not that much. It's more the other way around. Every time it's *Rakhi*, all the boys run away from me so I can't make them my brothers."

She threw her head back and laughed. I laughed with her as I thought of *Rakhi*, an Indian holiday celebrating brothers and sisters. Sometimes people choose "godbrothers" and "godsisters" during *Rakhi*. If any of Lovelina's male classmates did *Rakhi* with her—which involved exchanging bracelets and feeding each other sweets—they would always be there for each other, always protect each other. But they could never get married.

Joshua and I liked the holiday. Although there were a few myths surrounding it, most of the ceremony was not religious. Of the many Hindu holidays, this seemed one in which a follower of Christ could participate.

"I'm sure nobody wants to be your brother," I said. "They all want to marry you instead!"

Lovelina nodded and laughed. I smiled. Lovelina was striking and hardworking. She was helpful and cheerful. And even if she didn't always do so, she knew how to hold her tongue. She would be the perfect Indian wife.

"Would you rather choose a man or have your parents pick him?"

"I would never do that to my parents. Pick someone myself, I mean. I want them to choose for me." Lovelina often talked back to her mother and sassed her father. But on a deeper level, she respected her parent's wishes. She would push back on their decisions, but if she couldn't change their minds, she obeyed.

"Well, I'm sure your parents will find you a good man."

"Not all girls get married, you know," Lovelina said.

"Of course. I suppose some women would rather not. There's that whole family of unmarried sisters living down the path from here."

"They're different," Lovelina said. "Their father didn't want to pay a dowry for them. They'll tell you they didn't want to get married because they didn't want to get beaten by mean husbands. It isn't true. It's the dowry. But some women don't get married because they can't."

"Why can't they?" I asked. "Not pretty enough?"

"Sometimes. But not every time. Take my friend Darling, for instance. So pretty. So smart. But she'll never marry."

"Darling? You mean Amul's daughter? Why won't she marry?"

"She started getting possessed with an evil spirit when we were in high school. I saw it myself." Lovelina shuddered.

"Really?"

"Yes, really. Her parents have tried everything, but nothing works. She's not always possessed, but it comes over her sometimes. Nobody wants to marry her. Sometimes people can't get married or can't get pregnant because of demons."

"I see." I nodded. "The poor thing."

"Yeah. Anyway, let's not dwell on sad stories." Lovelina grabbed my hand and dragged me upstairs to her house for her family to see. Everyone oohed and awwed and took pictures with us just as though we were real brides. I fake-cried, and everyone laughed. Real brides in India cry when they leave home.

---

ONE AFTERNOON, Mrs. Opee dragged herself into our living room and lay down on a mat. Kneeling, I felt her head. "What's wrong, big sister? Are you sick?"

"I'm bleeding," she said. "I've had my period for over three weeks."

"You must feel so weak. Have you been to the doctor?"

"Yes. He gave me iron pills, but I'm still bleeding." She handed me her medical card.

"This card is from a new doctor," I observed. "Did you tell the doctor you have hypothyroidism? Your medication may need to be adjusted."

"I didn't want to bother him. There were a lot of people there."

"You must always tell the doctor all your symptoms and medical history," I said. "Even if he is busy."

"He won't help me if he's annoyed." Mrs. Opee sighed. Lovelina was doing all the cooking and cleaning these days. I'd offered to help, but Mr. Opee couldn't eat what I cooked anyway due to his janeo string.

Mrs. Opee knew I prayed for her. Maybe she'd let me share a story and pray with her. Raising an inward prayer, I began tentatively, "Sister, this reminds me of a story in the Bible. There was this woman who had been bleeding for twelve years."

"Hmm, twelve years?"

"Yes. And Jesus—"

"Do you have anything to eat?" Mrs. Opee abruptly interrupted. "I'm so hungry, and I have to wait until they bring food outside for me."

I brought Mrs. Opee a plate of muffins and a glass of milk. "So this woman had been bleeding, and—"

"I see you've moved things around in this room," Mrs. Opee interrupted again. She babbled for a while, then began cracking jokes.

"Jesus healed the woman," I blurted out when she took a breath.

"Interesting." Mrs. Opee continued talking.

*She doesn't want to hear!* I gave up and just listened as Mrs. Opee filled the awkward space with words. She'd been a big sister to me, taught me much of her language and culture. I loved her impromptu storytelling, constant laughter, even her need for attention. But loving Mrs. Opee was painful too like loving all the Parvata. Loving them meant wanting them to know Jesus. But I couldn't choose for them.

*God, please send Your Spirit to draw Mrs. Opee to You. And show me how and when to plant seeds in her heart that Your Spirit can water.*

---

ONE AFTERNOON, we went to visit the Momo Lady. She took Ashi's hand and led her into her shop. I stared at the scar on the Momo Lady's neck. It looked like a spiked choker from the nineties but flesh-colored. How had she received such a wound?

The Momo Lady showed Ashi the dumpling-like momos and her stove and the cabbages waiting to be shredded. Then she brought Ashi to a large poster of a Hindu goddess.

"Jai jai," she said in a baby voice. This means "victory" and is a common, simple way to worship an idol. The Momo Lady took Ashi's two hands and touched them to the feet of the goddess.

I immediately rushed in behind them. "Time to go."

I scooped Ashi up. As we left, I prayed that God would block Satan from using Ashi's unintentional "worship" as an excuse to bother her.

---

THE *RAKHI* FESTIVAL ARRIVED. Hearing the door squeak, I came out of the kitchen. Ajay was there, hopping from one foot to the other, asking to become brother and sister.

"All you have to do," he said, out of breath. "Is do puja for me. We'll feed each other cake, and I'll give you a pretty suit, and you'll put a bracelet on my wrist, and I'll keep it there until another festival. Oh please, oh please!" Ajay's voice was changing with adolescence. It squeaked. I stifled a laugh.

"I'd love to be your sister. But I can't do puja to you."

Ajay's face fell. "Why not?"

"Remember how we don't eat prasad, or bow to the devta?"

"Yeah."

"Well, that is part of being a Christian. I will not worship anyone or anything other than my Creator. Understand?"

"I guess." Ajay poked his toe at a speck of fuzz on the floor. He'd heard every day of his life that God is one. But for Hindus that meant something different from the Jewish or Christian declaration. It meant that God is everything and everything is God, including human beings.

"But we can feed each other cake," I said. "And I have an idea for how to become brother and sister. Sometimes followers of Jesus write the names of their family in the front of their Bibles. Would it be okay with your mom if I gave you a Bible?"

"Yes! I mean, I think so!" He ran off to ask Mrs. Opee.

"Yes, of course," she responded. "God is one."

That night I took one of our Hindi Bibles and wrote in the front of it. "To Ajay. From your sister, Abigail."

# 27

## ZABARDASTY

Ayushi was rearranging pillows when Joshua, Ashi, and I arrived for a visit. We stood in the doorway as she swept some knickknacks into a drawer. Slamming it shut, she huffed, "Guests are coming. They're trying to *zabardasty* my family."

"Oh, no," I said. "That sounds… intense."

"Believe me, it is!"

"Um, what is *zabardasty*?"

"Force," Ayushi said. "They're pressuring my parents to marry me off to their son."

"But I thought you wanted to wait for—"

"They want me to marry their son," Ayushi repeated. "And they're forcing my parents to agree to it. That's them now! Stay, please! I want you guys to stay."

We sat. A middle-aged man and woman walked in, followed by Ayushi's parents. Everyone namasted, and the couple sat. Ayushi and her parents left to prepare snacks.

"What are your good names?" Joshua asked. This was how Indians sometimes asked names in an extra respectful way.

The man scowled and spoke in a crisp voice. "In India, we do not refer to our elders by their names."

I felt my eyes widen. We never called elders by their names. It had been one of our first cultural lessons in India. But we always asked for their names. Nobody ever seemed to mind.

Ayushi returned. There was a lot of fake smiling and overly pleasant talking. The couple drank chai, ate sweets, gave sweets, and left. Once they were gone, Ayushi flopped down on a mat. "Ugh! They have been doing this for weeks trying to *zabardasty* my family."

"How exactly do they exert this pressure?" I asked.

"They bring cookies every week."

Joshua and I glanced at each other. I couldn't resist asking. "Cookies? Cookies are enough to force someone to marry off their daughter?"

Ayushi tried not to smile, but a tiny laugh escaped anyway. "It sounds funny when you say it like that. But it's cultural. They are putting social pressure on my parents. If you ask often enough, people just kind of break down."

I thought a lot about *zabardasty* in the coming weeks. I knew some people accused Christians of forcing conversions. That was why it had been so difficult to know how to use the money we were given to bless the Parvata. Money. Prayers. Spiritual blessings. According to Hindu extremists, all of these were used to bribe people to become Christians.

---

WE'D BEEN in India now for two full years, and the day had come for our ministry partners to arrive. Lars and Kay planned to stash their things at our house before embarking on a two-month exploration of the villages around Kushigaun. They too wanted to get out there, bond with the people, learn the language, and avoid foreigners for their first few weeks.

But I hoped they'd at least stay for breakfast. I strained my ears listening for Joshua's arrival with our guests. Then I heard Joshua and Lars's boisterous conversation approaching the apartment. Flipping the last pancake, I turned off the stove. We all met in the living room.

"We're here!" Kay said.

"You're here!" I responded. Then everyone was hugging, laughing, and exclaiming. Joshua and Lars shifted stuff around to make room for four waterproof duffel bags.

We sat on the floor and ate pancakes with peanut butter and honey. Lars's laugh boomed as he and Joshua discussed politics and religion. Kay's smile was quick and easy as we talked about her first impressions of India. Ashi toddled around with a big peanut-butter smile.

Mrs. Opee stopped by, jabbering to Lars and Kay. They smiled, then stepped back as though overwhelmed by the blast of a hose.

"They don't speak Hindi, do they?" Mrs. Opee asked me with a wink.

I smiled. "Not yet. But they will."

I turned to Kay. "I know our house is small. And I know you guys want to get out there and get started right away. But if you're tired, you're more than welcome to stay here tonight."

"Are you sure?" Kay asked. "Where will everyone sleep?"

"You guys can have the living room and sleep on your camping pads. We'll sleep in the kitchen. And tomorrow Ayushi has invited everyone to join her for the Bible study. Her parents will be there, too."

That night we fell asleep whispering as though we were all at summer camp and in the morning the adventure would begin.

THE NEXT DAY WAS WARM, but Ayushi's top-floor apartment felt like an oven. Ashi, wearing only a washable diaper that looked giant on her petite frame, played with a doll on the floor. Occasionally, she swiped at beads of sweat on her nose. I looked around the room. Ayushi's family sat listening to the Bible study. Just listening.

*Nobody is interacting!* Ayushi and her brother both tried a little too hard to look interested. They nodded too vigorously, leaned forward too far. I wondered if they'd heard a word I said. Their little sister yawned and scratched her head. Ayushi's mother and father wore faded perma-smiles, their eyelids drooping as they baked in the heat.

*Do they feel pressured to be here? Are they just being polite?* I wondered how I could show Ayushi's parents the freedom Christ gives us to choose Him—or not to choose Him.

Lars, Kay, and Joshua continued coming to the study each week. But the scenario repeated itself. Everyone was bored but too polite to say so. Would it be better to continue studying with just Ayushi and myself? What if Lars and Kay felt excluded? William and Mark had said the worst conflict on the mission field happened between former friends.

MEANWHILE, Lars and Kay continued sleeping in our living room and we kept bedding down in the kitchen. Joshua and I remembered the many times we'd felt overwhelmed our first year in the field.

"Maybe it all feels really real now," I said. "Maybe they're nervous."

"I'm not sure. Lars mentioned they might want to move into a house," Joshua said. "Let's help them look."

For days, the four of us searched for a home for Lars and Kay but found nothing. Kay worried they were wearing out their welcome at our place.

"Are you sure it's okay that we're still here?" She bit her lip.

"You can stay as long as you need to," I said. "But I know God will lead you to a home. Maybe we should look outside of Kushigaun."

"Let's take a walk," Joshua said. "There might be something in the next village."

Nervousness kept my shoulders tight as we walked. The straps of Ashi's carrier dug into my muscles. Lars and Kay were helpful, cheerful, and fun to be around. And we all wanted our friendship to stay strong. But living together in a house slightly larger than a king-sized bed might eventually strain things.

*God, please keep our team strong! And provide our friends with a home!*

Just outside Kushigaun, a man in a white taxi blared his horn. He passed us, swerved to the side of the road, and yanked the parking brake.

"How are you, my friend?" he called to Joshua. "Where are you going?"

"Amul!" Joshua jogged over and shook the man's hand. "Our friends are looking for a place to rent. Know of anything?"

I remembered what Lovelina had said about Amul's daughter Darling. *She'll never marry because she has a demon.* I sent up another prayer for her. If only we could introduce Amul's family to Jesus. Surely Jesus could help Darling.

The next day, Kay and I followed Amul to a three-story building in a neighboring village. The landlord led us to the top floor and unlocked a small apartment.

While Kay checked out the apartment, Amul and I stood gazing out over the apple orchards. Amul commented that he loved meditating in the outdoors.

"How do you meditate?" I asked. "Do you follow a guru?"

"No. I don't trust gurus. I'm too emotional. Gurus are human. If my guru made a mistake, it would crush me. I just worship my god."

"Jesus said something like that. Don't call anyone your teacher except God."

"You're a believer? I was a believer for ten years!" Amul became more animated. He described the wonderful time he'd had as a Christian, the testimonies he'd given, the friendships he'd cherished. "Then I realized my destiny was to be a Hindu. And I came home."

I knew that "coming home" referred to the controversial *Ghar Wapsi* movement, a Hindu extremist reeducation program. The group has been accused of kidnapping Christian and Muslim children to forcefully convert them to Hinduism. On other people, they use more subtle forms of social force —*zabardasty*.

"I see," I said. "So, umm, what is your life like now?"

Amul explained that he was dedicated to the goddess Durga. Durga was the same bloody-tongued goddess we'd highlighted in our fundraising presentation about India, the same goddess Ajay had said was one of India's "mothers." As I wondered what to say, Amul continued talking.

"I am an impatient man, an angry man." The whites of Amul's eyes were pink-tinged, and his nostrils flared a little. "I used to visit Mother Durga's temple every day for help with my anger. One day, she even spoke to me."

"Oh?"

"She told me not to come so often. She said I could handle my problems myself. That the answer is within me. Ha! What other god would say such a thing? 'Don't come to my temple.'" He smiled and shook his head like this was some wonderful, profound answer.

Just then, Kay came out of the apartment. "I like it. Let's see what Lars thinks."

As Kay and I walked away, I felt confusion and indignation wash over me in waves. What kind of *zabardasty* had it taken to push Amul away from the one true God and into this nightmare of family possession and helpless anger?

# 28

## COUNTING THE COST

L ars and Kay moved into their apartment. Over the following weeks, they
got settled and met their neighbors. Joshua and I moved back into the living
room and returned to life as usual. In the meantime, I prayed about the Bible
study. Nothing changed.

"I have an idea," Lars said at our next meeting. "We all want our friendship
to survive this mission. That means we have to keep bitterness from growing. I
propose we take out the trash at the beginning of every meeting."

Lars explained we'd open the floor for anything hard to say. If someone was
offended or needed to apologize, they could bring it up during trash time.

"They taught us this technique at the pre-launch training," Kay added.

I smiled. I knew that our organization's trainers were constantly developing
the pre-launch training, trying to make it as relevant as possible. I wasn't
surprised that Lars and Kay had learned a technique we hadn't.

"I like the idea of having a special time to talk about difficult things," Kay
continued. "Do you guys want to try it?"

"I have something." I cleared my throat. "But it's not exactly trash. I mean,
I'm not offended or anything."

"It would be okay to be offended," Lars said. "Although I don't get offended.
I just offend!"

We laughed. Joshua had known Lars a long time, and he'd told me it was
true. Lars wasn't easily ruffled.

"What is it, Abby?" Kay asked, her large brown eyes encouraging me. "We're
listening."

"It's about Ayushi. I don't think it's working to have everyone at the study."

There was a pause. Then Kay spoke up. "I said the same thing to Lars last
night. It's crowded in there."

"They do seem kind of bored," Joshua said.

I nodded. "When it was just the two of us, Ayushi shared her heart with me. But with all of us there and her whole family, no one is even listening."

"What do you want to do?" Joshua asked.

"I guess maybe continue the study by myself."

"I think you should do it," Kay agreed.

I let out a breath I hadn't known I'd been holding. Kay smiled. I knew she had to psych herself up before a confrontation, too. I went on, "I also want to pray about her family. I have a feeling they don't want to be there but feel pressured. I think that's another reason Ayushi is distracted."

"Let's remember Amul in prayer as well," Lars said. "We've been getting to know his family since we moved into the apartment. Crazy to think he used to consider himself a believer."

"Let's pray," Joshua said. We bowed our heads, and I felt as though all our thoughts and purposes united as we prayed.

---

LARS AND KAY turned their tiny apartment into a real home. Kay spread a quilt over the bed and hung jean-blue curtains.

Lars bought a clay pot and set it on the windowsill. Kay called it their Praise Jar. She kept extra pens and white slips of paper near the pot so visitors on Sabbath evenings could add their thanks to the jar. Sometimes Lars and Kay would turn the jar upside-down. The white papers would flutter onto the bed like snow, and we would read them all.

"Thank God for trash time," I wrote once. "And for good friends."

---

WHILE ASHI NAPPED ONE AFTERNOON, I went to see Ayushi. She made ramen, and we sat on the floor under the window to eat it.

"Whatever happened with the people who wanted you to marry their son?" I asked.

Ayushi grinned. "At first, my parents pressured me to agree. They were under pressure themselves. But I refused, so they told the family no."

"You must feel so relieved."

"I think they're relieved, too."

"There is strength in numbers, isn't there?"

"Yes."

"Ayushi, I wanted to talk to you about that. Numbers, I mean. What if we went back to studying by ourselves?" I studied Ayushi's face. She hadn't reacted yet. "I know you're eager to have your family learn. And they are welcome to join. But sometimes it seems they only come to be polite."

Ayushi looked down and sighed. "I know you're right. I shouldn't force them." "I think it's great that you invited them. And you should share your faith with your parents. But you know how polite they are. I'd hate them to feel *zabardastied*. Christianity is about your heart, your relationship with God. You can't force internal change."

"They are interested in Jesus—a little. But it's difficult for them. My father has spiritual responsibilities. Doing *puja* with my grandfather, for instance. And all the names of people and places in the Bible are so strange."

"I understand. I felt that way about Indian names when I first came here."

"Yeah." Ayushi played with the ends of her straightened hair. She was quiet.

"You're counting the cost, too, aren't you?" I asked.

"I guess so. I feel so stressed sometimes about my future that I get distracted. Do you think God has a plan for my life?" Ayushi's tastefully filled-in eyebrows furrowed.

"Of course He does. If you want His plan."

"People won't understand."

"Nobody will force you to follow Jesus. Do you think you still want to? Or have you changed your mind?" I tried to keep my voice soft, accepting. I wanted Ayushi to know I would still be her friend even if she wasn't a Christian.

"Of course I haven't changed my mind. I want to follow Jesus. I want to marry a Christian. I want to be a Bible worker!"

"If that's what you want, then pray that God will work out His plan for your life. And obey Him, no matter what He asks you to do."

"I'll try. I think the first thing I need to do is read the gospels. I never have."

"That's a great place to start. We have a couple of major stories from the Old Testament left. After that, we could read the book of Matthew."

"I'm going to get up at six in the morning every day," Ayushi said. "I'll read the same chapter every day until our next study. Then maybe I'll understand better."

"I'll be praying for you." That night, I emailed our angel dispatchers and asked them to pray for Ayushi every day at six a.m. India time.

———

ALTHOUGH SOCIAL PRESSURE was a real part of Parvata life, close friends tried their best to make us feel comfortable and accepted. Especially Mr. Opee, our tour guide to Parvata culture. Mr. Opee was always giving out unsolicited advice, and he had cheerful feuds with several neighboring families.

But the longer Joshua and I knew him, the more we respected Mr. Opee. He neither exerted nor was affected much by *zabardasty*. He warned us about food offered to idols and let his kids learn all they wanted about Jesus.

I knew Mr. Opee's pleasant indifference was a Hindu ideal, an unemotional acceptance of life and duty that eventually found its highest expression in Buddhism. But Mr. Opee was not devoid of emotion. He cared about people. He just didn't care whether they liked him.

Christmas came. Joshua and I purchased a large kerosene heater and charged up our laptop in case the power went out. In the end, we never lost power, possibly because a brand-new transformer had recently been erected in the village.

We made hundreds of cookies to give to everyone we knew. On Christmas evening, Ajay and his family joined us to watch *The Jesus Film*. A cousin of Ajay's said Jesus that was just like Sai Baba, a guru who once made a gold ring appear out of thin air. Ajay nodded, but I noticed he bit his lip like he was thinking more than he was saying.

Grandma shook her head. "Look what they are doing to that innocent man. It is wrong. He did nothing. He never sinned. Yet they accuse him. Look at them beating him! It is wrong. Wrong!"

# 29

## HINDU JUSTICE

"You should go to Pahargaun sometime," Joshua said one morning in January. "You know, get out of the house. Buy yourself some juice."

"We go all the time."

"You should go by yourself."

"Did you *hear* what just happened in Delhi?"

"Yes. But you can't let what happened in Delhi keep you from living your life."

What happened in Delhi was the brutal gang rape of a physical therapy student on her way home from the movies. Five men broke her male friend's leg and left her violated, mutilated, and struggling to survive. She was later life-flighted to Singapore. But a few days later, she died.

All over India, people protested. In one photo, schoolgirls in uniforms held signs: "I deserve to walk down the street and not have a stranger grab me against my will." People of all ages picketed, men and women, with slogans such as, "Don't tell girls not to go out. Teach men not to rape." In another photo, an old woman held a sign above her head, her mouth open in a shout: "We are ashamed. Save our girls."

The Opee family invited us over for lunch. Mr. Opee had just finished a Sanskrit scripture reading when we arrived. Joshua and I sat on mats on the floor with the family. Soon, we found ourselves discussing reincarnation.

"People don't remember their past lives," Mr. Opee said. "That's something you see in Western movies. It's not a Hindu idea at all. We can't remember. Only our soul remembers, and the soul can't speak."

"Then how does your past life affect you?" I asked.

"Everyone wants to know why bad things happen to good people," Mr. Opee said. "You can think of sin like mud getting on your pants. When you sin, some of that mud sticks to your soul. When you die, your soul is reincarnated into a new body, but the sin goes with it. When your new body suffers, some of that sin is removed."

"Does that mean Hindus believe everything that happens is related to their past life?" Joshua asked.

"In a way, yes," Mr. Opee said. "We believe there is a consequence for everything, maybe now, maybe later. The gods make everything fair. Reincarnation is one way they do that."

"How does reincarnation make things fair?" I asked.

"Listen, Abigail," Mr. Opee responded. "You know about duty. I have the duty of a Hindu, a Brahmin, a husband, a father, and a son. If I do my duty well and suffer a little, maybe in the next life I will be something better. But if someone doesn't do their duty or if they sin, their soul has to suffer. The gods write everything down and make sure justice is served by the physical body the soul inhabits. Maybe this body, maybe the next."

"What about the Delhi case?" I asked. "You don't think that girl was attacked because she sinned in a past life, do you?"

"No," Mr. Opee said. "What happened was wrong. So shameful. Personally, I believe the boys who raped her attacked her so they could be punished."

I heard my heart pounding in my ears. This made no sense to me. "How is that justice?"

"Surely the boys will be hanged. That is justice."

"And when someone hurts *you*?" I asked.

"If someone hurts me but I don't deserve it, the gods will make sure that person gets hurt, and it will be fair. Maybe now, maybe later."

"What about helping people?" Joshua asked. "Does that mess up the system?"

"You've noticed we sometimes give alms. But I would not do too much to help a poor man. He may need to suffer for his soul to be free."

"What about people who *want* to help the poor?" I asked. "Some people feel compassion and want to help. Will they be punished for interfering?"

"Let me put it this way. If you saw a dog in the street, dirty, hungry, and mangy, and you wanted to help it, it would be your duty to do so. The gods put that feeling in your heart, the feeling of wanting to help the dog. So you help, and the poor dog has a happy life from then on. That is the will of the gods. Maybe his suffering was complete. Or maybe you needed to do it to pay for your sins."

"In other words, good deeds change the balance, too," Joshua said.

Lovelina stopped painting her toenails and looked up. "When I was little, there was a man in our village who got stomach cancer. It was very painful. He tried and tried to figure out why. It could have been a curse, or maybe it was his *karma*."

"*Karma*?" I repeated. "You mean his bad deeds in a past life?"

"Yes. He went to a gur in case it was a curse and a priest too. They said he needed to do a big puja and give stuff away. He had a party. He gave away tons of clothes and fed everyone in the village. He thought maybe he could fix whatever he'd done in a past life."

"What happened?" I asked.

"He died anyway."

"But his good deeds were not worthless," Mr. Opee said. "His suffering, his good deeds, his death—perhaps all this worked together to pay the debt of his soul. Perhaps he will be born again into a rich Brahmin home or even become a god."

"A person can become a god?" Joshua asked.

"It's all a hierarchy, a points system. You do better, you're born better. It's better to be a god than a human, to be born high caste than low, better to be a man than a woman, better to be rich than poor, better to be healthy than sick."

"Wait, being a woman is a punishment?" I asked.

"Hey, don't shoot!" Mr. Opee put up his hands with a playful laugh. "That's just the way it is."

Mrs. Opee nodded, squinting her eyes to highlight her suffering. I understood it wasn't a joke. Women have babies and periods. They are unclean. They have to love children and husbands, serve in-laws and guests. All that loving and serving and giving is risky because there's no guarantee you'll be loved back.

"But what about science?" Joshua asked Mr. Opee. "Surely germs and genetics play into all this."

"Of course," said Mr. Opee. "But germs and genetics don't explain everything. Why was your soul born into those genetics? Why did you encounter those germs? That is justice."

Did the Parvata people think of their lives as a kind of purgatory over which they had almost no control? The Opee family seemed happy for living in purgatory. Yet I knew contentment was their duty. What was there to be unhappy about as Brahmins, anyway? They were at the top.

Despite the prescribed contentment, I began to notice how India fought to heal its wounds. There were strikes and rallies and speeches about rape and corruption and the abortion of baby girls. Yet as Shankar had pointed out, many people didn't notice their own contribution to the problem. People would justify a *small* bribe. It's not like they were embezzling *a lot* of money. It was just a little.

I thought about Psalm 115:8 again, how people who worship idols are spiritually blind, deaf, and mute. *No wonder Jesus's message focused on the inner person first! He knew it would never work to change us from the outside in.*

---

"SHANKAR IS GETTING MARRIED," Joshua said one day.

"Interesting," I said, thinking of Shankar's flirty smile too close to my face and the tales of his caste-crossed love life. "Who's the bride?"

"I don't know. We're invited, but they're keeping it small. You don't have to go." Joshua went to the wedding that morning with Shankar's sister, Mrs. Opee, and was back by early evening.

"I hadn't expected you back for hours," I said.

"It wasn't a big wedding."

"Did you get any pictures?" Drying my hands from washing dishes, I leaned over Joshua's camera. He was flipping through thumbnails.

"You weren't lying when you said it was small," I said.

"I've never been to an Indian wedding with less fanfare. They didn't feed the community. Only family members came. Shankar and Puja exchanged neck wreaths at the temple. We ate a small meal, and that was it."

"Strange," I said. "Was that Shankar's request? I mean, did he want a small wedding because he doesn't care about this relationship? Or did his wife want to get married quickly?"

"I have no idea."

I continued to flip through the digital images, zooming in on a picture of Shankar's new wife. She was beautiful, smiling like she'd won the lottery. She beamed as she clung to Shankar's arm. He looked tired and strained.

"Yeah, I tried to talk to Shankar about Puja, his new wife. But he just changed the subject."

"To what?"

"Politics. He even asked me to join him for a political rally. He's really into them, especially the anti-corruption rallies. Even out here in the Himalayas, there are demonstrations all the time protesting corruption in the government. Shankar said corruption is a big problem, and he wants to do what he can to see it changed."

"That sounds like a noble goal," I said. "So, you gonna go?"

"Maybe."

"Just try not to get yourself in the middle of any mobs, okay?"

"Will do."

# 30

## ANGEL DOG

Near our house was a seldom-used road that wandered up the side of a steep hill. It was a favorite walking spot of ours. One afternoon, Kay and I decided to take a walk there.

Ashi toddled along beside us for a while, stopping now and then to pick up a rock or stick. She soon tired. I put her in the baby backpack, and Kay and I picked up the pace.

We talked about everything and nothing. We discussed our beautiful *dupatta* scarves. So cute yet so inconvenient, constantly falling off our shoulders. Kay had resorted to tying hers on.

Kay and Lars had been visiting Amul's family every week. They were interested in being friends but not in talking about spiritual things. Kay's landlord's wife had miscarried twins, and Kay had been able to comfort her. I told Kay that Ayushi had a boyfriend and was wondering how to be a Christian if she married a Hindu.

After a couple of switchbacks, a golden-haired dog emerged from behind a tree. She flounced towards us. My heart pounded. Most dogs we met in India were feral and fierce.

Then Kay observed, "She looks friendly."

Sure enough, the dog's mouth was open in a grin and her tail wagged. She began trotting along beside us.

"Maybe God sent her," I commented.

"Maybe she's our angel dog!" Kay said. We chuckled. I shifted Ashi, who had fallen asleep on my back.

Half an hour later, we heard voices. I looked up. Four men stood on a ledge two switchbacks above us. They grinned down. One of them licked his lips.

"Hey there," one said. "Come on up here, honey."

"Yeah, we want to tell you something," another said. The others laughed. I looked around. There were no houses nearby. The village looked small below us. We were alone.

"Ignore them," I whispered. "Mrs. Opee says it's safest to ignore the catcalling."

"Okay," Kay said. "But let's turn around."

We did so. The men shouted after us, and for a moment I thought they would follow. But they went back to work. My legs shook as we speed-walked down the hill.

"Look," Kay said. "Our angel is still with us." The dog pranced close to Kay's side.

"Everyone around here is afraid of dogs," I pointed out. "Maybe she kept the men from following us."

"I guess we'll know in Heaven if she really was an angel," Kay said.

The dog walked ahead of us. When we were almost back to the main road, she stopped, turned around, and looked at us for a moment, her mouth hanging open like a smile. Then she disappeared into the brush. Though Joshua and I often walked that path, we never saw the dog again.

---

"SHANKAR and his new wife are here," Joshua called through the screen door. "Her name is Puja. You should come meet her."

I walked out the door. The sunlight glinted off droplets of water dripping from the roof. Shankar stood near the temple, leaning to one side with his hands in his pockets, talking to Mr. Opee.

Before I even noticed her, Puja embraced me. Then she plopped down in a plastic chair and patted a second. Lovelina joined us.

"Do you like our new aunt?" she asked in lieu of an introduction.

"She seems wonderful," I said. Puja beamed at me. There was a very short silence.

"I love traveling," Puja said. "Meeting new people, seeing new places. I just love to get out. And of course, I love my husband," she added, giggling.

Shankar sat down next to her, and she squeezed his arm. "I've been trying to get him to hurry up and marry me for years! I finally told him if he's going to marry me, do it now. Otherwise, call it off and let me be free to marry someone else. I'm not getting any younger."

She laughed. "Well, he married me, and I'm so happy. He's a great guy. We've been betrothed since we were kids, and I've dreamt of him since I was a little girl."

Shankar forced a smile. I glanced at him, then continued smiling and nodding at his new wife. "Well, congratulations. I pray you two will be very happy!"

Any time a new relative appeared, Puja stood. Putting her *dupatta* scarf over her head, she leaned down, reached toward the person's feet, then touched her heart. I had seen this before. When the Momo Lady touched Ashi's hands to the idol. When Chotu touched our feet before he left.

The gesture was a sign of deep respect known as "taking a blessing." Married women take a blessing from their husband's relatives, anyone who is not a child. Men take a blessing from older family members. Everyone takes a blessing from the idol.

There was an anti-corruption rally in town that afternoon, so Shankar and Joshua left to attend it, leaving Puja with his sister, Mrs. Opee. I helped the two women fold patus for a while. Soon, Mrs. Opee went upstairs to make tea. Puja turned to me.

"Listen," she whispered. "I want to know something. About pregnancy."

"Are you pregnant already?" I asked.

"Well, I want to know how to get pregnant. It's been a month and a half, and I'm still not. I've been eating almonds and garlic. Do you have any advice for me? Any inside information?" She giggled uncomfortably. I knew this was both a taboo topic and a favorite one for many Indian women.

"Sure, I can explain some things that should help." I explained a few missing details about a woman's reproductive cycle. Puja was surprised to hear that a woman is only fertile for a short time each month.

"Wow," she said. "I had no idea!"

"Let me show you something. It's one of the coolest things I've ever seen." Pulling Puja into my room, I set up my laptop, then loaded a beautiful video animation of the development of a baby. Mrs. Opee joined us. Everything grew quiet when the cells in the baby's heart began to pump at three weeks. The baby grew and developed before our eyes.

"I'm scared," Mrs. Opee whispered.

"Me, too," Puja agreed. The two women barely breathed as they watched the screen. It was the first time these two women had visualized the miracle of a child's development in the womb.

Finally, Mrs. Opee spoke. "To think people are walking around like everything is normal when *that* is happening inside pregnant women."

"Miracle," agreed Puja.

---

AT OUR NEXT STUDY, Ayushi was distracted. She fidgeted and kept glancing out the window. When I touched her arm, she jumped.

"What's up? You seem stressed."

"I had a nightmare last night," she said. "Sometimes my bad dreams come true. On top of that, the devta says I'm doomed to be single forever."

"Let me tell you a story." I told Ayushi a condensed version of the plan of salvation. I told her about how Satan and the fallen angels had coveted the worship of God and how they'd tried to get Adam and Eve to covet it too. I told her how the fallen angels were cast out of heaven. She immediately connected the story with the devtas, which she said she hadn't been worshipping lately.

"How can my people be the only ones who don't know they worship demons? Why doesn't someone tell them?"

"People all over the world want to tell them, Ayushi," I said. "There are people praying for India, whole churches, whole countries praying for India right now."

She shook her head. "Somebody has to tell them."

"Maybe you will tell them."

"Maybe I will. But what about my dream?"

"You're worried about your dream?"

"I had a nightmare about Ashi," she said. "Two of them. In the first, I saw the devta, and our village looked strange. Ashi was there. In the second one, you took Ashi out of someone's arms. You cried and cried, and I couldn't get you to stop crying."

"Ayushi, God is stronger than the devil," I said. "He will protect Ashi."

Ayushi chewed her bottom lip and glanced at Ashi, who was giving a stuffed robot a ride on the stuffed deer. "I don't know. My dreams come true, I'm telling you. I don't want to have these dreams. Sometimes I even wake up and feel like someone is in the room."

"You can command any evil presence to leave in Jesus's name," I said. "And you can ask God to take the dreams away."

"Okay. I'll try."

"Why don't we pray right now?" I suggested. We prayed together and began our Bible study. We had now finished the major Old Testament stories and were beginning the book of Matthew—Ayushi's first time reading the gospels.

# 31

# FINDING CHOTU

A yushi tried to read the Bible. But every time she did, she fell asleep. She told me she tried reading other things—her sister's homework, magazines. Nothing else gave her that lead-lidded feeling. Only God's Word.

"Sometimes people experiment with magic." Ayushi played with the edges of her crisp white tunic. "Especially teen girls. They want to see if they can gain a little control over someone. If they can cause something to happen. Maybe someone cursed me."

I thought about the Hindu system of reincarnation and duty. The way everything that happens is the will of the gods. Where did purposefully cursing someone fit into that? Maybe witchcraft was the loophole for the Parvata. A way to feel in control.

"I know dabbling in magic happens here," I responded. "But Jesus is stronger than curses. He's stronger than Satan. Pray before you read your Bible that God will block Satan's attempts to distract you and make you sleepy. He'll show you what to do."

Despite her discomfort and worry, Ayushi kept trying. Our angel dispatchers prayed, and we made it through the first three chapters of the book of Matthew. Then Ayushi asked to take a break. "I'm not sleeping well. Keep asking, and I'll say yes to the study as soon as I feel better."

I wondered if there were a more creative way to help Ayushi in her journey to Jesus. I gave her a Hindi audio Bible on an SD card and suggested she listen while scrubbing her clothes. She said she'd try.

Joshua and I collected hours of recordings from our Hindu friends. We recorded cultural stories and explanations of ceremonies. We asked about the biggest problems people faced and how they solved them. Joshua spent hours translating these recordings. Then one day, he thought of Ayushi.

"Translating could be a side job for her. It would save us a lot of time. And it would give her a chance to analyze her own worldview. It might even help her better understand the Hinduism she grew up in since most of our information is from Brahmins."

"Great idea. Let's ask!"

Ayushi said yes. After that, she spent her afternoons transcribing, then translating entire notebooks of text. She and Joshua would trade notebooks and audio recordings every few days. With Ayushi's help, the document where I wrote down our observations grew rapidly.

---

ONE COLD AFTERNOON IN FEBRUARY, I stopped on my way to the store to chat with one of the neighbors. She was slender with maroon lipstick that suited her mature face.

"We're going on a trip!" she said. "A *yatra*!"

"What is a *yatra*?" I asked.

"It's a religious trip. But you can come even if you are not Hindu. It's good for the health. I chartered a bus. We do this every winter. Please come!"

I smiled. "I should stay home with Ashi. But I think Joshua might like to go."

I couldn't wait for Joshua to come home that evening. I turned the heater on in the living room and tidied Ashi's toys. I heard a plop and a scurry. A giant but harmless spider had jumped off the wall onto the floor. As long as the spiders didn't drop onto my head as one had in the shower two days earlier, they didn't bother me.

Soon Joshua arrived, carrying two cloth bags of groceries. As we put them away, I told him of our neighbor's suggestion. "She called it a *yatra*. A bunch of people from the village are going. It'll be like a tour. They'll visit some of the holiest places in Hinduism. I don't want to take Ashi, but I think you should go."

"Sounds interesting," Joshua agreed.

"I don't know why," I went on. "But I feel strongly that you should go. Maybe you'll grow closer to someone who wants to know Jesus. Or maybe you'll get some good information for our cultural study. We're close to finishing it."

"I'll talk to the neighbor tomorrow. And to Lars and Kay. I think they'd be interested too."

It was decided that Joshua, Lars, and Kay would join the *yatra*. Then two days before the trip, it snowed. Powder muffled the roads. The power lines snapped.

"Should I stay?" Joshua glanced around at our dimly lit living room. The blue walls made it look like the inside of an ice cube. It felt that way too. Ashi stacked blocks on the floor wearing a snowsuit and a hat.

"No. We'll be all right. If it gets too cold, we'll visit someone with a tandoor."

"You can always light the Beast."

I glanced over at the black kerosene heater we'd purchased before Christmas. We called it the Beast because it was huge and lighting it made the house smell like bad eggs.

I crinkled my nose. "Yeah, there's always the Beast. You'd better go pack. I have a feeling the snow won't stop your trip."

I was right. The bus was delayed, but only by thirty minutes. Once they'd left, Mrs. Opee came to see if I was lonely or cold. She invited me to sleep in her house for the next two weeks while Joshua was away. I preferred to sleep in our own home but promised to eat with her. Ashi and I joined her for lunch that first day.

Mrs. Opee had lit a candle, and the flame made wobbling shadows on our metal plates. She poured a bright-yellow, tart curry over a steaming plate of rice. I stirred it with my fingers to cool it for Ashi. She used a spoon while I ate with my hand.

After eating, Ajay hopped off to nap under a pile of blankets in the unheated room next door.

"He reads the Bible you gave him every morning," Mrs. Opee said, swiping rice off the floor with her bare hands. "Says his sister gave it to him." She smiled, and I felt like I could fly.

Another day, we ate beans. After eating, I lay on a mat by the tandoor, rubbing my temples with my cold, stiff fingers. Ashi sat at my feet and played with Lovelina's old Blurbie, my word for an imitation fashion doll with its smeared lipstick and eyeshadow.

"Headache?" Mrs. Opee asked.

"Yes," I said. "Maybe I haven't had enough water."

"Your head hurts?" Ajay bounded into the room. He was used to helping his mother when she complained of pain.

"A little. I rarely get headaches, but I have one today."

"Let me help."

Ajay reached down and squeezed my forehead. I thought for a moment how strange this was. But it was normal in India for kids to massage their elders' heads or feet. Then I noticed Ajay murmuring something. His eyes were closed. He'd finished the mantra almost before I'd noticed it. I knew he was copying what his dad often did for his mother. He looked at me eagerly.

"Thank you for the massage," I said, smiling. I didn't correct Ajay. We'd had many important talks about religion and lifestyle. But this was not a teachable moment. It was just one human being trying to help another in the best way he knew how.

I did, however, have a time of prayer after that. If Ajay had invited any power into my life, I wanted God to block it. I prayed only His power and light would influence my mind.

JOSHUA CALLED every day to update me. I often heard the clanging of an Indian finger cymbal in the background. Singing is an important part of a *Yatra*. As the bus made its way into the plains, Joshua listened to his own music to prevent the catchy Hindu prayer songs from sticking in his mind.

Along the way, they visited temples. One temple reminded Joshua of a theme park. The fee to enter was expensive. The exhibits featured jewel-encrusted idols, hands held up in blessing to the worshippers. The crowds rushed in and out, eager to collect a blessing at each site. Once, two ladies ran out of a temple, squealing with excitement. An idol had moved, they insisted, though no one else had seen it. They believed a goddess had revealed herself to them.

Joshua's group arrived at Khumb Mela, a Hindu festival held every twelve years. Thirty-nine million people attended that year. At the time, it was the largest gathering of people in the world.

"I've never seen so many people in my life," Joshua told me. "It's crazy. Like a literal ocean of people."

We knew from research that bathing in the Ganges River is thought to atone for sin acquired in this and previous lives. Hindus say the waters are so pure and holy they can't be polluted even by the hundred thousand dead bodies estimated to be dumped into it every year. Some say ten lifetimes of sin are removed by a single dip. Others say ten sins.

At one point, Joshua stood on the shore of that holy river, watching the flow of people walk past him into the water. A sparkling-red sari caught his eye. A bony, old woman, bent over ninety degrees from her waist, held the arm of a young man. Wisps of white hair escaped her braid. Her head was up, eyes fixed on the river. If only she could touch the hem of that water, rippling like a garment in the wind. If only!

———

"ABIGAIL, I think I might be near Chotu's village," Joshua told me several days later. "We've traveled over a thousand miles. I'm looking at the map on my phone. If I go a few hours south, I think I'll be there."

"You should go find him," I said, surprising myself.

"I would have to leave the group. And I don't know exactly where he lives. There's no guarantee I'll find him. What do you think?"

"What if this is why you joined the *yatra*? I feel a strong impression that you should go."

"I feel that way, too. Let's pray." Joshua and I prayed together, committing our lives into God's care, promising to follow Him wherever He led.

"Okay," Joshua said. "I'm going."

———

THE NEXT EVENING, Joshua called again. "You'll never believe this, but I found Chotu's village."

"Praise the Lord! Did you find Chotu?"

"No. Chotu is working in another state. But I found his brother and sister-in-law."

"Did his brother recognize you?"

"Yes. It's a long story. But when he and his wife came out of the house... Abby, they were wearing cross necklaces!"

"No way!"

"They said they'd listened to the Bible stories. He's the only one in his family who can read, and he says he wants a Bible!"

"Amen! Then let's send him one!"

---

JOSHUA'S HOMECOMING was a joyous one. Just before his arrival, the power came back on. I aired out the house, then turned on our space heater. I made cornbread and a pot of chili. We had worship together, the three of us. Ashi crawled all over Joshua in her eagerness to see her daddy again.

"You said it was a long story," I said after Ashi slept. "What happened?"

Joshua reached into his bag and pulled out a piece of white paper. He stared down at it, re-creasing the folds with his fingers.

"The night I called you, I was about to leave for Chotu's village. But some local men stopped me. They said a terrorist group called the Naxalites is active in the area. They said I'd be kidnapped, maybe even killed."

I felt strange, as though listening to Joshua's words on a tape recorder. Had he been so close to danger?

"Everyone told me to wait until the next day when I could arrange police transport," he continued. "I felt burdened that night. You were back here all alone with little Ashi. But we'd prayed about it, and even you felt impressed that God wanted me to go. In my heart, God asked if I was willing to die for Him even if it cost my life. Would I trust you and the baby in His care? Finally, I decided to go."

Joshua rolled up his pant leg, revealing numbers written in permanent marker. "I wrote the number for one of our friends at the U.S. embassy on my leg. Just in case."

"I'm thankful nobody needed it," I said, feeling dizzy. "Did you get a police escort the next day?"

Joshua grinned. "That's the amazing thing. Just last year, the central government built a new road—straight to Chotu's village. The police reassured me I'd be fine. I took a taxi there and had no problem. I know Chotu's brother's name, so I asked around. The second person I met knew him. That person took me to Chotu's house.

"When his brother and bhabi came out, they were both wearing cross necklaces. I prayed with them and promised to send them a Bible. It turns out Chotu's brother somehow heard about Jesus while Chotu was still working for Mr. Opee. But they have no pastor, no church, not even a Bible. When Chotu came back with our SD card full of Bible stories and Christian music, it was an answer to their prayer."

"Joshua, that is beautiful," I said. "I'm so glad you're okay!"

"I'm glad, too. I think I needed to be ready to make the sacrifice even though it turned out I didn't have to go through with it this time. I wrote something for you girls, just in case. You can have it."

Joshua handed me the folded-up paper he'd been playing with. In his uneven, hurried scrawl, he'd written the following notes:

"My dearest Abigail, I love you so much. I know that God will comfort you. Hold on to Him."

"Ashi, Daddy loves you. I wish I could be there to watch you grow up. Always follow Jesus, no matter what."

"To the world: you may say that giving my life was a waste. But I've found something worth dying for. Have you?"

# 32

## DOUBLE CURSE

We'd been in India for two-and-a-half years, and I'd learned to make many Indian dishes. Dahl. Chapattis. Emerald-green *palak paneer* with golden chunks of Indian cheese. But not curry.

"You should ask Mrs. Opee to teach you," Joshua said from his post at our laptop.

I stuck my head out the door and smiled at Mrs. Opee, who sat on her porch looking tired. "Sister, I have a problem. Every time I try to make curry, the buttermilk separates. It tastes okay, but it looks terrible. What's your secret?"

"Easy. Don't add salt until the end."

"Tripti told me that, too. I tried, but it didn't work."

"Don't stir."

"Tried it. Maybe I'm missing something. Why don't we have a cooking lesson?"

"I'd love that!" Mrs. Opee bounded up the stairs. In my kitchen, she surveyed the ingredients sprawled on the counter. Tiny purple onions, diced to oblivion. A handful of garlic, minced. My spice container.

"Where's the *chana ka atta*?" Mrs. Opee asked.

I blinked. "Chickpea flour? I didn't even know such a thing existed."

"You have to have it to make curry!" Mrs. Opee screeched in the general direction of the door, "Lovelina!"

Lovelina soon arrived, then trudged upstairs to get the *chana ka atta*.

Mrs. Opee instructed me. Keep the flame low and don't be impatient. The onions should turn brown, but not burn. There should be plenty of oil to temper the spices. She scooted the sizzling onions to the sides of the pot and poured in another half cup of oil. Then she placed several spoonsful of spices in the center of the oil: yellow turmeric, brown coriander. She almost added chili powder, but I reminded her Ashi wouldn't like it too spicy.

"This is just garlic curry," she said, dumping in all the garlic and lowering the flame. "No potatoes or anything. Nice to make when you don't have time."

Then I learned the secret to Kushigaun curry: Mrs. Opee added several spoonsful of *chana ka atta* into a jar of buttermilk and mixed it with a wooden spoon. *Why didn't anyone tell me I needed this?* I wondered. Perhaps it was too obvious. The chickpea flour acted as a binder similar to cornstarch.

Mrs. Opee poured the buttermilk into the pan.

"Don't stir," she commanded. I obeyed. After a long wait, Mrs. Opee let me stir and add salt. Drool-inducing steam billowed into the room.

Mrs. Opee turned to me. "I have to go muck the stalls now. Tell me if it's good."

"Don't you want to eat with us?"

"Not this time. I have to cook for my family."

"Now I can make curry any time I want!" I said instead of thanking her.

Mrs. Opee beamed. "And I taught you!"

I brought a towel to the living room and spread it on the floor.

"Time for lunch?" Joshua asked.

"Yep. Hungry?"

"Starved."

"Mommy has hot food," I told Ashi. "Stay there."

I kept my eye on my little one lest she crawl over and I slop the hot liquid on top of her. Ashi still sat like a teddy bear, looking at a picture book. I set the curry on the towel and knelt next to it.

"Are you hungry?" I asked Ashi.

"Hunny!" Setting down the picture book, Ashi got into a crawling position. "'Poon!"

I looked up. On the far side of the curry was a spoon from Ashi's toy tea set. Ashi speed-crawled, eyes locked across the ocean of curry and onto that spoon. I lunged for her, but at the same moment, she stretched her arm across the curry. Before I could get to her, she lost her balance, her elbow plunging into the hot liquid.

She screamed. I grabbed her and rushed into the kitchen, yanking off her clothes. She yowled as I shoved her arm under the water, naturally cold at that time of year. Her skin was already blistering. "We have to go to the hospital! Get me a towel!"

Joshua was already at my side. He grabbed a towel and handed it to me. I wetted it and wrapped it around the burn. I didn't want infectious dust landing on the wound while we traveled. We rushed out to the main road, Ashi cradled in my two arms like an offering.

A passing vehicle saw us and stopped. They were on their way to Pahargaun and would take us to the hospital. Trees, people, and bridges sped past the window. I glanced down at Ashi. She'd fallen asleep, exhausted from the pain and crying. Why hadn't we just served ourselves from the kitchen? But this was how everyone in India ate, gathered around pots on the floor. Except in an Indian home, there are extended family members to hold the babies.

In the hospital emergency room, a blonde woman with a southern accent walked into our cubicle. I recognized her name tag: Dr. Sue. She was the doctor who'd saved Ajay when he was thrown in the trash as a premature infant. She was gentle and sympathetic as she bandaged Ashi's blistered arm.

"You'll have to come have it changed twice a day," she drawled. I shot Joshua a worried look.

"I'm not a doctor, but I have first aid training," Joshua said. "Could we do this at home?"

"Sure. I'll prescribe everything you need. Just do what I did today. But I'm telling you, it will be really painful for her every time you change it."

As we were leaving the ER, I turned to the doctor. "I've been wanting to meet you."

"Oh, really?"

"I don't know if people ever tell you this, but your kindness has done a lot to show people what Christians are really like."

"Well, praise the Lord," she said simply, avoiding eye contact and shrugging. She seemed to feel awkward about the praise. I understood and changed the subject.

"Well, we finally met," I said. "Though it would have been nice to meet under different circumstances."

"Poor thing," the doctor said, smoothing Ashi's fuzzy head. "It shouldn't scar. Kids are so much more resilient than adults."

---

WHEN WE RETURNED HOME, Ajay's family gathered to survey the damage. Ashi was well-bandaged from wrist to armpit. The white gauze was already smudged with dirt from the bus ride home.

I assured everyone Ashi would be fine. But Mr. Opee said something that jarred me. "Why did you let this happen?"

I already felt guilty. Now I felt hurt, upset, and confused on top of it. I stuffed down my impulse to respond defensively. "I was with her. We both were. We tried to stop her, but she went so fast. She just crawled right over and fell in."

"Well, be more careful now," he said, smiling and relaxed. Everyone dispersed.

I went to open the door of our house, still feeling dizzy from the shock of Mr. Opee's comment. My hand brushed a piece of tape stuck to the metal handle. "What's this? Tape?"

I looked for an end to peel it off. Then I noticed a hair underneath. Seeing Lovelina nearby, I pointed to the hair. "Hey, Lovelina. What's this?"

"A hair? Ha! ha!" Lovelina laughed, too loudly. "Must be some joke Ajay or Joshua played. I don't know."

But something told me she did know. Hair is used in India to curse people. Lovelina knew it. I knew it. Lovelina ran upstairs to her house. As I carried Ashi into our apartment, I thought of Ayushi's dreams.

*Did someone curse us? If so, why didn't God protect us? Who would hate us so much? And why did Mr. Opee blame me?*

Mr. Opee wasn't the only one. Over the next several weeks, everyone asked what I'd done to Ashi. I dreaded going out lest someone blame me for what happened. The whole world was against me, and my conscience didn't offer much relief. If only I'd done anything besides put that pot on the floor!

---

ONE MONTH LATER, Ashi's arm shone with new, pink skin. We went on a hike and picnicked in the sprawling woods beyond the river. We ate peanut butter sandwiches. Ashi ran about in the cute, high-footed prance of early childhood.

On our way home, we walked past a procession carrying the devta. I stepped in a ditch of dirty water, trying to avoid them. It was the first day of the *mela* celebration.

We'd experienced the *mela* before when I was pregnant and watched Mrs. Opee worship the devta and got food poisoning. The *mela* was one part spring-cleaning, one part family holiday, one part religious festival. Could we participate in the spring-cleaning and visiting without the idolatry? We prayed about it. Joshua thought it would be fine. I wasn't sure.

That evening, we visited Bablu's family. Their tandoor room was warm and smelled of wood and cumin. Everyone was merry, laughing, and joking. Joshua and I sat cross-legged in the circle of adults. Ashi and Bablu's daughter ran around behind us, playing with two of Tripti's *dupatta* scarves.

Then Ashi ran into the circle of adults. Her feet caught on the mat. She fell, and her face hit the tandoor. Everyone was gasping, shouting, screaming. Ashi cried. There was blood.

I ignored everyone's questions and comments, said she was fine, and carried her away. Joshua followed me. Somehow, I made it to our kitchen and set Ashi on the counter. "Open your mouth and show Mommy!"

Ashi stuck out a tiny tongue. It was split in half like a snake's. Once again I carried my firstborn child to the road, Joshua trying to keep up with me. During the *mela*, people are everywhere, standing on every square foot of the path. People stared. I ignored. Grief threatened to pull my heart out of my chest. We had to find a car. We had to get Ashi to the hospital. Again.

"What did you do to her?" Yog's eldest sister walked toward me on the path.

"Why do you people say stuff like that?" The words I'd swallowed for so long poured out of my mouth, my voice loud and trembling. "You think I would hurt my own child? How dare you say such a thing! Ashi is precious to me. What you just said is wrong and cruel. What mother hurts their child on purpose? Why do you speak to any mother that way?"

Yog's sister stared at me, shocked. Guilt for my harshness flooded in to join my grief at Ashi's pain. Somehow Joshua and I arrived at Rose's house. She called her father-in-law to drive us to the hospital.

It rained on the way to Pahargaun. The windshield wipers and the wheels were in sync. Ashi fell asleep. Rose's father-in-law glanced at the three of us in the rear-view mirror. "A lot of bad things have happened to Ashi. You know, we have ways of protecting our children from the evil eye."

"We *are* protected," I responded. "But some things happen without a spiritual cause."

He nodded and looked back at the road. The windshield wipers thumped and squeaked. I thought about Ayushi's dreams and the hair and all we'd learned about the Parvata. I knew what I'd said was not a good enough answer for this man.

"Brother, Christians are targets of God's enemy, Satan. Although God may permit bad things to happen, He has a hedge of protection around us. There is a point past which Satan cannot touch us."

"Oh." He nodded. "So being a Christian makes you a target?"

"Not of the evil eye. But of Satan? Yes."

"I see."

I winced. Had I just made Christianity sound unattractive? Why was God allowing this? Accidents happen. But why was He letting this accident confuse the very people we were here to reach? Should I have said something else?

I bowed my head. *God, this doesn't make sense. I don't have an answer for the Parvata or even for myself. I need Your help. Give me the peace that passes understanding. You promised.*

I waited, eyes closed. The windshield wipers continued to swish. Slowly, my shoulder muscles released. The knot in my stomach unraveled. I didn't know the reason or what would happen. But I had peace. A peace that makes no sense.

Even so, after that car ride my memories are a disjointed blur. Joshua and I called everyone. We paced. We asked people to pray. When they brought Ashi out of the operation theater, I noticed for the first time that the hot tandoor had also burned her upper lip and chin.

Then somehow, we were home. Morning came. The next day, Mr. Opee told me we should have put ghee on Ashi's tongue. That it would have healed fine without the sutures. I visited Yog's sister to apologize. She said she understood.

We had to travel on a visa run the day after the accident. Ashi lay next to me on the bus, her head on my lap. She didn't sleep all night but stared straight ahead, limp from the anesthetic, awake from something else. Maybe stress. Maybe pain. I stroked the wispy strands of blonde hair away from her forehead and looked at her tongue sticking out of her mouth. It looked like she'd eaten barbed wire.

We were under attack. Satan had systematically attacked each object Joshua and I had written about in our Himalaya song as testifying to the one true God. The crashing river was now a putrid stream. The mountains that should have pointed past the temples were now obscured by a temple in our own backyard. Then there was the line, "child of God who knows my Jesus." Joshua and I had spent months and months sick. Now our precious child had been injured twice.

My thoughts squirmed in my head. Was I making us a target by sharing Christ? Would we be safer if we just went home?

BEFORE LEAVING the country for our visa run, we met with a group of missionaries in another part of India for food and fellowship. I felt as burned as my daughter's smile, as though something inside me had been seared by a flaming arrow. I couldn't pretend to understand.

They were singing, now. Someone suggested *In Christ Alone*, a beautiful worship song written by Christian musicians Keith Getty and Stuart Townend. A smiling woman with a baby on her hip handed Joshua the lyrics sheet. Ashi sat on the floor with a couple of other children, stacking blocks. She stuck out her tongue from concentration. The stitches made it look spiky.

Joshua stood next to me, his shoulder touching mine. As the voices of the group rose around us, I stared down at the paper but couldn't read it through my tears. Looking up, I saw Joshua's red eyes. He gestured to the paper and covered his face with his hand. We stood there and held each other and cried. Not a single missionary in the room batted an eye as they all understood the significance of the words and our tears.

> *No power of hell, no scheme of man*
> *Can ever pluck me from His hand*
> *Till He returns or calls me home.*
> *Here in the power of Christ, I'll stand!*

## 33

## WHY?

Our visa run coincided with our organization's biennial retreat in Thailand. Thailand was bright-blue and tan with waving palm trees and smiling cat statues. We met with the other missionaries from Asia in a retreat center.

Joshua's *yatra* trip had proved invaluable to helping us finish our cultural study. We now had more than three hundred pages of personal research on the Parvata people. Joshua and I presented a few of our observations to the other missionaries.

"As you can see from this diagram, my task during culture study was to keep the baby occupied so the goose could lay the golden egg," Joshua said. He had created a silly graphic of a goose, a golden egg, and a tiny girl. A label under the egg read, "Cultural Study." The label under the goose read "Abigail." Everyone laughed.

I smiled and shook my head. Joshua was being modest. We had both asked questions, collected information, and analyzed. We had wrestled and researched until we understood the Parvata. I had just written it down.

"On a more serious note," Joshua said, "in the past three years I've learned a lot about myself and my wife. I haven't appreciated Abigail enough. She's been flexible and forgiving. We've grown a lot, and I want to appreciate her better from now on."

There were a couple of awws, and several missionaries nodded as though they understood. I remembered what I'd told Ayushi. When someone follows Jesus, they don't stay the same. I knew Joshua's relationship with God gave him the strength and humbleness to keep growing. And I was glad we could grow together.

We rented a bicycle. I put Ashi in front of me on a kids' seat. We went riding as often as I could get away from meetings. In the late afternoons, we went swimming with the other missionary families.

They had their own stories. Some had faced sickness, some evacuations. One family had been in a country affected by Ebola. When the news covered the story, a map showing the progression of the disease was all red in their country except for a small spot where it never reached: their village.

"We prayed," they said, "that God would put warrior angels around our village. We believe He did."

---

ON OUR WAY back from the retreat, we stopped to see Pastor Thomas and his family. Mrs. Thomas and I sat together on the couch in her living room. A ceiling fan shuffled the air. Her daughters swung Ashi on a hammock in the hot, damp shade outside.

"Do you like India?" Mrs. Thomas asked.

"Of course." People often asked if I liked India. I always said yes. And it was true. I loved India, many, many parts of it. But some things in India were scary images I saw when I closed my eyes. I couldn't love those.

I once read in an Indian newspaper that if some statement about India is true, the opposite will also be true. Although the longer I lived in India the less I considered myself an expert on it, I agreed. It was hard to believe that a rape crisis, rampant fear of kidnapping, and gangs of self-mutilating beggars existed in the same country as the many people who had helped, protected, and extended hospitality to me. But then, India was Earth. It was human.

And so I loved Mother India the way I loved any person, straining to see the good, praying grace over the wounds. The ones I inflicted and the ones I received.

"You should be careful," Mrs. Thomas said, interrupting my thoughts.

"Oh?"

"Yes, be watchful and stay on your guard. The area you live in is famous for witchcraft."

"But, *Didi!*" I called her my sister. "There is no magic that will prevail against Israel." It was a quote from the story of Balaam, who tried to curse Israel but couldn't.

"That's true. But read what happened after Balaam was unsuccessful. He got Israel to curse itself by tempting them to sin."

"I'm not familiar with that story," I said. "Though I'm sure I must have read it."

"Read it again," she said. "You and Joshua must be careful. Make sure your relationship is strong. And stay close to Christ. He is the only safety."

I thought a lot about Mrs. Thomas's comments. Was it possible we'd done something to take ourselves outside the protection of God? Were Ashi's accidents just part of growing up? Or was this a Job-like test of our faith?

---

OUR EXTRA YEAR in the Opee's apartment was up. We returned from our trip to find half his house torn down, the skeleton of a new one standing on our roof. This meant almost constant hammering and sawing and nowhere for Ashi to play.

We discussed the situation with Lars and Kay. It was decided we'd go to the mountains to fast and pray. I invited our angel dispatchers to pray, too, and we packed our backpacks.

We hiked in on a Friday night, bringing grape juice and unleavened bread with us. That night we ate our last supper before starting the fast. As I stared into the orange and yellow flames of our campfire, I longed to follow God wherever He led. Whether He told me to live in the Opee's apartment forever or move somewhere even smaller. I wanted to want God's will. I knew fasting would not change God's mind. But I hoped it would change mine.

Kay was eating for two now, so the next morning she fed herself and Ashi. The rest of us fasted. We lay on blankets in the sweet, brown grass and took turns reading scripture aloud. Lars read the last few chapters of the book of Job where God describes a huge, scaly beast. God says the beast is too much for Job. Was that God's way of telling Job it had been Satan all along?

I journaled, then took Ashi to play. She ran down a grassy knoll, falling into my arms at the bottom, then climbing up to do it again. She laughed at the weightless feeling. I loved her smile, so wide and easy now that the burns were healing.

---

WE WERE WALKING home after our hike back out of the mountains when a man we called Mr. Pandit invited Joshua and me into his shop.

"Do you want to rent our house?" Mr. Pandit leaned back in his chair. A prominent belly hung over his belt. His few teeth were long, and his eyebrows were gray below a local hat. "You've seen it. It's down the road from Mrs. Banana in the orchards. Three bedrooms and a tandoor room."

I remembered the house, the way the glassless windows let in the light. I had liked that house, though it wasn't finished. But I had figured we couldn't afford the rent.

"How much?" Joshua asked. The man gave the number we had prayed over.

"It's still under construction. It will be ready in four months if you're interested."

"We'll pray about it," Joshua said. We prayed and gave an advance on rent. Mr. Pandit promised it would be ready by the end of the summer.

I worried about telling Mr. and Mrs. Opee. What would they think? What would they say? Would it ruin our relationship as it had with Rose's mother-in-law?

One evening when Mrs. Opee came by, I broached the subject. "Sister, we love you like family. And we've loved living here."

"We love having you!"

"I know. You've been so hospitable. And . . . well, there's another house. It's bigger, and it's in the apple orchard. I want to stay near you, but I want to go where Ashi has a place to play."

Mrs. Opee nodded. "Do you like it?"

"Yes," I answered.

"Well, you can't help what you like."

"We like it here, too," I said. "We'll never forget our time here."

"We had hoped you would stay forever," she said. "After the second story is built, the courtyard will be a great place for Ashi to play. We'll have extra wood after our new house is done. We could put wood flooring in here if you like."

"Thank you so much," I said. Having boundaries felt like making too much noise near a sleeping tiger. But Mrs. Opee hadn't eaten me yet. "Please don't feel bad. But we plan to move in a few months once it's ready."

"I understand," said Mrs. Opee. "If you like it, you like it. Go and enjoy. But don't be strangers, okay?"

I was thrilled. Mrs. Opee would not disown us. We could stay family.

# 34

## A CURE FOR CURSES

When Ajay got the flu a couple of weeks later, he came straight to me.

"Bhabiiii," he whined at the door. "I have a fever."

"Poor thing! Lie down here on the mat." I covered Ajay with a patu and smiled to myself. He had grown a lot in the last year. His voice had changed. His feet looked huge, sticking out from under the patu.

"Ugh!" Ajay moaned. "Help. I feel awful."

I gave Ajay a hot foot bath and set a cool rag on his forehead. Then I knelt beside him and prayed. He slept.

"You play quietly, Ashi," I said. "Uncle Ajay is sick. He needs rest."

Several hours later, Ajay woke up. "Bhabi?"

"Yes?" I came out of the kitchen where Ashi sat on the floor stirring imaginary food. "Need anything?"

"I'm leaving," he said.

"Going home?"

"No. I mean, I'm leaving home. I have to go to priest school after a few weeks."

I felt my heart sink. Were my dreams for Ajay to be the first Parvata pastor unrealistic? "I see. Are you going to get your janeo string?"

"No." Ajay laughed. Then he coughed and sniffled. I handed him a tissue. "Mom said to wait another year or two. She knows I like raiding your fridge."

"You can still raid our fridge at the new house after we move. You're welcome any time you're on vacation." I paused. "How do you feel about going?"

"I want to go. I'm going to be like my dad. But who's going to take care of me? Who's will bake me chocolate chip cookies and give me hot foot baths?"

"I'll mail you cookies if you promise to share."

"Maybe Joshua Bhai can visit."

"I'm sure he'd love to."

"Things will change. It won't be the same after this."

"I know, Ajay. But I'll pray for God to bless you. And to guide your path."

"Thanks," Ajay said. Then he went home.

*Go after Him,* I prayed, swallowing back tears.

---

I VISITED Ayushi and watched her pound the dough for chapattis. "What is it? You seem tense."

"I told you," Ayushi said. "I have bad dreams, and then they come true. Why didn't God stop Ashi from getting hurt?"

I had wrestled with this question myself. I still didn't have an answer. But Job hadn't had all the answers either. "I don't know why it happened. Maybe it was even a coincidence."

Ayushi shook her head. "No. It was because of the hair."

I sighed. "Ayushi, I don't think it's a coincidence either. I don't have an answer. But I know one thing. There is a line past which Satan cannot touch us. We learned that from the story of Job, remember?"

Ayushi picked dough off her fingers. Had she assumed that Christians are untouchable, always kept safe from harm? Had she assumed Christians live lives full of blessings, never facing persecution or difficulties? Had I assumed that?

"I don't like it," she said.

"Neither do I. Your dreams were threats from the enemy to my family." I felt my voice rising. "And parts of your dreams seemed to happen. It's like Satan wanted to show off his power. To get us to back off and leave you alone. But you know what? There's one thing Satan has no control over."

"What's that?" Ayushi asked.

"You said in one of your dreams I cried and cried. That you couldn't get me to stop."

"I remember."

"There it is. The one thing Satan can't control. I will not cry forever, and I will not spend my life in grief and bitterness. No matter what happens, God will be with me. He's done it so far. He's proven Himself. And He will make everything right in the end, no matter what He allows me to go through." As I spoke, I felt my voice grow even louder, and the words seemed truer spoken.

For the next several months, Ayushi and I didn't talk much about spiritual topics. She seemed reluctant, and I didn't want to pressure her. Instead, we discussed her boyfriend and the beauty products she was now selling with an Italian skincare company. Ayushi feared the devta's prediction that she would never marry and seemed determined to prove it wrong.

---

I WAS eager to tell Rose about our upcoming move. Maybe she would feel more comfortable visiting our new place. When I arrived, I found Rose's mother-in-law Shanty standing in their courtyard, a dirty dupatta pulled over her face.

"Oh, Aunty! What happened?" I exclaimed. Huge sores covered Shanty's hands. She flinched as she removed her scarf to show me the sores on her face.

"Somebody cursed me," she said. "But we don't know who."

"I see." I was surprised at my empathy. It is easy for Westerners to explain away spiritual warfare. But sometimes there isn't an easy answer. I knew what Rose's mother-in-law must be thinking. Does someone hate me so much? What must I do to be saved from these sores?

"Aunty, there are many things that can cause boils. It could be a curse, or it could be something medical. You might want to see a doctor. Could I pray for you?"

Shanty nodded. I reached out and touched her shoulder. She flinched again. I moved my hand to her arm and felt her relax. I prayed.

"Wait here," I added after saying amen. "I have to get something."

I ran home. Joshua and I prayed together for Shanty. Then I grabbed a Hindi Bible and ran back. By the time I returned, she was gone.

"They're on their way to the hospital," Rose said. She fiddled with her ruby-red plastic necklace. I sat beside her, and we were quiet for a long moment, listening to the birds and neighborhood cows and the trickle of water in the nearby ditch.

"Jesus can cure curses," I said.

I saw Rose sit up straight in my peripheral. She said nothing.

"He can also cure anxious hearts," I continued. If Satan could try to use my daughter's injuries to hurt me, I would use the same to get somebody out of his prison of lies. "Remember the time Ashi got hurt?"

Rose nodded. "You cried. It worried me."

"I was very upset. I felt like I would go crazy. But I prayed, and God gave me peace. Another time when I was pregnant with Ashi, the doctor said I might miscarry. I was so afraid. But God gave me peace. In fact, I saw a picture in my mind of His two hands holding her tiny body as she floated in darkness."

"I never have peace," Rose whispered. "But I want it. I hope Jesus can give me peace."

"He can, Rose," I said. "Would you like to have a Bible? I can show you an easy place to start reading. Then you can get to know Him better."

"I would love that," Rose said.

I took out the Hindi Bible and showed it to her. She took it and smoothed the gold-leaf letters with her hand.

"I just have one question," she said. "What do you picture when you talk to God?"

"Picture?" I asked. "What do you mean?"

"Like the picture you saw when you thought you were miscarrying. What do you see with your 'third eye' when you pray?"

I knew the phrase "third eye" was sometimes used to signify the imagination.

Rose went on, "When I pray to one of our goddesses, I can picture the poster on my wall or a statue. But you told me before that you don't use images of your God."

"Yes," I said. "That's very important for Christians."

"But don't you picture anything?"

I looked up at the sky, trying to remember. What did I picture when I prayed? "I guess I talk to God like a real person. It's like talking with someone on the phone. I don't have to picture because He hears me and responds."

"I see," Rose said.

"But sometimes I picture Him as light. Or sometimes I think of a giant marble throne room in heaven. He is there on the throne, and I come and speak to Him." I smiled, thinking of how I imagined birds must nest near God's throne in heaven just to be close.

"Okay." Rose nodded and patted the Bible. "I will try."

I visited again a few days later. Shanty's sores had disappeared. Rose whispered to me that she believed Jesus had taken them away.

---

SUMMER CAME. Joshua prepared to lead his first tour group. They would be away for a month and a half.

After hugs with Ashi and me, Joshua bounced out the door with a backpack and camera. I watched him walk toward the gate, a hollow feeling in the pit of my stomach. I allowed myself a few tears as Ashi banged on the screen door. Her daddy stopped at the gate and waved.

"Dadddyyyy," she called out. "Bye, bye!"

Then she turned to me and put her arms up. I laughed through my tears and lifted her. "It's okay. We'll talk to Daddy on the phone. He'll be away for a while, but we'll see him again."

I knew this would be the first of many separations in the coming years. Joshua would have to work every summer for our friend's tourism company. It was the only way we could keep our business visa.

# 35

CHANGES

While Joshua was away, I tried to keep myself busy. I played with Ashi and visited friends, especially those like Rose who seemed interested in knowing Jesus.

Rose used to joke that our children should marry. They were very close in age, and with their short hair looked like the same child in different colors. They toddled about now in Rose's courtyard, each absorbed with a toy.

"I've been reading the Bible you gave me," Rose told me. "But every time I open it, I get drowsy. I can't keep my eyes open."

"Ayushi has the same problem," I said. "Even I have felt it."

"As soon as I put the Bible away, the sleepiness is gone. Why?" Rose studied my face, her brown eyes open wide. How could I answer in a way that made sense to her?

"You know about the *boori atma*, right?" *Boori atma* meant "bad spirit" and referred in a very abstract sense to a cruel, satanic power. It is the same power that Parvata witches are said to wield.

"Oh, yes," Rose said.

"It's like this. Satan doesn't want us to read the Bible. He wants to keep us away from God. I don't have all the answers. But I've learned that it's important to pray for God's protection. I wish we could know Jesus easily, but the enemy does want to stop us."

Rose looked down at the ground. I thought of something I'd learned in our missions training. *Always model. Don't just tell people. Show them!*

"Could I pray with you?" I asked.

"I would like that," Rose said, her voice low and solemn.

"Dear heavenly Father," I prayed. "Forgive us any sins that might keep us separated from You. Wash us clean in Jesus's blood so we have the right to come before You. Send mighty warrior angels to stand all around this house, especially

Rose's room. I pray that Your Holy Spirit would be near her to speak to her heart as she reads Your word. And I pray You would rebuke Satan's plan to make her too sleepy to read. In Jesus's name, amen."

"Amen!" Rose threw her arms around my neck. "Thank you!"

---

THAT AFTERNOON, Ashi and I walked to Ayushi's grandfather's shop. Ayushi was there, swishing at her phone with her thumb. She stood when she saw us. "Ashi!"

Ashi grinned and wiggled. I set her down, and she hugged Ayushi's legs before walking over to the yarn. She loved to squeeze the colorful skeins.

"How are you?" I asked. "How is your family?"

"We're all fine," Ayushi said.

"How's the Boy?"

"He's good." Ayushi blushed and smiled. "We talk on the phone a lot. Sometimes I leave him on the line all night. I sleep better that way."

"Still having trouble sleeping?"

"Something shoves me awake in the night," Ayushi whispered. "I'm afraid it's one of the devtas."

"I've been praying for you."

"Thank you. But it helps to stay connected with my boyfriend. If I get scared in the night, he hears me and comforts me."

I smiled, waiting for more. Ayushi glanced at Ashi and bit her lip. "There's one thing. The teachers at the school tell me I shouldn't marry him."

"Oh?"

"And part of me knows they're right." Ayushi sighed. "He isn't a Christian. What do you think I should do?"

"Well, if you want to follow Jesus, your friends are right. The Bible tells Christians not to marry non-Christians. I know right now it's all so exciting. But one day the feelings settle, and you find yourself going through everything with this person—trials, raising kids, big decisions, emergencies. You've got to make sure you have a solid foundation."

"He's interested in Jesus," Ayushi said. "And I've already said yes to be his girlfriend. I'm committed. I feel like I can't back out now."

I explained to Ayushi that dating is not the same level of commitment as marriage. But I knew it felt the same to her. Loyalty and honor were too much a part of Ayushi's identity to let her give up on this relationship.

"I can't tell you what to do," I said. "But I will tell you from personal experience that obeying God is the best way."

"Personal experience?"

"God once told me to break up with a boy."

"What did you do?"

"I said no."

"I don't believe you!" Ayushi tried not to smile. "You really said no to God?"

"It's true. I remember the moment He spoke to my heart, loud and clear. I regret that I didn't listen. I'm only glad I eventually chose God's way."

"Was it Joshua?"

"No."

"You're really lucky to have Joshua. He loves you and Ashi so much. He's a good man."

"Imagine if I'd continued going my own way. I'd never even have met him." The hair rose on the back of my neck as it often did when I thought of my own personal alternate reality.

"What you're saying is, God had a plan for your life and you could have missed it?"

I nodded. "He has one for you too, Ayushi. All you have to do is trust and obey. Make Him the foundation, and He will build you something that will last."

---

KAY WAS a blessed distraction from my too-quiet house. One morning, she called to see if I'd join her for a walk. She felt cramped sitting inside all day.

"I'd love to," I said. "And I have an idea."

"Ooh. What's your idea?"

"Do you remember 'Uh Huh!' the restaurant?"

"The one with the yak sign?"

"That's the one! I haven't eaten there, but there's a play area with an actual swing. Ashi would love it. Are you up for a long walk?"

"Pick me up on your way out of the village."

I held Ashi's hand, and we walked to the road. People waved to her from their shops. Yog beckoned us near, then gave her a handful of raisins. Once outside the village, I loaded Ashi in her carrier and trudged up the hill.

Kay was talking with a Parvata friend when I arrived outside her building. They hugged, and then Kay and I walked and talked. I wanted to write a book about my testimony. Kay was preparing for her first baby's birth. We commiserated over morning sickness in a foreign country. Why do you always crave what you can't have?

"Whew," I said when we reached the park at the restaurant. Setting Ashi free, I flopped into a lawn chair. "I haven't felt this tired in a long time."

A waiter appeared and handed us two menus. We both decided on the veggie burger and fries. When they arrived, Kay sniffed appreciatively. "It's so nice not to have morning sickness anymore."

We prayed over the food. Then I picked up my veggie burger. I took a tiny bite, then set it back on my plate.

"What's wrong?" Kay asked. "Not good?"

"I don't know. I was so hungry. I just... don't want it anymore. It doesn't smell appetizing."

"Oh?" Kay grinned.

"Wait, you don't think—"

"Could you be?"

"I guess it's not impossible. I mean, we said we'd be okay with another one."

"You should take a test," Kay suggested.

I shook my head. "I can't, at least not in our village. I know all the pharmacists. Man, the Parvata social shame is rubbing off on me!"

Kay laughed. "No problem. I'll buy it."

Back in my apartment twenty minutes later, Kay and I waited. I wandered around, dusted under things, scratched a paint blob off my desk. After a long two-minute wait, I had my answer. My heart fluttered as I turned to Kay.

"Two lines! Bright ones! I'm pregnant!"

# 36

## ANYWHERE WITH JESUS

"Awww, congratulations!" Kay hugged me. I called Joshua. He announced it to the people on his trip, and I heard a loud, muffled cheer in the background.

But just one week later, nausea and exhaustion took over. Mrs. Opee noticed first. "You're pregnant! I knew that's why you wanted to move."

She looked down at me where I lay in the middle of our living-room floor. Ashi sat on a pile of clean laundry, coloring her leg with a marker. "I'll send Lovelina."

Lovelina came and folded our laundry while I wallowed in guilt for needing help. Later, I called Lars and Kay. "Um, I hate to ask you this, but . . . can you come cook my dinner?"

"We're on our way!" Kay and Lars soon arrived. Ashi's half-made meal sat on the counter.

"I started making it," I told them. "But the smell tried to kill me."

"Leave it to us!"

Lars and Kay could be hospitable even in someone else's house. It was their spiritual gift to bring the feeling of home wherever they went. Soon Ashi was fed and asleep. Lars and Kay prayed with me. Then they walked the two miles back to their apartment.

---

I WAS WASHING dishes when I heard our screen door creak. Just as I reached for a towel to dry my hands, an arm tinkling with bangles slipped through mine.

"Puja!" I exclaimed. It had been several months since we'd seen each other.

"Abigail, I'm pregnant," she whispered.

"Are you serious?" I turned around. "I am, too!"

Puja gasped. We laughed and hugged. We compared due dates. Hers was just a few weeks after mine.

"Where is Shankar?" I asked.

"Pahargaun," she said. "Another political rally."

"He must be so happy."

"He is. Shankar is busy a lot. Our marriage hasn't been the storybook I dreamed of growing up. But the baby will change everything. We'll feel like a family, now. I just know it."

---

JOSHUA RETURNED, and Kay's due date drew near. Lars' and Kay's mothers, eager to become grandmas, braved the long flight from the states to visit. They set about cooking, folding, washing, and shopping. In between vomiting and trying not to vomit, I packed our things in preparation for the move to our new house.

In the midst of all this, our laptop gave up its electronic ghost. The closest repair center was in Delhi, so Joshua left. He would spend a week in Delhi getting the computer fixed and connecting with friends there.

"Kay," I said over the phone just a few hours after Joshua left. "I'm so sorry. Listen, I know you will literally have your baby any minute. But I need help. I haven't been able to keep food down for two days. I was wondering if I could come stay in one of the apartments near you guys, and maybe someone could just bring food for Ashi."

"Of course," Kay said. "Come on over."

As I packed Ashi's things, despair seized my mind. I was not a fun mother anymore. All I could do was stay horizontal next to a bucket. This frustrated Ashi, and it frustrated me. Now I was about to crash Kay's party. I felt heavy as a burden on someone else's back.

I hitched a ride to Kay's in an autorickshaw. Kay's landlord rented me a furnished room near hers. I handed Ashi some toys, knowing they wouldn't hold her attention forever. Then I collapsed on the bed. *Jesus, I need You! I'm drowning.*

Was I allergic to pregnancy? Why couldn't I stop vomiting? Why couldn't I stop thinking? I closed my eyes and could just see Bablu's mother's silver hair and proud face. His grandmother sitting in the corner of the room. Tripti dressing Ashi in a tiny patu dress. They had been one of my Parvata families, had fed me and taught me their language. But things had changed.

Tripti's favorite deity was Durga, the goddess with the bloody tongue. More than once, I'd seen her dance for the goddess with her dupatta scarf tied around her waist. She and her family had no interest in Jesus, and this grieved my heart. But it wasn't their lack of interest that had changed things.

It was Ama's poison tongue.

Ashi could understand now what people said in both English and Hindi. I saw her listening. Saw her worldview beginning to form. I didn't want Ama's words to settle in her thoughts.

"Men are stupid. They are useless, worthless. The low caste are trash." I could hear Ama's cracked voice, see her in my mind. She seemed to detest the taste of her own words, scowling as she said them.

So I'd decided. I would visit Bablu's family by myself. But I would not bring Ashi there again. I knew this would greatly reduce my visits. But I had to do it—for Ashi and her little sibling. Besides, what if the baby was a boy?

LARS TOLD me later they could hear my constant retching during their porch picnic. His mother came to my room. She entertained Ashi for a while. Then she sat on the edge of the bed.

"I got really sick when I was pregnant. Sick and depressed. I couldn't do anything. I know how hard it is." She handed me a granola bar. "Try to eat it."

It tasted great, but it didn't stick. Soon, Lars came by. "Try this. Mom says they give this to ladies with hyperemesis in American hospitals."

He handed me a packet of pills. I looked online, my hands trembling. Hyperemesis was the medical term for nausea that tries to kill you. The drug Lars had given me turned out to be safe for pregnancy.

Within an hour, I could keep food and water down. Joshua came home. Kay had her baby, a girl as beautiful as a little flower. They named her Posy. Soon they moved into a larger home thirty minutes south of ours by bus. This way our team could broaden our contacts with the Parvata, and Lars, Kay, and Posy could have space to live.

IT WAS time to move into our own new place. Some of our Nepali friends helped us move, carrying our belongings from ropes slung across their foreheads.

As I walked into our new living room, I frowned. Why was it so dark? Glass hadn't been installed the last time we'd visited, but why would that make a difference? I whirled around. The windows were one-way mirrors. We could look out, but nobody could see in, and the light coming in the windows was a midnight blue color.

I strode into the other rooms. Each had the same window treatment. *Oh, God*, I prayed. *They've blocked the light!*

A few nights later while making dinner, I felt my belly tighten, gently at first, then hard. I doubled over and grabbed a chair for support. *I'm only nineteen weeks. This can't be happening.*

I felt cold and hot and sweaty but tried to smile as I put Ashi to bed. Joshua noticed my pained expression. "What's wrong?"

"I don't know. I'm having contractions and not just Braxton hicks. I don't know what to do. I . . . I think I'll call your mom."

"I'm so sorry you're going through another trial," Mrs. Follows said tenderly after I explained what was happening. "I'll ask my OB/GYN friend to call you."

He did call. He suggested I lie down and drink water. If I was going to miscarry, I was going to miscarry. If not, the pain would subside on its own.

I lay on my left side and stared at the wall. Moths circled a fluorescent wall sconce above me. Mrs. Follows was right. Joshua and I had been through many trials. Trials in our marriage. In our home. With our child. Trials with our health.

Now here was another trial. Yet something felt different this time. Our circumstances hadn't changed much. We still had more questions than answers. The hospital wasn't going to get any closer, cleaner, or more high-tech. We still had mold to fight even in the new house. But something was different.

My heart pounded. *Something in me is different! I've changed. I've learned something. But what?*

The answer was clear and wonderful. God had proven Himself to me. Now as I faced the possibility of losing our baby, I knew that God would see me through this trial, too. Whatever happened, He would be with me and give me the strength to handle it. As I thought back over nearly three years in India, I surprised myself. I was thankful, not just for life and healing and happy memories but for the fire.

Just then, the baby moved.

"Oh, sweet little one," I said aloud. "Are you scared? There, there. It will be okay."

I had to be strong. I had to use the faith I had earned. I began singing a favorite hymn.

> Anywhere with Jesus I can safely go,
> anywhere He leads me in this world below.
> Anywhere without Him dearest joys would fade.
> Anywhere with Jesus, I am not afraid!
> Anywhere, anywhere, fear I cannot know.
> Anywhere with Jesus I can safely go.

The baby's movement slowed.

"There, there," I said again, stroking my belly, speaking to us. "Everything will be all right."

---

THE DAY of the threatened miscarriage sank into night. The next morning was Sabbath. I awoke to soft pink light creeping up over the mountains. I stretched. The baby kicked. There was no pain.

# 37

# BORN IN A TAXI?

O ur third anniversary of moving to India arrived. We had fulfilled our first set of goals: to learn Hindi, bond with the people, complete a cultural research project, and switch to a business visa. Our organization provided us with another round of training, during which we prayed and discussed the best way to share the gospel with the Parvata.

During this training, I dreamt I gave birth behind somebody's couch. I cried out for deliverance, but nobody cared. It became a recurring nightmare.

"You have nothing to prove," a fellow missionary mom comforted me. "Why don't you just go home to have the baby? Why would you do that again, knowing what it's like?"

I wanted to listen. To tell Joshua I needed to go back to the United States to have the baby. Since we'd been in India for three years, we were technically eligible for a furlough. But we'd already spent several extra months away from the Parvata project. It made sense to wait another year and go the following summer. Besides, what might God do in the coming months if we stayed?

After training, I received a phone call from another missionary. She'd felt impressed to give me a message God had laid on her heart. "I've been praying for you, Abby. And I think if God gives you peace, you can trust Him to take care of you. If you feel called to have your second baby in India, you should do it."

So it was decided. We would stay and take our furlough after the baby was born.

---

ALTHOUGH THE MISSION hospital in Pahargaun had a new and competent OB/GYN, their policy still didn't allow husbands in the delivery room. So we kept looking. We discovered one of the Chotashaher hospitals also had a new

OB/GYN. I privately referred to her as Dr. Wonderful due to her kind, warm demeanor with the worried pregnant women who came into her office. Her husband was a pediatrician, and the two of them attended births together.

*I wonder if she'll end up delivering this baby, after all,* I often wondered. *Will we even make it to Chotashaher?*

I'd read that women often give birth more quickly the second time. My first labor had taken just over six hours. What if it was shorter this time? What if the taxi was late? When I packed our hospital bag, I included everything needed for an emergency road-side delivery, down to a black trash bag to cover the back seat of a taxi. Just in case.

---

SUMMER TURNED INTO AUTUMN. We began to see Nepali men descend into the apple orchards below our house, scarves over their mouths, jet-pack-like canisters on their backs. Standing under the trees, they'd aim a hose into the air, and a white cloud of chemicals would billow up to settle on the apples.

Whenever we saw the sprayers, Ashi and I rushed into the house and slammed all the windows shut. Then we'd stayed inside for several hours. Later as our family walked through fields swaying with yellow mustard flowers, we'd find empty pesticide containers. The chemicals listed on the labels had long been banned in the United States.

During spraying season, neighbors complained of asthma, pneumonia, and constant coughing. Chemical containers, used sanitary napkins, and uncapped syringes were among the garbage washed down into the fields via ditches running from the road to the river. On our walks, I fussed over Ashi. Don't touch that. Don't go there. I tried to breathe around the poison molecules, willing oxygen to make it untainted to my baby.

*Just relax,* I told myself. *Let Ashi run and live and breathe. Don't teach her to worry. Don't let the baby feel your fear.*

---

I FOUGHT my fear over the next several months as we waited for the baby to make his appearance. The apples and mustard flowers were harvested. We bought wood for the *tandoor*. Friends from the hospital visited for Thanksgiving and Indian friends attended another Christmas showing of *The Jesus Film*. Soon only one week remained until my due date.

"I wish we could just go to Chotashaher now," I told Joshua. "We could stay in a hotel and be near the hospital. It might even be relaxing."

"Nah," Joshua responded. "It's more convenient to cook our own food."

"I guess that's true," I admitted.

Joshua left to do some errands. After doing a few chores, I knelt. *God, maybe Joshua is right. But I keep thinking we should go to Chotashaher. If this is an impression from You, give me confirmation!*

Just then, Joshua walked in, his cell-phone to his ear. "Here she is. Abigail, Mom wants to talk to you."

I took the phone. "Hi, Mrs. Follows!"

"Abby, listen… I have to tell you something. You need to go down to Chotashaher today, okay? You need to go and stay in a hotel. Can you do that?"

"Did Joshua say something?"

"No. I had a dream about you last night. And I think you'd better go."

Packing our things, we called a taxi to take us to Chotashaher. During the drive, I called Lovelina to ask about caring for Ashi while I was in labor.

"I can't," she responded. "But Mom says she can."

I felt my eyebrows shoot up. Mrs. Opee? As tender and loving as Mrs. Opee was, she was not the calming presence I'd hoped to have around my toddler during the birth of her sibling. "Okay. I'll let you know if I need her."

---

JOSHUA, Ashi, and I booked a homestay. The owners said they'd be happy to drive us to the hospital when it was time to have the baby. We found a place to eat, a cafe owned by an Indian pastor and his wife. The following three days in Chotashaher turned out more relaxing than expected. But we still hadn't found anyone to help with Ashi.

"Rose's mother-in-law won't let her," I told Joshua. "Lars and Kay just left for language school. Ayushi is visiting her brother in Delhi. And I don't want Mrs. Opee here. Joshua, you'll just have to stay with Ashi yourself. I'll be okay alone."

"I have an idea," Joshua said. "Remember Pastor John, the one who owns the café? He and his wife Martha said to call on them if we need anything. They live near the hospital."

I hesitated. I didn't know these people well. But I knew Someone who knew them. "Okay, then. When it's time, we'll call John and Martha."

We knelt and thanked God for providing someone to take care of our precious firstborn.

"Lord, You are so good," I prayed. "We trust you… to…"

"Abby? You falling asleep?"

"Call them now," I said through clenched teeth. "I'm in labor!"

The contractions came so quickly I had a hard time walking the five meters to our homestay owner's car. Though they barely knew us, Pastor John and Martha took Indian hospitality to a whole new level. Though they had a six-year-old daughter and a newborn baby, they bundled themselves up and met us at the hospital, ready to care for Ashi.

Just two hours and thirteen minutes after the first contraction, our son was born. I watched the pediatrician, Mr. Dr. Wonderful, whisk him to an incubator to check his vitals. Then the room began to look strange. I heard Dr. Wonderful's voice. "We've got a bleeder!"

I heard clinking and clanging and nurses rushing. Dr. Wonderful leaned in close. "Abigail, you are bleeding badly. I have to give you a pain killer so I can fix it."

The doctor worked quickly to stop the bleeding. It seemed I was observing something outside myself.

"I feel woozy," I said.

"It's okay," the doctor responded. "You'll be okay, now."

Someone wheeled my gurney towards a room. Meeting us in the hallway, Pastor John placed a warm hand on my arm. I felt strength and comfort and love radiating from his hand into me. He said nothing, but it was as though my own father stood there with his hand on my shoulder. I knew I'd be okay. Pastor John was praying for me.

---

THAT EVENING, I called Joshua's mom to tell her all was well with sweet baby Arav.

"I didn't want to scare you," she said. "But now that it's all over, I want to tell you about my dream. You were in a taxi with the door open. Joshua was standing outside, trying to cut open a black trash bag to put on the seat so you could have the baby. Then I woke up."

"How did you know I had a black trash bag in my hospital bag? Did I tell you that?"

"No. I didn't know that," she said. "But God must have."

I calculated. Chotashaher was two hours from Kushigaun, not counting the ten-minute brisk walk to the road from our house. My contractions had been too strong for me to walk quickly. If we hadn't stayed in Chotashaher, I would have given birth in a taxi.

My head spun as I thought of the implications. If I'd given birth in a taxi, there would have been no one to stop the hemorrhaging. I could have died. The hair stood up on the back of my neck. God was near. He was still the God who sees me.

*Thank You,* I prayed.

---

JOSHUA'S PARENTS CAME. For two weeks, they played with Ashi, cuddled Arav, and helped around the house. By then, Joshua and I were accustomed to the lack of sleep and had developed a good parenting rhythm. After another beautiful baby dedication, Mr. and Mrs. Follows went home.

Then I remembered Puja. She must have had her baby by now. I bundled up the children, and we headed down to Mr. Opee's place.

"Come in, come in!" Mrs. Opee took Ashi's hand to help her up the stairs. "I haven't seen you since Arav's dedication two weeks ago!"

"We've missed you," I said. "And wished we could come."

"I know you're busy now. Two babies in less than three years. It's a lot of work!" Smiling, Mrs. Opee made noises at Arav. I found it jarring how the Parvata snapped and clapped and spoke to babies as though they were hard of hearing. But the babies loved it. Maybe it made them more social or helped them sleep more soundly. Culture and mindset are molded by experience even in infancy. Perhaps my children too would have a mix of Indian and American world-views.

"I brought some baby clothes for Puja," I said. "Arav outgrew them so quickly. Has she had her baby yet? I know it should be any day now. I'm so excited for her!"

Mrs. Opee stared down at Arav but no longer smiled. She was silent. A prick of discomfort twisted into me. Mrs. Opee was never quiet.

"She had her baby." Mrs. Opee sighed. "But he died."

I felt my heart fall through my stomach. "What happened?"

Mrs. Opee shook her head. "She just labored and labored for hours, and nobody even checked her."

I thought of Dr. Wonderful with her competence and smiling encouragement. I thought of my dream of laboring behind a couch with nobody to care. "What hospital was she at? What do you mean nobody checked her?"

"She was at the government hospital in Chotashaher. A nurse checked the baby's heartbeat at the beginning, and a doctor saw her once. Someone checked the heartbeat again when she was pushing, but it was too late. The baby came out blue."

In my mind, I saw the rows of narrow cots and women laboring on the floor. "Didn't they even try to save him?"

"No use. He was already gone. My mother said he was a beautiful boy. Fat like Arav."

We walked home, Arav asleep in the baby carrier, his soft, chubby cheek against my neck, Ashi's little hand clinging to mine. From my other hand swung the bag of outgrown baby clothes.

———

AS SOON AS I COULD, I visited Puja. She was the only one at home. We sat cross-legged on her bed and drank chai, talking with soft voices, savoring the quiet afternoon. Soon the topic turned to the child she had lost.

"Did you name him?" I asked. "I mean, I know it isn't your custom to give a name if a child doesn't live. But before he was born? In your heart?"

Puja gestured. "See that jar up there?" I looked up. On top of Shankar and Puja's steel locker was a jar half-full of coins. "Shankar put that there. He was so happy about the baby. It seemed to knit us together, you know? He'd come home every day and put a little money in the jar, saying, 'This is for Lucky.' So we were calling him Lucky."

Ashi and Arav grew. Joshua and I spent the next several months as usual, connecting with people, looking for natural ways to talk about spiritual things. Any time the kids outgrew something, I gave it to neighbors in need. But I saved that first bag of Arav's clothing. That summer when we went on furlough, I brought the bag with me to give away—the clothes that Lucky should have worn.

# 38

## GOLIATH

**B**ack stateside, Joshua and I planned our mission presentation for our supporting churches. Joshua shared facts and Biblical wisdom, the bones of the sermon. I fleshed it out with stories about Ajay and his family, Chotu, Puja's baby, and others. We wanted our angel dispatchers to understand India's needs and to feel they knew the Parvata people.

One Sabbath after church, Joshua got into the passenger's side of our car. "You drive. I'm beat."

My smile covered a sense of dismal foreboding. "I'm a bit tired myself. Don't you think you should drive?"

"Nah. It's not far." Leaning the seat back, Joshua stretched. "You can do it, Abby."

"I really don't want to."

"But you can."

"But I can't! Please don't make me drive."

Things heated up from there. I drove, angry. Something in me knew this wasn't logical. Grown people take turns driving. But wasn't it better to have the more capable person drive? Someone sturdy who could save us all in an emergency? That wasn't me. I was the jumpy person who envisioned us all dying in a car crash and should definitely sit in the passenger seat. Probably for the rest of her life.

That night as we lay awake in the dark, Joshua said something that would change everything. "Abigail, listen. This has to stop."

"What do you mean?" My stomach tightened into a knot. "What did I do?"

"It's like you have this bubble around you, and you're only safe inside it. And that bubble is getting smaller. You exercise in the house. You don't want to drive."

The silence was loud and ringing in my ears. He was saying I had a problem. An anxiety problem. A mental problem.

"Just think about it. Fewer and fewer places feel safe for you. Your circle of safety is shrinking." Tears pooled in my eyes as he went on. "Pretty soon, you'll be stuck at home. Nowhere will be safe."

*What's so bad about staying home?* I almost argued. Women all over the world stayed at home. They stayed home in Saudi Arabia. Some women in India stayed home. Their husbands brought the vegetables home from the market. And the socks and the new bras, too.

Then I remembered. I didn't *want* to be that kind of woman. The woman who has to wait for life to happen to her. My pride fought to stay alive. *Don't let him tell you what to do. He has no idea what it's like to be you. He underestimates the risk. He—*

"You're right," I said. I thought about my mother. For years, I'd looked at my beautiful mom like a good dream that might disappear. Depression had kept her, as she'd put it, "in a box, in a box, in a box, in a box."

And I had been determined never to live in that box. I had squinted suspiciously at my emotions, worried they might betray me. If I noticed anything vaguely resembling a mental disorder, I reined myself in with positivity, poetry, and prayer.

God had brought me so far, taught me so much. I'd always thought if I just trusted Him and avoided getting too stressed, I'd be okay.

But if I saw stress as a giant ready to crush me, Joshua saw me as David with his sling and smooth stones. Joshua believed I was perfectly normal, sane, and capable of handling stress. Sometimes I found his generous view of me annoying. Now I saw it as a lifeline. And I was ready to reach for it.

"What do you think I should do, Joshua?" He squeezed my hand.

"You've got to fight it. Do stuff you're scared to do. Believe that God will give you the strength to handle whatever happens. Otherwise, that bubble will keep getting smaller and smaller. It'll paralyze you, Abigail."

I had thought anxiety was something you get cured of, like cancer. But anxiety is not like cancer. It's like alcohol. It's an unchosen addiction to worry, to control. You have to stare it in the face and say no every time. Even when you're tired. Especially when you're tired. Otherwise, it takes over and convinces you that you'll never feel happy unless you avoid "just this one thing." It destroys the faith you've worked so hard to build.

"You're right. I know you're right," I said. And that was the moment I stopped pretending I was fine, the day of the death of my pride.

---

THE REST of our furlough was full of baby steps. I tried jogging, driving, shopping in crowded stores, letting Ashi slide down way-too-tall slides, and other life-threatening activities. Soon it was time to return to India.

Because of road construction, our bus ride from Delhi took even longer than normal, nearly nineteen hours. The first thing we noticed when we walked into our yard was that our house was no longer just a one-level building. An unfinished floor with an outside entrance sat on top of our formerly flat roof.

Joshua unlocked the front door, and Ashi ran in to find all her old toys. Arav crawled after her. Joshua and I set down our bags, then walked back outside to survey what had been our roof.

"Looks like our landlords have been busy," Joshua said.

"Wonder when they'll move in," I said.

"They've still got a good six months of work left here. Maybe more."

---

WE SETTLED back into life in Kushigaun. One October day, I was standing on our porch watching the fog move through the trees when I heard a shofar-like wail in the village. Then drumming filled the air. After four years in Kushigaun, that sound meant something to me. It meant someone had died.

My phone rang. It was Joshua. "Bablu and Tripti's grandma died this morning."

I didn't know what to say, think or feel. I'd just seen her! As soon as Joshua arrived to take over kid duties, I grabbed a coat and ran. The drumming grew louder, and soon I could feel it in my chest. When I neared the house, I saw a group of men, each carrying a log. Ahead of them, up the road, four men carried a pine box heaped in silk scarves. They were on their way to the bank of the river to cremate the body.

*Jesus, please be with me!* I prayed as I entered the courtyard. It was crowded with women, some weeping, some staring at nothing. I spotted Tripti. Her eyes were so pale, she looked as though she'd cried all the color out of them.

"Look! Your *sehali* is here," someone said, referring to me as a close friend. Tripti collapsed into my arms. She screamed into my shoulder, the loudest, saddest sound I had ever heard a human being make. I held her and wept.

The women allowed a few minutes of crying, but soon gathered around Tripti, demanding she regain composure. One neighbor got right in her face and forced eye contact. "Take courage. Get yourself together for your own sake."

Inside the house, Ama, Bablu's mother, sat on the floor, back against a wall, silver braid hanging down her front like a fraying rope. Sometimes she cried out or moaned.

Other women in the room chatted among themselves about whether Tripti's grandma was now in heaven. I knew from our cultural studies that these thoughts didn't express the teachings of classical Hinduism. But something was comforting to these women about the idea of a heaven.

"I've heard you go to heaven if you're really old when you die," someone said.

"I think it's only if you've been good," said another. "Then you don't have to be reincarnated."

As I walked home, I tried to sing our *Himalaya Song,* but choked on the words:

*O, Himalayas, white with snow fall,*
*Sparkling like the stars above,*
*Singing sad songs for your children,*
*For what they see when they look up.*
*For in your peaks they see the eyes*
*Of a deity you've not known,*
*While the hands that carved your surface*
*Long to break their hearts of stone.*

Had I done the wrong thing by visiting Bablu's family less often? Had my fear of offending someone, making a mistake, even getting kicked out of India rendered me less bold than I should have been? Rather than my stressors, my anxiety was the giant in my life. And now that giant was in the way of the Parvata people's access to the gospel. *God, help me. Give me the strength to take down Goliath!*

---

MY FIRST STEP in the battle of Abby and Goliath was to go to Pahargaun by myself. I had still never done so without another adult. I felt vulnerable and exposed as I walked to the bus stop alone and climbed aboard. The bus was full of people I recognized as Joshua's friends. And I found that Joshua's friends were my friends, too. They looked after their bhabi on the bus, and I felt a new connectedness with the Parvata.

Some weeks later, Joshua gave me another anxiety-busting assignment. "You should ride a bike."

"Nah. Too many cars."

"It's awesome to ride a bike. You'll be passing cars!"

I gave in. For several weeks, I went to Pahargaun every day by bus or bicycle. With my eyes no longer glued to Joshua's back, I looked around and saw Pahargaun for the first time. I learned the roads and where to find things. I brought back small items: socks for the kids, batteries, toilet paper.

On cycling days, when I pulled on my black leggings and blue tunic, tied my shoes, and tucked in the laces, I would panic. Just a little.

"Cheer for Mommy!" Joshua would say. Ashi would shout and wave. Arav would clap his hands. I'd push the bike up the rough cement path, my mind still frantic. *What will happen to the kids? What if they're half orphaned by the end of the day?*

No, better to be a well-adjusted mother who takes risks than one who hides from life. I would not teach anxiety to my children!

Once, I was just strapping on my helmet to return home after a trip to Pahargaun when I happened to look in the opposite direction. The road wound up a hill through mountain villages and past shops where you could rent 1980s snowsuits or buy ramen. I turned my bicycle in that direction. My legs tried to give up, but I wouldn't let them. *Just go.*

Women in patus and headscarves watched me as I pumped up the hill.

Reaching a snack shop, I paused to drink some water. Then I turned my bike around and set my feet on the pedals. No need to use them. Gravity would take me home.

Soon I was zipping down the road. I was going too fast to be afraid but not too fast to control the bike. There weren't many cars. Gripping the handlebars, I heard and felt nothing but wind. I was flying over the road, and nothing was stopping me. Not even me.

---

THE NEXT DAY, I brought Tripti a photo of her grandma. She stared at it for a long time before gently placing it on a shelf. I sat by her and held her hand for a while. She told me she was having trouble sleeping and that her blood pressure was high. For the first time, I offered to pray with her.

"No pressure," I said. Tripti looked at me a long moment, eyes searching my face.

"Yes, please pray." I prayed and shared a psalm, then showed Tripti how she could find the psalm through an app on her phone.

"Keep coming, okay?" she said as I got up to leave.

"I will," I promised.

# 39

## DARSHIKA

Not long after their grandmother's death, Bablu and Tripti's mother died. I could see Ama's face in my mind. The bitter smile. The coarse laugh. The once-beautiful face framed in silver hair. Cancer took her quickly, knocking the wind out of Tripti in the process.

I brought Tripti a new psalm written on a folded-up piece of paper. We sat in her living room, the only two people there. "How are you?"

"Still not sleeping since Grandma died. Now Mom."

We talked for a while. She forgot to bring tea. I didn't remind her. I prayed for her and told her I felt her sadness and grief in my bones. Then I offered her the piece of paper. "I brought this for you. It seemed you liked the other one. Maybe reading this would help you sleep. It helps me."

She looked down at the paper, then up at me, her chin raised in defiance. I sucked in a silent breath. In that moment, Tripti looked just like her mother.

"Some people try to force others to become Christians, you know. I think it's wrong."

"You know I'm not like that," I said. "True Christianity is about choice. God honors our choices. I . . . I just wanted to comfort you."

"Good. I'm glad you don't believe in force. Because nobody should force their religion on someone."

Putting the folded paper in my pocket, I walked home past people I knew and people I didn't. So much death in such a short time. More of our Parvata friends had died than seemed interested in Jesus. Had my anxieties kept me from being bold? Or did boldness just push people away?

I envisioned the Holy Spirit moving over the land like a purple-clouded storm, causing the seeds we'd planted to germinate. Without water, I knew a harvest was impossible.

"ARE YOU COMMITTED TO BEING HERE?" Joshua asked later as we sat on the floor near our *tandoor*. "I mean, are we committed?"

I fiddled with Ashi and Arav's blocks and tried not to cry. "I don't know. We work so hard to avoid being deported. But sometimes I almost wish we would get kicked out. Then we could leave, and the pressure would be off."

"I've thought about that. But wouldn't it be better to do what God has called us to do? To finish the work and then go home?"

The tears I'd been holding back pooled in my eyes. "Of course. But how? How is the work going to get done? After we finished the scrapbook, we were so excited to start sharing more. But every lead we've had has fizzled out. And they're not just leads. They're people we've loved."

Shankar had asked Joshua to give a class comparing the Bible and the Bhagavad Gita. Yog had said he'd be interested in a Bible study. But despite Joshua's prayers and invitations, nothing had materialized. Were they just being polite?

Meanwhile, Ayushi struggled to let go of her non-Christian boyfriend. Ajay was away becoming a Brahmin priest. Tripti had made her choice clear. So had many others.

"People love to talk about religion," Joshua said. "But their hearts aren't open. I thought if we bonded with the people and contextualized the gospel, they would accept Christ. But now I see that liking us—even loving us—isn't what will bring people to Christ. The gospel isn't a popularity contest. And it isn't an easy choice for them, no matter how relevant it is."

"I know," I responded. "Sometimes I imagine someone trying to tell me how to become a Muslim or a Buddhist. How that would feel."

We were silent for a while. Then I spoke. "There's something else I've been meaning to talk to you about. We've been so absorbed trying to fit into this community that we've lost our identity. We're just not *us*."

Joshua nodded. I knew he was remembering all the times we'd canceled our plans to adjust to someone else's schedule. "I see what you mean. We don't have to drop plans to do something as a family just because someone comes over."

"Exactly. It's like we think every social engagement is connected to someone's eternal salvation. But our kids need us too. This book I've been reading says the family is a light God uses to reach into dark places. The health of our family will show people what God is like. But our family can't shine unless we care for it."

"I want that too," Joshua said. "I want us to be one hundred percent committed. To our family and the mission."

"I'm willing," I said. "If we're going to recommit ourselves to reaching the unreached, let's do it right. Let's prioritize our family."

"And let's make prayer the centerpiece of our mission," Joshua added. "I know we pray. But we haven't prayed like we need to. We've relied too much on ourselves."

That evening, Joshua and I recommitted ourselves to reaching the Parvata for Christ by His power. All our effort and strength wouldn't do what Jesus could if we allowed Him. We would fast and pray, not to move the arm of God but to remind ourselves that without Him we could do nothing.

I emailed our angel dispatchers, and Joshua and I set our alarm clock to 5:30 a.m. We would begin each day with an early morning prayer time.

---

DURING OUR FIRST couple of years in India, neighbors would sometimes hear the music from our family "church" service and drop by. But not many people came now that the newness had worn off. Chayana was the exception.

Chayana was a short woman with green eyes and a big smile. She visited several times a week and made it a point to visit on Friday evenings when we welcomed the Sabbath. She even sang with us. Joshua and I prayed for her every morning.

One afternoon, Chayana let herself in, a bag of knitting in one hand, a paper sack in the other. I motioned to a mat near the tandoor. "Betho, Aunty." Chayana smiled and handed me the sack. It was full of apples.

"For Ashi."

After serving Chayana a hot cup of mint tea, I sat next to her on the mat. There was the usual discussion about the weather, relatives, and sickness. Soon Chayana's life story came tumbling out. She'd married young and had two sons.

"My older son, he could sing like you wouldn't believe. And he was intelligent. He was excellent in his studies and made everyone laugh. But not now."

"Oh?" I asked.

"Something happened to my son. He was in the third grade. We asked him to write, and he would just write 0s and 1s. He couldn't read anymore." Chayana said she'd recently taken her son to a mental institution. She dabbed at her watery eyes. "I didn't want to, but he beat me up. My husband died when the children were young. All I have now is my younger son. I really want things to go well with him."

Chayana went on to explain that she had *greh*—astrological bad fortune. Greh was all about the stars you were born under, a topic I'd compiled data on for our cultural study. If only I could do something to help Chayana. But to help her, I needed time. And to have time, I needed help.

---

LIVING TAKES LONGER in a developing country. Everything must be cooked and baked from scratch since there's nothing ready-made to buy. Carpets must be swept twice daily. Mopping is done on hands and knees. Clothing must be hung out to dry, then taken in if it rains. Blankets are stomped in tubs of water.

Keeping the house ready for guests to drop by at any moment is a full-time job in itself. Since terror wasn't keeping me at home now, we were always behind on chores. Joshua did his best to help, but it wasn't enough. We both watched kids, cleaned, ministered to local people; everything but get enough sleep.

Joshua thought we should hire someone. "Abby, if you weren't cleaning all day, you could do more visiting. And you would be less stressed."

"I know," I agreed. "I've barely had time to visit anyone. Rose, Mrs. Opee, Ayushi, the Corner Woman. And our kids need me, too."

"Maybe we could hire someone for a little while."

"Maybe. Let me think about it." I braced myself for the second death of my pride. Was it resurrected every morning? Or were only parts of it withering each day, like the dying leaves of a weed without water?

---

ON HER NEXT VISIT, Chayana found me in the kitchen washing my way through a stack of dishes. Ashi and Arav sat by my feet, playing with a pile of toys. "I see you're busy!"

"I've been wanting to visit you," I said. "But there's all this!"

Chayana grinned. "You need help, my daughter."

"Joshua thinks so too. I just wish I could do it myself. I don't like relying too much on others."

"I know someone. She's a good worker. But she's been through a lot in life, so she's a little different. I'll bring her tomorrow."

Too tired to protest, I just smiled and nodded. The next evening, Darshika arrived. It didn't take long to recognize what Chayana meant by "different." Swinging open our door, she strode to a mat and plopped down. Her phone rang. "Hellooo?"

Soon she was holding the phone out in front of her, screaming at it. I looked at Joshua. "She's feisty."

Darshika concluded her phone conversation with a popular invective. "Fine. Eat ash!"

"Who was that?" I asked.

"My aunty."

I swallowed a laugh, and we discussed the help needed—someone to be at our house about four hours a day to do dishes, laundry, sweeping, and other chores. Darshika leaned forward, hand to her heart. "I will do good work. And I can learn anything you teach me."

Crawling into the room, Arav put a chubby hand on Darshika's knee. He was instantly in her lap, playing with her jewelry, laughing at her as she made silly faces at him.

"I've never seen him take to someone like that," I said to Joshua in English. "Let's hire her."

---

I FOUND it difficult to be someone's boss and avoided giving orders. But Darshika worked energetically without needing direction. Though she'd lived in our village for ten years, we'd never seen her. She was a loner but called everyone by a familial name—aunty, uncle, brother, or sister. People said she'd been married seven or eight times. She said she'd been married once. I reserved judgment.

It was almost Christmas. Lars and Kay came, and we sang carols. We included a few Hindi songs for Darshika's benefit. She sat next to me on the floor, staring at our Hindi songbook. She eventually admitted she couldn't read.

Kneading dough for chapattis, she explained, "My mom died when I was five. After that, I had to go to work. I did the dirtiest jobs you could imagine, cleaning people's toilets, giving them foot massages."

She wiped a stray hair from her forehead, leaving behind a streak of flour. "Bhabi, if I even glanced at their food, they would scold me. I got the old stale bread or nothing at all. Nobody has ever treated me like you and Joshua do."

I urged Darshika to continue her story. "When I was thirteen, my dad sold me. He just sold me." She spat out the words. "He married me off to a man twenty years older than me. Didn't even give me a dowry. That family gave my dad five thousand rupees, and I became their slave."

My stomach twisted as Darshika described the abuse and terror she had suffered for eight years. When she fled, she didn't bring her two young children with her, for she had no guarantee she could keep them safe as she worked. They now lived with her ex-husband's relatives. She rarely saw them.

I thought of the gossip I'd heard about Darshika. She had heartlessly abandoned her children. She'd had multiple marriages just to satisfy a raging lust. Darshika knew people talked about her. In India, people can say anything they want about someone with no family. There is no consequence, no one to stand up for you. So Darshika avoided visiting people lest she be accused of something worse. But that didn't stop the rumors.

"I've worked in a lot of homes," she continued. "And I've never seen a man treat his family like Joshua treats you. I've never heard him yell, not even when the kids are being loud or naughty."

"We're not perfect," I assured her. "But we try. We pray together. We talk about problems and try to figure things out."

"No, you're different."

One day, Darshika washed breakfast dishes while I rolled out chapattis for lunch. Seeing the flour sprinkled over my dark-green countertop gave me an idea. "Come here, Darshika. Look at this."

I used my finger to write out some Hindi letters, voicing their sounds. Darshika copied what I'd written in another smattering of flour. She squealed and hugged me. "Maybe you could teach me to read!"

As winter snow began to accumulate again, our village crawled under a blanket of fog and hibernated. In our small living room, the tandoor radiated warmth. The yellow paint on the walls enhanced the coziness. Often when Darshika finished her work, she would sit near the wood stove, pull her thin knees up under her chin, and close her eyes.

What was she thinking?

# 40
---

# WITNESS

Christmas morning, the sky was a bright, cloudless blue. White snow sparkled in the sunshine, and the village smelled of burning wood. When Lars, Kay, and their daughter Posy arrived at our house, I was busy putting together a special presentation for the kids.

Joshua's parents had sent me a tiny bottle of perfume for Christmas. Its shape reminded me of the gifts of the wise men, so I decided to tell the gospel story through the objects of gold, frankincense, and myrrh. The perfume would represent myrrh. For gold, I found a bronze coin. For frankincense, I wrapped one of the kids' blocks in wrapping paper.

Staring wide-eyed at each tiny treasure, Ashi, Arav, and Posy listened to my story without a fidget. As I finished the story, I got an idea. *What if I shared this with one of the Parvata people?* Rose had asked me what to picture when she prayed. Maybe these objects would help her understand the story of Jesus.

I tucked the items in a box and walked to Rose's house. Rose had become like a little sister to me, and I truly loved her. Over the years I'd prayed for her, prayed with her, and given her a Bible. But I hadn't done the most important thing of all: simply tell her the story of Jesus.

Thinking back, I realized I'd been afraid to tell that story. I knew Rose would never turn me in to the police. But I didn't want to lose her as a friend or have her think I only spent time with her because I had some proselytizing agenda. I didn't want her to feel as Tripti had felt.

Still, what kind of friend would I be if I didn't try to share the most precious gift I'd ever been given? Ultimately, I couldn't see into people's hearts. I couldn't know who was ready to hear about Jesus and who wasn't. I would have to obey the Holy Spirit's promptings and leave the results in God's hands.

Rose and I sat near her *tandoor*. The room was bright from the sun's reflection on the snow outside. Rose was curious about the box. Opening it, I used the mock gold, frankincense, and myrrh to tell her the story of Jesus's birth. Then I shared God's plan of salvation as simply as I could.

Rose smiled. "I like this story."

"Rose, would you, um... would you like to know more about the Bible? If you wanted, I could come once a week, and we could read together."

"Sure. I'd like that."

"You would?" I couldn't hide my surprise.

Rose laughed at me. "There's just one thing. I don't think my in-laws will like it. I'll text you when they go somewhere, and you can come."

"Okay. I'll be waiting for your text!"

---

A FEW WEEKS after Darshika started working for us, she flounced into our kitchen and announced that she was getting married. "His family knows everything. I told them my whole story, and they still want me! They took pity on me. They understood it wasn't my choice to marry so young. They're a good family. I'll have a new life!"

I hugged Darshika, too happy to speak. In India, it is rare for a woman to remarry. It's hard to describe how important it is for an Indian family to find a "fresh" bride, a *kuvari*, a virgin. This is one reason many rapes go unreported. Even unwanted sexual contact can ruin a girl's prospects for marriage.

But here was a family whose humanity was touched by Darshika's story. They had chosen her to marry their son. The next morning she would travel to the home of the groom's uncle. Her wedding would occur the following month.

That evening, Darshika came again to say goodbye. As usual, she arrived talking on the phone. "You swear to God you won't drink? Promise you'll never hit me."

Darshika ended the call, her brow wrinkled with anxiety. "I went to see the devta. He said if I get married, I'll go crazy."

As Joshua and I sat with Darshika on the floor, my heart began to pound, and a familiar sense of prompting brought butterflies to my stomach. This was it. The opening. The moment for boldness. The moment for obedience.

"Darshika, let me tell you a story." I told her about creation, the fall, and Satan's desire to be worshipped as God. I told about Christ's death and resurrection to cleanse us from sin. Darshika nodded, leaning forward. When I finished, Joshua read her Jeremiah 29:11 in Hindi.

"For I know the plans I have for you," declares the Lord. "Plans to prosper you and not to harm you. Plans to give you hope and a future."

Darshika stared at our Hindi Bible, full of words she couldn't read. "Is the story you just told me in there?"

"Yes," Joshua and I said in unison. "It's all there."

"I believe you." Everything in my body froze except my heart. I felt my blood surging through my veins.

"I believe you," Darshika said again. "All these gods just want people's worship. They fight over people's devotion. I've seen it myself. Why should we honor them when our Creator made us?"

"I'm not saying you should or shouldn't get married, Darshika," I said. "What I'm saying is that you shouldn't trust what a devta tells you."

"I will only serve the true God from now on," she said.

We ate. Then we took pictures. Soon it was time for Darshika to leave.

"Bhaia," she said to Joshua, "I need help to move some of my stuff in the morning."

"No problem." Joshua pulled out a five-hundred rupee note (worth about eight dollars) and handed it to her. "If your new family turns out to be not so great . . . I mean, if something happens . . . just don't spend this, okay? Keep it on you all the time, and if you have to run away, use it."

Darshika stared at us, looking suddenly small and vulnerable. She blinked. Then she burst into tears. Burying herself in our arms, she cried into my shoulder. Her sobs were loud, the kind you hear when an Indian bride leaves her home. "Goodbye, Bhabi."

---

IN JANUARY, heaps of snow buried the valley in silence. Once again, the power lines snapped. After a week without power, we packed up and hitched a ride to Lars and Kay's.

Lars and Kay's home was warm and cheerful. Their *tandoor* stood in one corner of a large living room. A bright-red patterned carpet covered the rest of the room. After dinner, Lars brought in three buckets half-full of warm water and set them near the tandoor. "Bath time!"

Soon three rosy-cheeked children sat in the buckets, laughing. Lars brought in extra towels to mop up splashed water. After putting the kids to bed, we had a team meeting by candlelight.

"We have to pray for Ayushi," I said. "A few weeks ago, her brother became possessed. When the family tried to help, they became possessed, too. Ayushi was the only one unaffected. She's grateful that Jesus protected her but very confused."

"What about your Bible study?" Lars asked. "I know you had taken a break. Did that ever start up again?

"After the possessions, Ayushi said she wanted to do studies again. She even said her family wanted to join. But then her grandparents saw all the trouble they've been having. They said they wanted to talk to the devta first."

"Oh! What happened?" Kay asked. I looked at Joshua. He'd recently visited Ayushi's uncle and heard the whole story. He sighed, remembering.

"The devta demanded a ceremony, so they gave it one. There was the usual shaking and screaming. Then the gur pointed at Ayushi's uncle, the Christian one, and said everything was his fault because he'd left Hinduism. The devta said he lives under the house in a giant rock, and he's angry that the family built the house before asking permission. The family offered a sacrifice."

"Tell them what Ayushi's uncle told you," I said.

"Oh, yeah. I asked her Christian uncle if he took part in the sacrifice. He said, 'God is one,' just like a Hindu would say. But he looked really confused."

While Christians and Jews also say God is one, the Hindu proclamation means something very different. It means that God is everywhere and in everything. It means that it doesn't matter who you worship or what you believe because God is everything and everything is God.

"He's been a Christian for eighteen years," I said. "But I guess when you hear something enough times, you wonder if it's true."

"Did Ayushi go to the ceremony?" Lars asked.

"She did," I said. "She said they made her. But she didn't eat the food offered to the idol. She said she still wants to follow Jesus."

"We need to pray," Joshua said, and we all nodded. This was not just a philosophical or mental battle. It was a spiritual one. No one spoke. Each of us felt our helplessness and need of Christ. Only He could win. We prayed together for Ayushi, Rose, Darshika, and all our Parvata friends. Then we slept.

---

THE SNOW MELTED, but the world stayed gray. I hadn't heard from Rose or Ayushi, and Darshika's phone was switched off. So I rode my bike to visit my friend Naina.

Naina had a gentle voice and careful, polite mannerisms. But she was also a fiercely independent woman. She'd worked at a school for the blind and was into women's rights. She had a son Ashi's age and another child on the way.

Naina understood me in a way that many other Parvata didn't. She was always trying to figure out how to save the world and make a difference. She thought of people as people, not as colors, castes, or countries. And she liked to hear about Jesus if only as a point of cultural interest.

This day over mint tea and peanuts, Naina confessed that her morning sickness made it difficult to eat.

"I know how you feel," I said. "My second was worse, too. You just sit tight. I'll be back in an hour."

Joshua had recently figured out how to make ginger-ale. I thought the spicy, sweet, tingly drink would hit the spot for my friend. So I rode home, where Joshua and I mixed up the homemade syrup, ginger juice, and club soda in a bottle.

"Mmm," Naina said when she tried it, smacking her lips. "Thank you so, so much! This is great!"

Several weeks later, Naina told me her son had been bewitched. It surprised me to hear an educated woman say such a thing.

"Really?" I asked. "What makes you think so?"

"I know it sounds old-fashioned," she said, embarrassed. "But the woman next door... well, my son just loves playing with her daughter. At first, I thought it was cute. But now he cries and cries if he isn't allowed to go there and wants to be there all the time. He almost can't sleep, he's so obsessed."

"Sometimes kids get fixated on things," I said.

"But he's not the obsessive type, you know? Something seems strange about it. I just wish I'd never let him out of the house."

"I don't think you're old-fashioned," I assured her. "I know spiritual things happen that we don't always see. I've had some experiences with Ashi, too. And I believe we can ask Jesus for protection. His power is great enough to provide it."

"I had no idea you'd gone through something. Ashi is a beautiful child. People get jealous."

Naina and I both looked at our eldest children as they played together on the floor.

"Would it be okay if I prayed for your son?" I asked.

Naina nodded. "Yes, please. Pray for me, and my son. The baby, too."

We bowed our heads. While Naina namasted the sky, I prayed for the blood of Christ to cover us and our children. When I finished, Naina looked at me. "Thank you. I feel a kind of peace after that prayer. It was refreshing."

Soon the topic turned to Naina's secret wish: to learn to ride a bicycle. Ashi, at three and a half, had just mastered her tiny bike and offered to loan Naina her now-unnecessary training wheels. They were, of course, too small for Naina's husband's extra bike. Naina installed them, anyway.

"Turn the handlebars the way you're gonna fall, Aunty," she said. "That's what Daddy says." Naina laughed.

"What a helpful girl you are, Ashi," she said. "Thank you!"

---

OVER THE FOLLOWING WEEKS, I had trouble sleeping. I tossed and turned, a sinking feeling whirling in the middle of my stomach. I searched my heart and prayed. Something wasn't right.

"Joshua," I said one night. "I can't stop thinking about Darshika."

"Me too," he said, fully awake.

I sat up. "It doesn't make sense. Why would that family want her? She has no dowry. Family and dowry are almost like a pedigree here. She has already been married and had kids. According to the rural Indian mindset, she's a second-hand bride."

"I've been thinking the same thing. I've tried calling her every day this week. But her phone is switched off."

The next morning, Joshua searched online for information about bride trafficking. He discovered that our area was a major exporter of brides. And the city to which Darshika had said she was moving was a major importer. Sometimes brides are trafficked to become indentured housekeepers. Others are used for more sinister purposes. All are lured by the promise of a new life.

"Did we just send Darshika away to become a slave again?" I asked. "Do we have any other phone numbers for her?"

"None of them are working," Joshua said.

We found an agency that specialized in rescuing people from bride trafficking and submitted Darshika's details. While Joshua filled out the forms, I went to the kitchen to try calling Darshika's phone again.

"The number you are calling can't be reached right now," said a woman with a British accent. "Please call again later."

"Joshua, listen." I walked back into our room and held up the phone. "I'm scared. She can't even read well enough to catch a bus. We have to do something. We're all she has. She doesn't even—" I stopped. Joshua sat in front of his laptop, his face in his hands.

I knew how he felt. Darshika had lived enough pain and trauma to ruin several lives. What if this "new start" was just a bullet point in a long list of betrayals? This could snuff out the first fire of hope that had ever burned in her heart. I wiped a tear off my cheek.

Joshua took a deep breath and began typing on the computer again. "Thank God we took pictures of her before she left."

# 41

# EMERGENCIES

By February, the snow melted, and the power came back on. But it was still cold enough to see our breath, even indoors. We bundled up and used both *tandoor* and space heaters. But the constant cold was hard on our kids, who were already thin from frequent bouts with worms.

"Arav doesn't look so good," I told Joshua one afternoon, pacing back and forth with our year-old son limp in my arms. "I'm worried."

"Maybe we should take him to the mission hospital," Joshua suggested.

"They'll probably just tell me to have him breathe steam. Maybe I'll try that first and see if his cough and wheezing get better."

I barely slept that night. As I cradled Arav, the crackling, dragging sound of his breathing caused my chest to tighten. I prayed for his safety and hoped I was just being a worried mom.

Early the next morning, I bundled Arav in a wool wrap and trudged down the path toward the bus stop. The only shop open belonged to the Grumpy Shopkeeper, as we'd nicknamed him due to his cranky expression and gruff voice.

"Namaste, Uncle. Arav is sick. Could I sit here while I wait for the bus?"

"Of course." The Grumpy Shopkeeper looked at me as though he knew exactly how I felt. Arav stared down at some birds, who pecked at a discarded biscuit on the ground. It seemed the bus would never come. Forty-five minutes later, it did.

By now I knew the mission hospital ER well. A doctor came and listened to Arav's lungs. "He has pneumonia. I want to admit him. And he needs a chest x-ray."

I took Arav down a dimly lit hallway towards the x-ray area. The technician told me to hold him down on a little bed. He dashed behind a lead-lined wall, giving me only seconds to wonder whether I should ask for protection. *Oh, well. Protect me, Lord!*

"I'd like a private room," I told every staff member I saw as we were ushered upstairs. But the tiny room into which we were led was definitely not private. It contained two gurneys. On one lay a woman and her preschool-aged son. Around them, several men sat on chairs. I swallowed. Germaphobia mingling with claustrophobia threatened to turn the lump in my throat into full-on tears.

"We don't have any private rooms now," a nurse told me.

"Okay." I tried to smile as I eased Arav onto the other gurney. It would serve as bed for us both. I didn't want my new neighbors to know I'd give anything not to be in a room with them right now.

"Namaste," I said to the family. A man I guessed to be the young boy's father gathered up a large, soft blanket. He turned towards me as though addressing his sister and not a stranger. "It's cold. Take this blanket. We have several."

Despite my long underwear, wool suit, and down jacket, I felt cold. I looked at my watch. The public buses were no longer running. How had it gotten so late? I knew Joshua would find a way to get to me if he had to. But I also knew he'd likely already put Ashi to bed.

Accepting the blanket, I tucked myself and Arav in and tried to rest. But soon I was swept up into a conversation with our neighbors. Their son also had pneumonia and had been in the hospital for four days. Right on cue, he launched into a coughing fit.

When you go to the hospital in our area of India, you are responsible for acquiring any necessary materials and medicines. That means if you need a syringe, IV antibiotics, cough syrup, and/or saline, you go purchase them. If the nurse needs gloves, you go get them. My new roommates offered to care for Arav while I collected the necessary medications. Since the pharmacy where I would buy these things was nearby, I accepted their offer.

When I returned, the boy's mother told me not to worry about dinner. A few minutes later, a relative brought in a home-cooked meal of chapattis, fried vegetables, and dahl. It was warm and delicious.

"Everything will be okay," the woman said as I ate. "Don't be scared. Your boy will be fine."

After dinner, I prayed with Joshua over the phone. Then I said goodnight to my roommates and pulled a thin curtain between our gurneys.

"Mow," Arav said his word for milk. My heart melted. Arav hadn't been able to nurse well for days, and the hospital staff had only been able to keep an IV in his tiny vein for a few minutes. He needed nourishment and hydration.

I tried to breastfeed. But Arav couldn't breathe through his nose and had a hard time catching his breath between gulps. What was I going to do?

"Didi?" I poked my head around the curtain to address the other boy's mother, using the familiar term for sister. "Would you watch Arav again for a minute?"

"Of course."

Setting Arav on the gurney, I walked down the hall to a small hospital cafeteria. I bought a paper cup and plastic spoon, silently thanking God they came sealed in their own pieces of plastic wrap. Back in our cubicle, I washed my hands and pulled the curtain closed again. Expressing my milk into the cup, I fed it to Arav with the spoon.

The night seemed endless. Light from the hall shone in our room, and a nurse kept coming in to nebulize Arav or the sick little boy next to us, never at the same time. The little boy was about four years old and kept having to go pee. His mother and father were tender and patient with him.

The next morning we had visitors. Word travels fast on packed buses and crowded streets. It turned out that the Grumpy Shopkeeper's adult son was also in the hospital. His daughter-in-law came to visit as well as several other people from our village. They sympathized with me, encouraged me, and offered to bring me whatever I needed.

Eventually, Joshua and Ashi came with a change of clothes for me and Arav and a sleeping bag. That night, I sat on our gurney with Arav in my lap surrounded by my roommates' relatives, who now claimed me as theirs, and a few people from our village.

*I want to be with these people for eternity,* I thought. *Lord, reach these precious unreached people!*

By that afternoon, although the nurses had been unable to keep an IV in Arav for more than a few minutes at a time, the small amount of IV antibiotics he'd received had made a difference. His lungs were clearing up. The doctor agreed to let us go with instructions to nebulize him every couple of hours. Joshua and Ashi came on the bus to accompany us home.

Joshua shook the hand of the sick boy's father. "Thank you for caring for my wife when I could not be here."

"No, don't say thank you," he responded. "You are family. What else could we have done?"

We took a taxi home. The driver was a friend of a friend. He chatted with Joshua while I watched the familiar sights out the window. First was the bridge, encrusted with colorful Buddhist prayer flags. After that, the road opened into a beautiful view of the valley in every shade of blue and green, white mist outlining the evergreen treetops. Our taxi rocketed around a bend, slowing down here and there for cows or people, stopping to pick up someone the driver knew.

*This is how you get home,* I thought. One day you just look around and realize that all these people aren't "them" anymore. That bend just before our village, the one with the chicken shop, wasn't the road to adventure anymore.

It was just the road home.

# 42

## HOPE DEFERRED

The following months were busy ones. All the hidden vegetable seeds in the fields sprouted, and the apple trees blossomed. The rainy season came, growing seedlings into plants. Arav learned to walk, and I took the children to collect fistfuls of yellow mustard flowers.

Joshua visited Ajay at his Brahmin priest training school, where Ajay eagerly introduced him to all his friends. Even when we were apart, Joshua and I continued getting up early every morning to pray and spent as much time as we could with our Parvata friends and neighbors.

Around this time, Ashi lost patience with the Indian habit of squeezing the cheeks of cute children. During our recent furlough in the United States of Hands Off Other People's Kids, Ashi had experienced a culture completely new to her. And she preferred the hands-off of American culture to the face-touching of the Parvata culture. Upon our return to India, it didn't take her long to develop the unfortunate habit of growling and baring her teeth at passersby.

"They don't mean to bother you," I crooned down at her. "But you can say no if you don't like it."

Joshua and I taught her how to say in Hindi, "Please don't touch my face."

One evening, Joshua took Ashi to a wedding. I stayed home so Arav could nap. When they returned, Joshua's flared nostrils gave away his anger. "You will not believe this!"

"What happened?" I asked.

"She tried saying, 'Don't touch my face,' like we taught her. But they just touched her again to hear her speak in Hindi!"

"What did you do?"

"I grabbed one lady's hand and said, 'She asked you not to touch her. Don't touch her.'"

"Good for you!"

"Yeah, well, they laughed it off, but I don't think they'll do it again."

"This is getting ridiculous," I said. "I don't even want to take her out of the house anymore. Everywhere we go, people try to touch her face."

"We've got to be the ones to protect her. If somebody does that, just grab their hand and say no."

"I keep thinking I'll do that. But at the moment, I just can't. I know people aren't doing it to be rude, and I know they will be embarrassed."

"But we have to protect Ashi," Joshua said. "Who cares what they think?"

For years, we'd cared so much about what people thought. Now we were supposed to stop. I wanted to be strong for Ashi. But I understood the Parvata a little too well to forget how they would feel if I shamed them. *What is it going to take for me to be able to be mean?*

---

DESPITE ASHI'S disdain for having her face touched, there were many people in Kushigaun she loved. Rose. Lovelina. The Momo Lady. And especially Yog, who kept a marker just for Ashi at his shop and let her draw all over his inventory.

One afternoon, I took Ashi to see the Momo Lady. Lovelina was there helping out in her shop. I'd seen Lovelina several times since we'd moved, but she was in college now and always busy. This week she was on vacation. She wore an oversized hoodie and looked tired.

The Momo Lady set a plate of momos in front of Ashi. Handing one to Arav, she complained, "I'm having one of those days. Everything is going wrong."

"Be thankful you're not having one of those months," Lovelina said. "I've been miserable for five weeks straight."

"What's going on, Lovely?" I asked, using her childhood pet name.

"Lovely's upset. Aren't you?" the Momo Lady asked.

"My friends all abandoned me." Lovelina wiped away a tear. "They're all talking smack about me. I didn't do anything wrong. They're just jealous. They're liars."

"Oh, Lovelina, I'm so sorry," I said.

"I wouldn't cry if I were Lovelina." The Momo Lady laughed at herself. "I'm too angry to cry. Can't help it. I just fly off the handle, you know?"

I rubbed Lovelina's back as the Momo Lady talked about her angry streak. Even when the Momo Lady was angry, it was a sort of cheerful anger. She gestured to the scar on her neck I'd wondered about for years. "Got this one when my ex tried to kill me. I guess I had to get mad to survive."

I nodded, thinking about Darshika. She'd had to get mad to survive too. I sent up a silent prayer for her, hoping she was okay. Lovelina snuggled her head into my shoulder and played with the strings on her hoodie.

"Lovelina, do you remember the video you used to watch with us every Christmas?"

"*The Jesus Film?*"

"Yes. Remember Jesus? He was a good person and only tried to help people.

Yet they bad-mouthed him. He didn't have to go through that. But He did it just to show us that He understands what it's like."

Lovelina sniffled. The Momo Lady said with a sigh, "Sometimes you're happy because you're looking good one day. Then someone comes along and sees you, and it's all ruined."

By now I'd been in India long enough to know what she meant. "You mean, the evil eye. Someone looks at you with the evil eye, and it ruins your day. Some people might even curse you on purpose. Right?"

The other two stared at me for a moment before exploding into conversation. "Yes! That's right! How do you know about that?"

I told them about Ashi and the curse someone had tried to put on her. I knew Lovelina remembered. "I've been a Christian my entire life, and I'm still learning about how wonderful God is. After Ashi got hurt, I really started praying. God loves us and wants to protect us. That's why Jesus died and rose again. He conquered Satan and proved to us He has authority over death and everything else."

As Lovelina and the Momo Lady stared at me, I added, "Would it be okay if I prayed with you?"

"Ooooh! That would be so cool!" Springing out of her seat, the Momo Lady closed the door to her shop. She grabbed a scarf, put it over her head, and took a deep breath. "Okay, go!"

I prayed that the Momo Lady would find peace and joy, that Lovelina would be comforted, and that God would show both of them His plan for their lives. Lovelina sobbed into my shoulder.

"That was great," the Momo Lady said when I finished. "I like praying to Jesus!"

"Me too," I said. "Me too."

Lovelina sniffled and wiped at her tears. We'd now been in India four and a half years. What was the alternate universe if I'd never become a missionary? If I'd moved out of the Opees' house too soon? If I hadn't taken the time to understand? If I'd stayed too timid to pray with people?

---

I HAD the privilege of being with Lars and Kay as Kay delivered their second child, a boy they named Elijah. Birth involves so much effort, pain, and hope. But then the child, hidden away for nine months, is born. The love of the parents, held in their hearts for nine months, becomes tangible. It is the moment you finally see something that was invisible.

Sometimes waiting for the Parvata was like waiting for a baby to be born. I kept expecting Rose to be ready to do a Bible study, but she was rarely left alone at her house. I kept expecting to see Lovelina's faith in Christ blossom, but she got back together with her friends and seemed to forget about our prayer. I expected Joshua's friends with all their spiritual talks to realize how much they needed Jesus. But nothing happened.

Sometimes Joshua and I would sit by our tandoor with our guitars and play our song, *Hope Deferred*. As I pressed into the pain of waiting for what God had promised, I would think how true were the words of that proverb written so many centuries ago:

> *Hope deferred makes the heart sick, but a longing fulfilled is a tree of life.*

PROVERBS 13:12

I just hoped that we were waiting on the Parvata and not the other way around.

# 43

## TOO EXPENSIVE

On her next visit, Chayana asked about Darshika. I said we still hadn't heard anything. "She always does this," Chayana said, shaking her head. "Just runs away. I should never have introduced you. Do you know how many times she's been married?"

"Once," I answered. "She's not as bad as people say, Aunty."

"Poor thing. I tried to stop her from leaving, but she wouldn't listen. Who knows what will happen?"

"You did what you could. All we can do is pray."

"The gods know. Why don't you come visit, daughter? I'll make you *malai kofta*. You said you'd never tasted it."

"I'd like that. I've been wanting to try it. Everyone says the *malai kofta* you cook is delicious!"

That afternoon Chayana brought me to her house. At three stories tall it was one of the largest local homes I'd seen. As we drew near, Chayana's dog yanked on his chain, barking and snarling. Ashi cowered.

"It's okay, Ashi. He's tied up."

"Calm down, Nero," Chayana said. "It's just us."

We climbed a steep wooden staircase to the third floor. On the wall was the usual giant poster of a multi-armed goddess. A sign declared, "Shiva is the head of this house, the unseen guest at every meal, the silent listener to every conversation." I'd seen similar words written of Jesus in Christian homes in the U.S.

"Neel is helping me today," Chayana said as I lay a sleeping Arav on a nearby bed.

I looked around, curious what Neel looked like. The stairs from Chayana's loft kitchen creaked. I stifled a gasp. It was the large, lumbering man who'd shoved a cookie into Ashi's mouth in the market. I remembered how villagers had scolded him as they might shoo away a dog. Now here he was in Chayana's living room. Her son.

Setting two plates on the floor in front of us, he tried to smile. "Here are the plates, Mother."

"Don't clink them. Don't you know how to do anything?" Chayana turned to me. "I'm sorry."

"No, it's okay. He's doing a good job." I knew Chayana loved her son and spoke harshly out of her pain. "I'm sure he's a good helper. It must be nice to have a man around to lift heavy things."

"He breathes so loudly it sounds like an animal. He's like a baby in a grown man's body. Even crawls up into my lap and cries sometimes."

Neel's brow furrowed in concentration, his tongue held between his lips, as he set cups by our plates. Then he disappeared into the kitchen. Chayana huffed. "It's embarrassing. But what can I do? I've tried institutionalizing him. He doesn't stay."

"I'm sure it's frustrating for him too. He must know there's something different about him. But different doesn't have to mean less. He seems helpful."

Neel brought out the food. I tried to compliment his service. But his mother's bitterness had landed on him hard, like salt on a fire. Or a wound. Deep compassion for Neel welled up inside me. He wasn't too slow to know his mother was bitter about his condition.

*God must want to heal this man. Isn't there anything I can do? What if we prayed and God healed him? God, is healing Neel a part of your plan?*

---

WE VISITED LARS AND KAY. Ashi played with their daughter Posy in the dirt. I held Arav's hand as he toddled over the soft ground. Nearby, Kay's vegetable garden was beginning to sprout. I stooped to admire an eggplant seedling. "I've always wanted to garden. You should teach me."

"I'm not an expert," Kay said. "I just love it."

"Yeah, but your plants live."

"There is that."

"Here's a question. According to the backs of seed packets, you're supposed to thin plants. Couldn't you just plant them further apart to begin with? It seems an awful waste to pull them up."

"I just plunk them in the ground somewhere else," Kay said. "I suppose some people throw them away. But I say, why not try? If they grow, they grow."

I stood. We walked into Kay's kitchen. Kay stirred a pot of lentils, tasted them, then added salt. "I've been getting to know my neighbor, Saachi. I've been praying God would reveal Himself to her. In my devotions, when I read a Bible verse I think she'd like, I write it down. I have quite a few. I'm just not sure when I should give them to her. "

"I'm still praying for Ayushi, too," I said. "Her family and her faith are pulling her in very different directions. And then there's the boyfriend. Ayushi said he's interested in learning about Jesus and asked us to send him some information. I hope she'll be strong enough to do whatever God calls her to do."

Kay and I talked about giving up things for God, how it's always worth the sacrifice. After lunch, we had a team meeting. Joshua asked for prayer requests.

"We got an e-mail from one of our supporters," Kay said. "Abigail, she read what you'd written in your prayer bulletin about Chayana and felt impressed that God wants to heal Chayana's son. She's committed to pray for Neel every time she nurses her new baby."

Suddenly my heart was on fire. "I think God wants to heal Chayana's son too. That's just the confirmation we've been praying for!"

Joshua and Lars shared their prayer requests. Then we all knelt together. We prayed God would send His Spirit like rain to bloom the desert. We prayed for each of our Parvata friends by name. We prayed for ourselves that God would make us faithful.

The next time Chayana visited, I was ready. "Aunty, I want to have a special prayer for your son. I believe God wants to heal him."

"Do you really think so?"

"Yes," I said. "Joshua and I will fast and pray for the next three days. You can have this New Testament, if you're interested, and read through it. After three days, come again. That will be Friday evening. We will pray together for your son then."

"Thank you so much." Chayana took the small, black Hindi Bible from my hands. "I will read it."

Each time hunger twisted my stomach over the next three days, I remembered God's longing to bring healing to the Parvata and asked Him to heal Neel. I prayed that the Holy Spirit would fill our home and us. On Friday, we fed the kids and put them to bed early. I had no idea whether demons would come flying out of this guy, but I wanted the kids asleep when we prayed.

"With God, nothing is impossible." The words of a children's scripture song playing on our laptop spread into every corner of the house. My heart jumped into my throat, and my eyes stung. *Nothing is impossible for God.* This could be the moment Chayana saw the power of Jesus for the first time.

I checked again to make sure everything was perfect. Then I found Joshua. We held hands and prayed that Christ would be victorious.

Chayana came. With her were her two sons, Neel and his brother Daksh. They came in smiling and normal as though we were just having dinner. I ushered them into the tandoor room. Neel sat on a mat, and his mother and brother sat on another. My heart skipped a beat again as I looked at them.

"We've asked you here today because we believe it is God's will to heal Neel," Joshua said. He held a brown, threadbare Bible. "Before we start, I'd like to pray."

Joshua prayed, then read aloud the story of the demoniac among the tombs Jesus had healed (Mark 5, Matthew 8).

"Oh, he doesn't have a demon or anything. It's just brain damage," Chayana said with a nervous chuckle. But I knew the truth. Chayana believed Neel was cursed and haunted by a demon. It just hurt her pride to admit it.

Chayana adjusted her pink headscarf. On her forehead, she wore a soft, powdery orange smear. I didn't think much of it. Hindus consider the forehead one of several spiritually significant points on the body and draw all kinds of things there. There is the *bindi* dot to show a woman is married or even just for fashion. Then there's the anointing received after going to a Hindu temple or after a family member does *puja* at the family shrine. There are even shapes to show devotion to various gods.

"Don't worry, Aunty," I said. "We wanted you to hear this story so you would know Jesus has authority to heal Neel, whatever the cause of his problem."

"*Aacchaa,*" she said, "Okay."

Joshua knelt in front of Neel. I joined him. Neel's eyes were red, and he wore an absent, silly grin. Joshua put one hand in the air and one hand on Neel. I did the same. Joshua raised his head. I bowed mine.

"In the name of Jesus Christ," Joshua said, his voice rising. "May your mind no longer be like that of a child. Be healed in the name of Jesus!"

There was silence. I opened an eye and peeked at Neel. He still sat grinning as though watching a cartoon. I glanced over at Daksh and Chayana. They watched, emotionless. I bowed my head again.

As Joshua and I prayed for Neel, I began to feel pins and needles in both my hands. I shifted, thinking perhaps I had been in one position for too long. The burning sensation increased. I glanced over at Joshua.

"Let's sing," I said. We sang and prayed again and read a few verses. I asked God to forgive Neel of any sins he may have committed.

"I think we should be done," Joshua whispered. "We have presented our request to God. It's time to wait in faith and see what He does."

"Okay." I felt disappointed and unsure, but I closed with prayer. "Dear God, thank You so much for Chayana. She has been like a mother to me here in India. Please bless her and bless her sons. May Your will be done in their lives, and may they know Your power and love. In Jesus's name, amen."

I turned to Chayana, using the Indian expression for mother. "*Amaji,* I prepared food. Please stay and eat with us."

I fed our guests in the traditional Indian way, waiting on them until everyone had finished. There was a peaceful, joyful atmosphere despite the fact that Neel remained unchanged. *Maybe God will do something in the night. Maybe Neel will wake up normal.*

Chayana and her boys left. Joshua and I stood inside the house, shoulders touching. We were silent for several minutes, staring at the back of the heavy wooden door.

"Maybe God will heal him in the night," I said.

"Maybe," Joshua said.

"What are you thinking?"

"Did you notice that Chayana wore a *tilak*?"

I stared at Joshua. For a moment, the word *tilak* did not register in my brain. Then I remembered the orange smear on Chayana's forehead.

"Yes, I did!" I gasped. "But that means they visited the temple!"

"I see the *tilak* so often, I didn't give it much thought. But a fresh *tilak* definitely means they visited the temple today."

As we went over the events of the evening, I was surprised to hear Joshua had felt an electric tingling in his hands, too.

"What if the power of God was present to heal," I asked, "but there was no faith to receive the healing?"

---

THE NEXT DAY, I called Chayana on the phone. She admitted she and her sons had visited the temple on the way to our house. "I just wanted to give him the best chance to be healed. To make sure our gods are on the same page."

I told Chayana about the tingling and the conviction we and others had been given that God would heal her son. She answered, "It's all right, daughter. I already knew it wouldn't work. They prayed for him at the Christian school when he was eleven. They said we'd have to follow Jesus or the problem would return. But we don't want to do that."

Several days later, Joshua took his Bible and went to visit Chayana and Daksh. Neel was away. He had disappeared after our prayer session. Back at home, I interceded for Joshua, kneeling on the floor, my head bowed down over my Bible. I begged God to speak to Chayana, to heal Neel, to save them, for they had shown me kindness. I felt impressed to open my Bible. This is what I read:

> But to this day whenever Moses is read, a veil lies over their hearts; but
> whenever someone turns to the Lord, the veil is taken away. Now the
> Lord is the Spirit, and where the Spirit of the Lord is, there is
> freedom. But we all, with unveiled faces, looking as in a mirror at
> the glory of the Lord, are being transformed into the same image from
> glory to glory, just as from the Lord, the Spirit.

2 CORINTHIANS 3:15-18

Although I knew this verse was about those who rejected Christ as Messiah, the spiritual principle was the same. Those who turn away from God cannot see Him. *Oh, God,* I prayed. *Let them turn their hearts toward You!*

Joshua returned several hours later. I rushed to him, eager to hear what had happened. "Well? What happened?"

"We talked. Chayana and Daksh were there. It was a good talk. I told them God will not share His glory with another. I explained that God wants us to know He is the true source of healing. Going to the temple first may have been part of the reason nothing happened."

"What did they say?"

"They said they didn't expect anything to happen, anyway."

"She told me that, too!"

"Yeah. I talked with them about the importance of faith. I told them about the spiritual battle over people's hearts. I told them who the devtas are, that they're evil angels coveting the worship of the true Creator. I've never been bolder."

"What did they say?"

"They said it might be true."

"That's amazing!"

"Yeah." Joshua hesitated. "They said it might be true, but it's just too expensive."

"Too expensive?"

"That's the word she used. It costs too much. They'd have to give up their remaining status in the community to follow Jesus. Chayana's not willing to do that. Daksh took a Bible, though. He said he'll read it."

I felt heartbroken for Chayana. Especially when she came to visit me later.

"It's okay to count the cost of following Jesus," I said. "He tells us to do that. You just take your time and keep praying about it."

Chayana patted my arm as though she felt sorry for me. "I could never follow Jesus, daughter. My husband was an important man. I don't invite the devta to my house. It just comes. Every time there is a festival, it stops at my house. It's my duty to do puja for the devta. And I know to follow Jesus I would have to give that up."

I nodded. As a widow with a cursed son, doing puja was the last honor Chayana had. She sighed. "I can't do it."

"I still care about you like a mother," I said.

"It's just too bad about my son," she said. "I guess he'll have to stay this way forever."

I grieved for Chayana. Yet I knew I'd done everything I could. Missionaries and preachers the world over do their best to make the gospel attractive. They sing it into modern music. They translate it into different languages. They squeeze their square-shaped selves into the roundness of another culture until it hurts. They try to balance being bold and avoiding any hint of *zabardasty*, or force.

But despite the lengths people go to and the natural beauty of the gospel, missionaries and preachers cannot lessen the sting of dying to self. And dying to self is a requirement for the Christian. For the next few days, an old gospel song put itself on repeat in the back of my mind even as I prayed that Chayana would learn what I learned again every day—that giving up everything for Jesus is worth every penny.

> Jesus walked this lonesome valley;
> He had to walk it by himself.
> Oh, nobody else could walk it for him;
> He had to walk it by himself.
>
> We must walk this lonesome valley;
> We have to walk it by ourselves.
> Oh, nobody else can walk it for us;
> We have to walk it by ourselves.

You must go and stand your trial;
You have to stand it by yourself.
Oh, nobody else can stand it for you;
You have to stand it by yourself.

# 44

## TANGIBLE

I received an e-mail from the president of our mission organization asking if I'd be interested in writing a scholarly article on spiritual warfare to present at a seminar the following October.

I loved telling true stories to encourage and exhort people. But spiritual warfare? Although we had received some instruction in spiritual warfare, I hardly felt an expert on the topic. Especially after what had happened with Chayana's son.

"But you have experience with it," the president reassured me. "That's important." So, I got a list of books to download and began studying.

---

AT SOME POINT, Darshika's groom realized we'd given her name to the police as the possible victim of bride trafficking. As she later told me, a general panic ensued. We got a phone call inviting us to come and see for ourselves that Darshika was safe.

"I hope Darshika's new family are as nice as they sound on the phone," I told Joshua as we packed our bags. "I hope we're not putting ourselves in any danger by visiting."

"Don't worry, we'll be fine. If anything, they're a little scared of us. This will be fun. Darshika said there's a courtyard where the kids can run around."

The journey to reach Darshika took three buses and eight hours. The first two hours were fine. Then the air grew increasingly hot. Arav rubbed his red, sticky face on my arm and whined. Ashi's hot body slumped over my lap.

I was grateful for how patient Indians are with children. We'd now been in India for five years. Our children were four and two and had traveled extensively, often on long bus rides such as this. Usually they were troopers, but they were human. They wiggled, giggled, and whined. Yet not one Indian person had ever scolded or glared at us.

Finally, we arrived in Uskigaun. Farmland bursting with greenery stretched out on every side. A dirt path extended up the side of a hill. Dusty from the journey, Joshua and I lugged Ashi, Arav, and a few backpacks up the path. After passing a house and its accompanying buffalo, we found ourselves in a spacious courtyard. The jangle of wedding anklets sounded from around a corner.

"Namaste!" Darshika threw her arms around me. I hugged her, and she kissed my cheeks. The family gathered, all grinning and namaste-ing. Two dogs did laps around the group, barking their welcome.

Darshika's new mother-in-law had a soft, easy smile. A rose-colored scarf framed her light-brown hair. Her father-in-law sat in a plastic chair, knees pulled up, his slender frame wrapped in lean muscle.

"It is good you came," he proclaimed, nodding his white head. The dirt on his hands and feet, the well-kept farming tools leaning against a wall, and the neat rows of plants nearby told me they were farmers.

The family fussed over us. Were we tired from the trip? Would we like to have our feet washed? How about a massage? Darshika's new family embodied the Indian saying, "the guest is god."

The next morning after a breakfast of fried spinach and corn cakes, Darshika motioned to her father-in-law. "Shall I do *puja* now, Papa?"

"Yes. It is time."

I watched. Did Darshika remember our talk about God? Would she be true to her decision to serve Him only? She began to sing as she gathered items from around the courtyard. "*Prabhu ka dhanyavad karo.* Praise the Lord, oh my soul."

Over and over, she repeated that one line of a song she'd learned in our home. She lit incense and candles. Noticing me watching, she smiled and said in a whisper, "I'm taking the Lord's name."

That meant she was worshipping God, receiving His blessing into her heart. When we left, Darshika's mother-in-law gave me a Punjabi suit, yellow with red and purple polka-dots, and a matching scarf. They walked us to the road. As we waved goodbye from a taxi, I looked around. All around us, the young wheat in the fields swayed. The harvest would be great that year.

---

WHEN WE GOT BACK from visiting Darshika, Kay called me. Her friend Saachi, for whom she'd been collecting Bible verses, had experienced a great loss. Her new baby, at just a month old, had died. Kay visited Saachi and told her she'd been praying for her. Then she handed her a stack of papers covered in handwritten Bible verses. "I think God wants you to have these."

Saachi cried and hugged her. Kay had prayed for months that this woman would experience God in a tangible way. That tangible way turned out to be Kay's handwriting.

I knew Kay asked God every day what He expected of her. Our families had expectations of us as wives, sisters, daughters, mothers. The world had expectations of us as women. But if we fulfilled God's expectations, we could always know it was enough. Kay taught me that without even knowing it. So, I prayed that God would make me a blessing too, and show Himself to the Parvata through me. And I decided to check with Rose about our Bible study.

As Rose seated me in a plastic lawn chair, a door creaked. A thin woman wearing tinted lip balm and a long, thick braid emerged from one of the guest rooms. She held a black book. Rose pulled me up from the chair and towards the woman. "This is my friend Jyoti. She's living in the homestay while her husband works at a bank."

I smiled. "Namaste." I'd always loved the name Jyoti, which means light.

Nodding toward the black book Jyoti held, Rose whispered, "We've been reading the Bible together. We're both interested in Jesus. Since she lives here, we can sneak to each other's rooms when we have time. Nobody knows."

"We love the Book," the woman said, smiling.

A lovely pain pulled at my ribs as I looked from Rose to Jyoti. "See how wonderful God's plans are? He arranged it so you would have a friend to study the Bible with! I'm so happy."

Rose came to our home the following Sabbath for our family church time. She and her son enjoyed the simple Sabbath school I'd prepared for my Ashi, Arav, and her son. But her in-laws didn't like her visiting a Brahmin home. After that, she contented herself with her time with Jyoti, and I prayed and visited when I could.

---

ONE NIGHT, as we had so many times before, Joshua and I knelt and interceded on Darshika's behalf. Images of her laughing, singing Christian songs, and namaste-ing towards the sky filled my mind. Then the phone rang.

Joshua's looked at the screen. "Guess who?"

"Darshika!" I sprang off the floor.

Joshua's eyes grew wide as he listened. "Here, tell your Bhabi."

He handed me the phone. I listened to Darshika's excited voice. "Bhabi, I couldn't help myself! I couldn't keep it inside! After you left, I sat on my bed and cried. I took out the pictures you gave me and was looking at them, remembering the stories."

We'd given Darshika a set of laminated pictures, each depicting a different Bible story. "I was looking at those pictures and crying when my mother-in-law came into my room. And I told her, Bhabi. Everything I know about Jesus. How He has changed my life. How I want to follow Him but don't know if they will let me."

I looked at Joshua. He grinned. Darshika went on, "She told me it's okay for me to worship Jesus! And she let me pray for her arthritis. I just know that if Jahne's family hears Jesus's stories and prays to Him, they will want to follow Him, too."

My heart was out of control with adrenaline. This was a miracle! Darshika added, "There's more. The other night I was feeling lonely. It's hard to be the only one who doesn't worship idols. As I was singing my worship song, I felt a presence in the room. I looked towards the door, and I saw Him. I saw Jesus! I couldn't see His face, but I knew it was Him. He was wearing a white robe. I didn't feel afraid. Peace came from Him into my heart. Even though I'm alone, now I know I'm not alone. He is with me!" I felt like crying, but was too happy. God was showing Himself in a tangible way.

And not just to the Parvata.

# 45

# DASHBOARD MIRACLE

Joshua got several phone calls from Chotu over the coming months, always from a different number. He now worked as a laborer, traveling wherever work was available. Joshua visited him several times. Once they shared a meal of fried greens, eating off one plate, the only dish Chotu owned. Our Brahmin friends would have been horrified at the spiritual pollution of sharing a plate. But Chotu was touched.

"You really are different," Chotu told Joshua.

Later, Chotu called Joshua to invite him to his wedding. Joshua traveled for days by bus and train to get there. It was summer and well over a hundred degrees Fahrenheit in Chotu's brother's mud hut. When Joshua called me on the phone, he sounded exhausted. "It's just really hot. There's no electricity or anything. They've got Chotu's nephew constantly fanning me with a piece of cardboard."

"Don't get heatstroke," I said.

"Don't worry, I'll be fine. Hopefully, I can take a bath in the irrigation ditch again tonight with the guys. We did that yesterday."

"Sounds sanitary."

"At least it cooled me off. Hey, I noticed something interesting. Things have been kind of high-stress around here with the wedding. I'm not sure why, but nobody is smiling at all."

"Might be the heat."

"Maybe. But it was so striking to me that nobody has been smiling. Until Chotu's brother's wife, the one who is a Christian, came from her hut down the road. She had the most sincere, peaceful smile on her face."

Several days later, Joshua witnessed the wedding of a child bride. Chotu explained that marrying off the thirteen-year-old was one way her family could protect her from rape. A man was less likely to rape a married woman as her husband might retaliate. Perhaps her young age explained the tension in the family.

Shortly after Joshua returned from Chotu's wedding, I asked him to watch over Arav during his nap so Ashi and I could go visiting.

"Who will we visit, Mommy?" Ashi asked in her sweet, high voice.

"*Mausi* Rose," I said, using the term for "mother's little sister."

"I'll play with her clothes. She has pretty clothes."

"Hello!" Rose came to meet us at the gate, already laughing about something. "Come in!"

We stepped into Rose's room. I sat on the big bed she shared with her husband and son. Ashi found a sparkly tunic on the back of a chair and pulled it over her head. Rose brought a box of rings and bangles for her to try on and stuck a *bindi* on her forehead.

"I'm the queen," Ashi said, clomping around in a pair of heels. "I'm Queen Esther."

Rose smiled and nodded. She didn't know any more about Queen Esther than she knew about Cinderella. "Where's Arav?"

"Napping. Joshua stayed home so I could come." Rose and I talked for a while about kids and life. I had no idea what would happen in the future. Would Rose keep following Jesus? Would her husband's family ever choose to join her? Something in me told me I'd played my part in Rose's story. It was time for me to just be a friend, to wait and pray and hope. But I had one more thing to share with her.

"I have a gift for you," I said. Reaching into my bag, I pulled out a softbound journal. Its faux suede cover was dyed purple and embossed with tulips. This was how I pictured Rose—a bulb planted in the hard, cold ground waiting for a season of warmth and rain to coax her into the light.

"Oooh, pretty," she said.

I opened the soft, floppy pages and handed her the book. "It's called a prayer journal. I like to write my prayers because reading them later helps me remember all God has done for me. Read here, on the first page. I wrote you a message." Among other things, I had written that I knew Rose would find God if she searched for Him with all her heart.

I watched Rose's eyes as they searched the words back and forth. Looking up, she put her hand over her heart. "I hope I *will* find Him."

"You will. He promised." I suggested Rose write in English so nobody else could read her prayers. Soon it was time to leave. Rose gave Ashi a couple of gold-painted tin rings and a bindi dot sticker.

"Bye-bye, Mausi!" she called behind her. "Bye!"

———

WE OCCASIONALLY VISITED our nearest Adventist church, the one that was four hours away by bus where we'd first seen a demon cast out. One evening, the pastor of that church called Joshua. "We enjoyed the sermon you preached last time you came. My wife says your wife also likes to preach. Would she be willing to share this Sabbath?"

"I'm sure she would." Joshua asked Rose's father-in-law to drive us to the church. It would take less time and be easier with the kids. He agreed.

The night before the sermon, I was so nervous I typed the entire thing on our computer and printed it out. The next morning when we arrived at the church, I looked at Rose's father-in-law as he opened the car door for me. "You're welcome to stay for the church service. I'm sharing the message."

He looked over at a clump of sunflowers nodding nearby. "I think I will join you."

I thanked God that I'd written out the sermon as I was now ten times as nervous. Taking the children by their hands, Joshua and I turned toward the church.

"Oh, no," I heard behind me. I turned back. Rose's father-in-law was kneeling by one of his tires. "Flat tire. I'll have to get this fixed."

"It's okay, Uncle," I said. "Next time."

I preached. As I glanced up from reading, I noticed a slender, pale girl hunched next to her mother. Her eyes looked large and pale over dark circles. After the service, her mother helped her to the front of the church. They spoke to the pastor. Then the pastor spoke with me. "This young lady is suffering from a demon. She wants you to be here when we pray for her."

I felt like throwing up. I didn't want to be there during their exorcism. The girl smiled at me, a weak, frightened smile.

"Okay," I said.

Joshua took Ashi and Arav out of the church, and I sat on the floor with half-a-dozen other ladies. The pastor led the girl to the middle of the circle. Resting his Bible on her forehead, he began to pray. The girl began to scream.

The women shouted and pleaded in prayer. The pastor's voice rose above theirs. The girl screamed as though bereaved, her head swaying back and forth. At first, I just watched, eyes wide, breath suspended.

Then I too began to pray. I prayed for freedom for the girl. I prayed for the women, that they would stop screaming. I prayed for the church, myself, my children, and India, that God would deliver us all from the power of the enemy. Then I sang, "My peace I give unto you."

Everyone stopped shouting. They stared at me. I kept singing. "Not as the world gives, give I to you." The women continued praying, quietly now, but the girl stopped screaming. After some time, the pastor ended his prayer.

"You must not take her into any temples," he told the mother. "Don't let her eat food offered to idols. Let her have this Bible and let her read it every day. Come back next week."

When I walked out of the church, I saw Joshua and the kids standing with Rose's father-in-law near a mossy baptismal tank.

"What happened in there?" Rose's father-in-law asked. "I heard screaming."

"A woman was brought here with a demon," I said. "We prayed for her, and it left."

"Do demons have to listen to Jesus?"

"Yes."

We all ate in the pastor's home. He shared with Rose's father-in-law about Jesus' power over evil spirits. Then we got in the car. I commented, "Glad you got your tire fixed. Praise God you noticed it was flat."

"Strangest thing," Rose's father-in-law said, putting the car in reverse. "I was out looking for a place to change the tire when a man walked up to me. He handed me this book."

He pointed to the dashboard. There sat a black book with shining gold letters. "It's a Bible. After hearing that exorcism, I want to read it. I'll keep it in my car and read when I have time."

A Bible? A man in the mountains of India had given Rose's father-in-law a Bible? But how was that possible? Did Rose's father-in-law know he had a miracle in his car? Did he know his daughter-in-law had her own secret time with Jesus?

Some weeks later, we visited the church again. The girl with the big eyes was there. She smiled shyly at me, and I noticed her cheeks had a healthy glow. I learned she had remained free of the demon and now came to church regularly.

---

# 46

# THE SEEDLING

"**B**habi, I want to come stay with you," Darshika said over the phone. "Just for a little while. I need an operation, and I want to recover at your house."

"You're always welcome here," I assured her. "When do you want to come?"

"Soon. I know Jahne's parents will let me. He's going to pay for part of the surgery. And I have my own money for the rest. I gave it to my uncle for safekeeping, and all I have to do is pick it up."

"I see. Are you sick?"

"No." She lowered her voice. "After my first two kids, a mobile clinic came to our village. They were offering free surgeries to stop pregnancies. I had the surgery. Now Jahne and I want to try for a baby, so I want the doctor to fix it."

Darshika came a few weeks later. She bear-hugged Joshua and me. Then Ashi and Arav dragged her off to play. After the children slept, she recited her to-do list. "I need to get my surgery. And my in-laws need a copy of my government card. Do you still have the documents I gave you for safekeeping?"

"Of course. They're in the safe where we keep our passports." Going to the safe, I retrieved a stack of papers that included Darshika's medical records, a court document, and a bank card.

"Ah-ha! Here it is." Darshika pulled her government ID from the stack. It bore a pixelated black-and-white photo of her. Suddenly, she frowned. "Um, this is not good. My ID still says 'Darshika, wife of Rohit.'"

"That's okay," I said. "You can get a new one at your *panchayat* when you go home." The *panchayat* is a village-level government.

"I can't!" she moaned. "My in-laws can't know I was married before!"

"Wait. I thought you said you told them everything."

"Well, I told *him* everything." Darshika hung her head. "I thought he'd told his family before we got married, but he didn't. If I tell them now, Jahne says they'll kick me out and revoke his inheritance."

"Look, Darshika, they seem like good people. Couldn't you at least tell his mom?"

"I tried, sort of. I told her my story as though it were someone else's."

"What did she say?"

"She said if she were that woman's mother-in-law, she'd kick her sorry behind out on the streets. It's not like I want to lie, Bhabi, but I can't tell them. It will hurt Jahne."

My mind reeled. Darshika was caught in a game of chess, and she was not a powerful piece. And now *I* knew about the lie too. I felt as though a giant spider was throwing its sticky webs around me.

"Besides," Darshika continued. "It's not their business, right? A man and wife should have some things they keep private."

That was true and biblical. But did it violate cultural rules? Did cultural rules even matter? What was right and wrong in this situation? Darshika hadn't lied. And she hadn't asked to be part of withholding the truth.

"He said it's just between us," Darshika added. "Our secret. We're going to have a new life. He even cried when he heard my story."

I hoped Jahne was as big-hearted as he seemed. "Well, I'll pray for you. It's always better to tell the truth. Then you don't have to hide things. But this is your business and Jahne's, not mine."

A thought suddenly occurred to me. "Wait a minute. That's why you need to have the surgery here, isn't it? So they won't know you've had kids before and had your tubes tied?"

She nodded. "Yes."

"Ugh. You are in a big mess, girl!"

"Maybe I could use my sister's card. Couldn't Bhaia edit it on the computer so it has my name and picture?"

"That's not possible. See this number?" I pointed to the ID card. "It's unique to you. Your sister's card has her number. Not every village uses a computer, but in a computer somewhere is this number, and it says, 'Darshika, wife of Rohit.' You have to change it in the system if you don't want them to know."

"What am I going to do? My divorce papers aren't here, either. I need them for my new ID." Closing her eyes, Darshika namasted upward. "God in Heaven, hear the sound of my voice. Help me!"

---

JOSHUA TOOK Darshika to visit her family, who lived halfway up the side of a mountain. They drove partway, then hiked in on foot. Every few hundred feet, Darshika stopped to pray.

"Oh, Lord, I know I'm a dumb sinner. But You are so merciful. You sent people to tell me about You. Please open a way for me. Help my father to cooperate so I can get my documents. Please, I'm begging You!"

When they arrived at Darshika's childhood home, her father, old and stooped, squinted at his daughter. "Darshika? I thought you were dead."

"I need some papers," Darshika said.

At first, her father insisted he didn't know where her stuff was. But he eventually opened a large trunk. There beneath a pile of winter clothing was a stack of documents, including a photocopy of Darshika's divorce papers.

When Joshua and Darshika walked in the door that evening, Darshika was all smiles. God had answered her very first real prayer.

---

DIVORCE PAPERS IN HAND, we all drove down to the *panchayat* near Darshika's childhood village. The secretary there shook her head when Darshika handed her the divorce decree. "This is not a real divorce. This paper is a cheap, fake divorce from some phony lawyer."

"What!" Darshika moaned. "You mean I'm not even divorced?"

"No."

"Can't you just change my ID card?"

"Not without proper divorce papers."

"How do I get those? Can you make them?"

"You're going to have to get your man and go see a lawyer about this. We don't do divorces."

Darshika turned pale. My own eyes widened involuntarily. Her man? Her ex-husband—or, apparently, her husband?

*I'm living in a soap opera!* I thought as we drove home. But there was nobody else in the world willing to care about Darshika. I just wished it wasn't all so messy. Still, God hadn't turned away from my own messy heart. Jesus was willing to eat with prostitutes. The least I could do was help an honest woman have a new start in life.

Darshika called a cousin who called another cousin who called the friend of a cousin of her ex. After several hours, Darshika's husband agreed to meet her in Chotashaher the next day. If he agreed to the divorce, there shouldn't be a problem other than the usual time-sucking bureaucracy. If he didn't, we could be in for a court battle. We sought God with extra fervor that night and encouraged Darshika to trust Him.

Our first stop the next morning was a lawyer's office. He agreed to accompany Darshika and Joshua to meet with Darshika's husband. The husband turned out to be as old, stooped, and gray as her father. He did not object to officially finalizing the divorce.

"God did a miracle for me," Darshika said as we got back in the car.

---

DARSHIKA WAS NOW eager to have her surgery. I took her to Pahargaun, but the doctor didn't want to operate.

"Come back with your husband," he told Darshika.

"But my husband works," Darshika said.

"Why does he need to come?" I asked.

"We don't want to get involved in messy family matters," the doctor said. I understood the sentiment.

That night, Darshika cried herself to sleep. A few days later, we went to Chotashaher again, this time to see Dr. Wonderful. She said she would operate and gave us a printout of the cost. She patted Darshika on the arm. "Don't worry, sweetie. I think you have a good chance of getting pregnant after the surgery."

As we returned home, Darshika poured out her excitement. "First, God protected me from my ex and prompted him to let me have the divorce. Now we've found a doctor who will do the surgery. I've been crying my eyes out to God these past few weeks. He is hearing me!"

"God does hear you, Darshika. He created you. He loves you. He has promised to give you hope and a future." I asked Darshika if she'd like to do Bible studies once a week. She said she wanted to study every night. Knowing this might be our only chance before she returned home, I agreed.

Although both Joshua and I had spent hours teaching Darshika to read, she couldn't read well enough to understand the Bible. So, I decided to do the study another way. We would pray, then I would tell her a Bible story. She would repeat it, then tell me what she learned.

The story of Noah became an instant favorite. "I get it! Jesus' way is just like that boat. There it is, free and open, and you can go in and be safe from the flood. But not everybody chooses to get in."

I hardly needed to teach Darshika. I just had to pray with her and tell her the old, old story. The Holy Spirit spoke to her, and she heard His voice loud and clear.

Another story Darshika loved was Jesus' parable of the sower. One day she said, "I am like your little seedling. You planted the seed, and now I'm growing!"

I knew, though, that God had planted the seed of faith in Darshika's heart long before we came. Darshika had told me about an Indian Christian known locally as the Jesus Teacher. He had lived in her village when she was first married. The villagers disrespected and made fun of the man mercilessly, yet he continued witnessing. Another time, a tourist visiting Darshika's village told her the handful of stories about Jesus she remembered from her childhood. Darshika had treasured these things in her heart. When we came, we only poured water on a dry, dormant seed.

I began referring to Darshika in my prayers as "my seedling," and would ask God to grow her in His grace and love. She liked this, sometimes calling herself a seedling in her own prayers.

---

IT WOULD TAKE several weeks to change the information on Darshika's card and several more to get a physical replacement. In the meantime, she had a surgery to undergo. She just needed the money she'd earned some years before as a maid, money she had left with an uncle for safekeeping.

Darshika called the uncle to tell him we were coming. When we arrived at his concrete block of a house, an old man emerged, puffing on a cigarette. He chuckled when he spotted Darshika. "So, you're back!"

"Namaste, Uncle Ji," Darshika said. "How are you?"

"Fine. How's the guy you married?"

"Fine. Uncle, I came for the money you've been saving for me."

"What money?"

"I gave you thirty thousand rupees when I came back from working in the mountains, remember? You said to leave it with you for safekeeping."

"Ha! Well, I don't have thirty thousand. I can give you ten."

"But I'm having an operation. It's expensive." Darshika's eyes darted about like a bird looking for a way of escape. "I need money."

"Don't we all?" The man flicked his cigarette. I pulled Ashi behind me. Joshua picked up Arav. "Look, I came to your second wedding. I gave you a gift. That's a lot of money."

I could no longer hold myself back. "So the bride pays you to attend her wedding and then pays for her own gift? Is that how it works? The money Darshika gave you wasn't yours to spend."

Joshua interrupted me in English under his breath. "He might not give her anything if we're too rude." The man chuckled and walked toward Darshika.

"Come on. You're making me look bad." The man thrust some money at Darshika. "Here's your ten thousand. Hope you get your 'surgery.'"

The man disappeared into the cement block, leaving Darshika frowning down at the money in her hand. Joshua stared at the money, too.

"Exactly what kind of work does your uncle do, Darshika?"

Darshika bit her lip and stared at the ground. "He sells hashish." Looking over her head at Joshua, I motioned with my eyes that we should get out of there. Ten thousand rupees in hand, we left at a faster pace than we'd come.

# 47

## POISONED

Darshika emerged from my room with red eyes. She handed Joshua her phone. "Jahne wants to talk to you."

"Namaste." Joshua listened for a long time, then said, "Let me talk to Abigail. I'll consider it and let you know."

Once we were alone, Joshua explained, "They want to borrow the rest of the money needed for the surgery. The equivalent of a hundred bucks."

"I don't know." I felt uneasy at the thought. "I can't help thinking of those who say Christians pay people to follow Christ. This is exactly the kind of thing that could get us kicked out of India."

"Darshika helps around the house as though she's still working for us," Joshua responded. "But since she thinks of us as family now, it would be insulting to pay her. Maybe this is a loophole."

"Why does generosity have to be so complicated?" I asked.

"We need to pray."

We prayed. The next day, we told Darshika we'd loan her and Jahne the amount they lacked for the surgery. She cried.

---

DARSHIKA HAD HER SURGERY. When they wheeled her out of the OR, I was waiting.

"Bhabi," she mumbled, "Bhabi."

"I'm here."

"Okay. You're here." Her eyes rolled back, and she fell unconscious again.

The doctor emerged a few moments later. "The surgery was successful. But were you aware Darshika has tuberculosis?"

"I knew she'd had it in the past," I responded. "But she was treated for it."

"Yes, well, I saw evidence of damage from tuberculosis. Once she heals from surgery, she should try to get pregnant as soon as possible. If she waits too long, she'll lose her chance."

"Thank you for letting me know."

I stayed that night with Darshika in the general ward where patients occupied open cubicles. A baby yowled two cubicles down. After several sleepless hours, I thought back to when Arav had pneumonia. I remembered the family who'd shared blankets, food, and comforting words with me. I stood and followed the sound of the crying baby. Peeking into the cubicle, I saw a woman about my age rocking the crying baby, trying to shush him. Her husband sat by a tray table heaped with medication. I recognized a boxed drink given to combat dehydration.

"Namaste," I said, looking with pity on the baby. "I have two kids. I know how tough it is when they're sick. If you need anything, I'm in the cubicle in the corner there." The man smiled.

"How did you learn Hindi? Where are you from? We have two kids, too. Our daughter is with her grandmother."

The man and I chatted for a while. I tried to engage the young mother in conversation, but she gave me a narrowed, unfriendly stare and didn't answer.

"It's amoebic dysentery," her husband said. "Very bad."

As if on cue, the baby wailed louder. I turned to the woman. "I'm so sorry. But the pediatrician here is wonderful. You'll be out of here in no time."

"Uh-huh." She looked me up and down. I felt my cheeks flush. Had I done something wrong?

"Well, I'd better go take care of my friend." I turned to leave.

I rested for an hour. Then Darshika needed to use the toilet. I eased her into the bathroom. One "squat pot" was filthy with excrement. We found a cleaner stall. When Darshika finished, I looked at the sink. There was no soap. I hadn't yet been in a hospital in India that had soap. Did people steal it? Was it too expensive?

A woman with a squeegee mopped down the bathroom, including the offending toilet. Picking up the rag, she plopped it into the sink and ran the water over it. I thought of the toilet and the baby with amoebic dysentery and decided it would be safer not to wash my hands.

The next morning, Joshua brought the kids to visit. Under my breath, I told him, "Don't let the kids use the toilet here. Trust me!"

"Bua!" Ashi and Arav crawled onto Darshika's bed, calling her their father's sister. She patted them and smiled at the little drawings they'd made her.

Ashi ran out of the cubicle. I went after her. Another little girl was there, with curly black hair and a dark smudge above her cheek to ward off the evil eye. Ashi took her hand, and they walked around together.

The man from the night before appeared. He nodded toward the little girl. "This is our daughter. I think our girls are friends!"

"I'd say so," I said. "How nice!"

Darshika called my name. I went to her, then hurried back to check on Ashi. She walked out of the sick baby's cubicle, still holding her new friend's hand.

"Joshua," I said. "I love seeing you guys, but could you go? It's so dirty."

"Okay. Hope you can get out soon."

"So do I."

---

WE REJOICED when Darshika was discharged from the hospital a few days later. But soon Ashi began to feel ill.

"Mommy, I have a headache." I rubbed her forehead and kissed it. No fever. She played, but every twenty minutes she complained of pain, which soon migrated to her stomach. I gave her water and took her to the bathroom. She continued to grow worse.

"Mommy, I don't feel good," she cried.

I touched her forehead with the back of my hand. It was flaming hot. By evening, her fever was 103. I gave her a fever reducer and tucked her into bed.

Darshika knitted. Joshua budgeted. I had just picked up my guitar when a thought as loud as speech entered my mind. *Go check Ashi.*

*Don't be paranoid,* I told myself. *You're just being a worried mom.*

*Go check Ashi.*

*She'll be fine,* I reasoned. *I just gave her medicine.*

*Check her now!* I felt as though someone pushed me towards Ashi's room. Once there, I checked her temperature. It was 105 degrees.

"Ashi? Ashi, are you okay?" I couldn't rouse her. I threw off the covers. She was unconscious, and there was a mess on the bed.

"Joshua!" I yelled. "Call somebody! We have to get Ashi to the hospital!"

I was already yanking one of Arav's pull-ups onto Ashi's limp body. Grabbing a wet rag and bottle of hand-soap, I carried her to the road. Our landlord's son drove us to the mission hospital in Pahargaun. I sponged Ashi's face and chest and fanned her.

In the ER, a nurse checked Ashi's temperature and said it was 102 degrees. I spoke to the head nurse. "You need to teach your nurse how to read a thermometer. My daughter's temp is 105, and she's unconscious. Please do something!"

The head nurse gave Ashi a shot of ibuprofen, then commanded another nurse to bring ice. Together we sponged Ashi's thin body.

"Symptoms?"

"Head and stomach ache all day. Now this fever and diarrhea."

The nurse took a stool sample to the lab. About fifteen minutes later, the ibuprofen kicked in, and Ashi woke up. She looked across the room where a small boy wiggled and screamed as a nurse tried to set his broken arm. "Are we in the hospital?"

"Yes, sweetie," I said. "We're in the hospital."

"We should pray for that little boy."

Ashi's results came back: amoebic dysentery. I tucked Ashi into a gurney as a nurse put in an IV. Once admitted into a blessedly private room, I put my hand-soap in the bathroom. All night long I slept in five-minute stretches, taking Ashi to the bathroom, washing both our hands and falling into bed again.

The next morning, I left Ashi with a nurse friend of mine and went to the cafeteria. I bought a bowl of oatmeal and an apple, hoping to tempt Ashi's appetite. It was 7:00 a.m., and the hospital staff had gathered for worship. They were singing a hymn called *Trust and Obey*:

> But we never can prove
> The delights of His love,
> Until all on the altar we lay;
> For the favor He shows,
> And the joy He bestows
> Are for those
> who will trust and obey.

Those words burned in my heart as I walked back up the stairs to Ashi's room. She lay awake, staring at the ceiling. That afternoon, an Australian doctor who recently arrived in India came to see Ashi. A tiny koala bear hugged her stethoscope. Ashi loved both the doctor and her koala.

"I just wanted to say I heard you all singing this morning," I told her, choking up. "Trust and obey. That means a lot, because . . . you know, it's not always easy being here."

"No, it isn't." She paused a moment as though remembering, then went on, "Your daughter will be okay. But she must stay another night and day. She needs IV anti-parasites and antibiotics."

That evening Joshua traded places with me. During the night, a new nurse came in and woke Ashi. Joshua assumed she was there to check Ashi's vitals. Instead, she whipped out her cell phone to take a selfie with Ashi. When he called me the next morning to tell me what had happened, I was shocked and angry. But I wasn't surprised. Everywhere we went, people tried to take pictures of our kids.

It was a happy day when Ashi finally came home from the hospital. After a few hours of playing, she asked to lie down. I knew if she asked for a nap, she was still not feeling a hundred percent. Tucking her in, I lay down next to her. "Mommy's so glad you're back."

"Me too." Ashi stared at the ceiling, her voice small like a kitten's mew. "Mama, I know why I got sick."

"Why, Ashi?"

"I drank something."

"What did you drink?"

"Alcohol."

I snuggled closer. "Oh, sweetie, no. You've never had alcohol."

"Yes, I did." Her voice wobbled. "Somebody gave me some, and I drank it."

"Oh?" I tried to sound casual, but I was now on full alert.

"Yeah. A grown-up gave me some alcohol."

"Well, it probably wasn't alcohol, and it's probably not what made you sick.

But you don't have to eat or drink anything that isn't from Mommy or Daddy. Remember?"

Ashi burst into tears. "They - made - me - drink - it! I - didn't - want - to!"

"Wait, what do you mean? Where were you? Who made you?"

"I don't know. It was at Bua's hospital. The people with the baby. I said no, but they put it in my mouth and made me drink it. I got sick, and I know that's why!"

My mind jerked back to the hospital in Chotashaher. I saw each detail of the scene. The crying baby. The talkative dad. The mother's narrow, angry eyes. The juice box. The little girl walking about with Ashi. The short interval when I didn't see her.

Then my mind flashed forward. Ashi in the hospital, unconscious. The screaming boy with the broken arm. Sponging Ashi's hot body. The doctor's diagnosis: amoebic dysentery.

I cuddled and comforted Ashi, promised to take care of her, prayed over her. Eventually, she fell asleep in my arms. But one thought pulsated through my mind. *Did someone poison my child?*

It was a question to which I'd probably never know the answer. But one thing was certain. My child thought she'd been poisoned, and that was enough.

---

DARSHIKA PRAYED for Ashi and worried. She felt guilty, as though it was her fault for having the surgery and needing my help.

"Dear God," she prayed. "Please heal Ashi's heart and bless her, oh my Lord. And my holy Father in Heaven, please, give me Bhaia and Bhabi for a brother and sister-in-law for my next hundred lives. Amen!"

I couldn't help smiling. Seeing me, Darshika asked, "What is it, Bhabi?" Then she smacked her forehead. "Oh, I forgot that reincarnation isn't in the Bible. It's just so easy to think that way. I'm sorry!"

I laughed and hugged her. "Don't be sorry. We all have ways of thinking that Jesus has to change. Be patient with yourself and others too. Trust that people who follow Jesus don't stay the same. It's one of the only things I know for sure."

---

IT WAS time for Joshua to lead another tour. Darshika's husband gave her permission to stay longer to keep me company. Each evening, we continued our Bible studies.

Ashi and Arav loved Darshika, and she played with them a lot, enjoying their crayons and stuffed animals and tiny teacups. Sometimes she joked, "You have three kids. Ashi, Arav, and me!" She often called me *Bhabi Ma*, meaning: "My brother's wife who is like a mother to me."

When I played with my kids, there were only two games Ashi wanted to play: Hospital and Monster.

In Hospital, one person takes a turn having a terrible disease while the other two give injections and prescribe medicine. Ashi set up elaborate scenes complete with makeshift IV lines. We'd been playing Hospital for over a month now.

"Could we play something else?" I suggested. "How about Restaurant?"

"No," Ashi said. "Let's play Monster."

In Monster, a bear, enemy soldier, or other Scary Thing is coming to get Ashi and Arav. It's my job to make it go away.

"Go away, Bad Thing!" I would command. "You can't get my children! I won't let you!" Ashi and Arav would shriek, run around, and laugh until I defeated the monster.

In college, I'd written a paper on the role of play therapy in healing from trauma and grief. Now long-buried memories of what I'd learned tugged at me. Was Ashi playing to deal with her fear? Had all her trips to the hospital traumatized her? Was it believing someone had poisoned her? Or was it the constant disrespect of her boundaries, the picture-taking and hated face-touching?

Over and over, Ashi asked me what happened the night she went to the hospital. I told her how an angel had whispered to my heart to check on her. Later, she dreamed that she'd lost us in an airport and the doctor with the koala stethoscope found her and brought her home.

# 48

# UPSTAIRS NEIGHBORS

I often visited a new neighbor, the Corner Woman. She had a bunch of kids, and like Joshua, her husband traveled for his job. One afternoon, she said, "Joshua will be home before you know it. Just be careful with your kids. You know there are kidnappings in India. Even around here."

I knew. I'd recently seen news footage of a man stealing a toddler from the arms of her sleeping mother on a crowded train platform. The child was never found. I shuddered. "Yes, Sister. I only let my kids out of the house when I can watch them."

"Good. And call me if you're ever scared in the night."

At about 3:00 a.m. the next morning, I jolted awake. Sitting straight up in bed, I listened. I could hear a rustling sound outside my window, then footsteps. I called the Corner Lady. "Sister, I need help! Someone is breaking in!"

"I'll send the neighbor's husband. Sit tight, okay? Whatever you do, don't go outside!"

"Got it." I hung up. The footsteps rushed off the porch into the bushes next to the house. Grabbing a couple of walking sticks from under the bed, I strode to Darshika's bed in the tandoor room. "Darshika," I hissed. "Wake up!"

Darshika always slept with her head covered by a blanket. It's a wonder she didn't smother herself. I poked her. She flopped the blanket onto the floor and sat up. "Bhabi, what's wrong?"

I handed her a stick. "Someone was at the house."

She jumped out of bed. "Just let them try to get in here! I'll kill them!"

We checked all the doors and windows before going up the inside stairs that used to lead to the roof. Now they led to our landlord's new home. The only thing left to do before they moved in was to install a door between our floors.

Darshika and I stood back-to-back in Mr. Pandit's living room, holding our sticks like ninjas. Darshika shouted, "Get back here and fight like a man! I'll knock your head off!"

I checked the front door. It was unlocked. The windows were open, probably to air out the rooms. Someone could have easily come inside the house from the outside stairs, then down into my house through the inside stairs.

I locked everything, and Darshika and I went back downstairs.

"I'd like to sleep now," I said, "but I don't know if I'll be able to. I'm still shaking thinking of that open door. What if I hadn't woken up when I did?"

My phone rang. I jumped. It was the Corner Lady. Her friend's husband had checked around the house. Whoever had been there was gone.

"Thank you so much for your help," I said. "Do you want me to come sleep there?" she asked.

"No, it's okay. I have Darshika. We'll be fine."

"Let's pray," Darshika said when I hung up. Together, we knelt on the rough wool carpet and asked God for peace. Then in a miracle greater than the first, we slept. A sweet, deep sleep that lasted until morning.

When we took the kids for a walk the next day, I learned that two of our neighbors had been robbed in the night. For the next week, homes were robbed, one or two per night. One family lost all the money given them at their daughter's wedding. It was a terrible financial blow as they'd provided her with a dowry worthy of a princess.

When Joshua returned, the children pounced him. He filled one room with mattresses, pillows, and blankets, and we played David and Goliath. "Goliath" would fall off a chair into the soft mound, and "David" would chop off his head, raising his pillow sword in triumph.

---

THE DAY our landlords moved in upstairs was a happy one. Kids were running around everywhere, ours and theirs, dodging laborers carrying furniture.

The family patriarch was Mr. Pandit, a sought-after puja expert and Hindu priest who presided over the ceremonies of important politicians in our state. He sauntered up the stairs to his new domain like the important person he knew himself to be. Behind him strolled his wife, Mrs. Pandit. She screamed at her grandchildren not to knock over the workers, then turned to smile at me.

Their son, whom we called Pandit Jr., passed by with a bag full of odds-and-ends. He was the one who'd driven Ashi and me to the hospital when she had dysentery. His wife Sarala walked behind him with their baby Neenoo, who was just a few months younger than Arav. Their daughter Dee was a few years older than Ashi.

"We're all one big, happy family," Sarala said to me before walking up the stairs. "We'll be living together, after all!"

The door at the top of our inside stairs now opened directly into Mr. Pandit's home. Both sides were kept locked, though Mrs. Pandit occasionally knocked on her side of the door, calling for us to open up. Then she'd give us treats like cream, milk, or apple-mint chutney.

Darshika took a liking to Sarala and spent hours upstairs chatting with her and her mother-in-law. Joshua and I visited as well. We promised to be extra careful about ritual purity. To refrain from eating meat and eggs. To rinse off with our clothes on before entering the house if we'd visited the bereaved. After these promises, the Pandit family accepted our invitations to eat in our home and allowed us into theirs.

One evening, we sat in Mr. Pandit's *tandoor* room, watching TV with him and his family. The show was a retelling of *The Ramayan*, one of two major Sanskrit epics.

Leaning back against the wall behind him, Mr. Pandit commented, "My daughter-in-law has been talking with Darshika. Let me ask you something. Is it true reincarnation is not in the Bible?"

"Yes, it's true," Joshua responded.

Mrs. Pandit turned down the TV, and the entire family began asking questions about the Bible and Christianity. They explained why they believed in caste and reincarnation. They shared several things they found confusing in Hinduism.

"There's one thing, though," Pandit, Jr. said after about an hour of discussion. "We know you can't worship other gods. We could worship Jesus just like we worship any god. We could even come to your house for church. But don't ever go thinking you could make us into Christians!"

The rest of the family nodded. I explained, "Christians believe in freedom of choice. It would be against our religion to force anyone to do anything."

There was a collective sigh, and the friendly discussion resumed. Pandit Jr. added with a smile, "One thing I do like about your religion is your Sabbath. No Hindu god would ever tell us to rest. We never get a break!"

Over the following weeks, we had many similar discussions with our landlord's family. During our early morning prayer sessions, we prayed for them and for ourselves that God would speak through us.

In addition to being a Hindu priest, Mr. Pandit was a fortune-teller skilled in cursing and reverse-cursing. People came at all hours of the day to seek Mr. Pandit's help for their problems. The door between our homes was thin, so I often heard him upstairs performing various ceremonies.

---

ASHI GREW thin and complained of headaches. While Arav chowed down on whatever was on the menu, Ashi picked at her food. She had terrible nightmares and night terrors, screaming at me in the night as though I were something unreal. She was angry all the time and naughty on purpose. Other than a select few, she didn't want to see any Parvata people or go out of the house.

This concerned me. For Ashi's first three years of life, she'd been social, laid-back, and cheerful. At four and a half, she seemed a shadow of that person. Joshua soon left for his second month-long trip that summer. I let Ashi sleep in my bed. She slept better there.

I was still reading about spiritual warfare, still working on my paper for the upcoming conference. Inspired by my research, I decided to fast. For three days, I ate nothing. Every time I was hungry, I prayed. I prayed during quiet time and when the kids went to bed. Darshika helped me cook for the children, and I spent the extra time I gained to talk to God and read His Word.

*God*, I prayed. *Is this PTSD? Is it worms and poor nutrition? Is it spiritual warfare? Could it be all three? Show me what to do!*

Maybe it was the face touching. I knew Ashi needed me to make the "monsters" stop touching her face. Why couldn't I just be mean? Darshika, who loved my children like a fierce mother bear, had no problem being mean. One day I told her how disappointed I was that I couldn't stop people from touching Ashi's face.

"Let me coach you. Be stern. Loud. Make a scene and don't apologize!" Darshika demonstrated. "Now I'm the face toucher. Come on. Tell me off."

I marched over and grabbed her hand. "Excuse me! Isn't the head holy in your culture? Well, my daughter's face is part of her head. So hands off!"

Darshika nodded. "That was good. You talk like that and nobody will lay a hand on Ashi."

"I just hope I can say it in real life." I sighed. "I need to pray."

"Go on, Bhabi," Darshika encouraged. "You pray tonight. We'll skip our study this time. God will do something!"

Even after praying, I barely slept. Scooting closer to the thin, hot body sleeping next to me, I prayed again. *God, heal my child. Heal the trauma in her heart. Fill her with Your peace and joy, not the fear and sadness of the world. I trust her into Your care, God. And I trust You to grow me into the kind of mother she and Arav need.*

Mrs. Pandit came to visit the next day. I made popcorn for her and the children. As we sat on the floor chatting, hunger stabbed at my middle. Mrs. Pandit looked at me. "Eat!"

I knew that fasting is not something done to show off. But Jesus did say to let your light shine. "I'm fasting, Aunty."

"Christians fast?" Mrs. Pandit looked surprised. "How do you do your fast?"

I explained there was no prescribed method, but that I had committed not to eat for three days. I was drinking water, however.

"We fast for Mother Durga," she said. I thought of the bloody-tongued goddess and tried not to cringe at the thought of her being anyone's mother. "We only eat at night. It lasts nine days and is done to honor her. And you? Why do you fast?"

"I'm seeking wisdom from God," I said. "I want to know His will for me and my children. I want His will to be done in my life."

"Huh! Interesting." A few days later, Mrs. Pandit told me she'd found a Bible and was reading it.

"I'm just curious," she said.

---

JOSHUA and I had new supervisors with our mission organization. Retired university professors, Bob and Hazel had served as missionaries with their young children in an African country for several years. When they came to visit us, it was immediately clear they hadn't lost the missionary spirit. Though they didn't speak Hindi, they loved the Parvata people and took every opportunity to connect with them. Darshika felt that love and adopted them as her aunt and uncle.

Before our landlord's family moved in upstairs, we enjoyed living in an idol-free home with no dark spiritual influence. Now the house felt different. Though I opened all the blue-tinted windows to let in the sun and the air, the atmosphere grew darker and more smothering each day. I began having nightmares that people were breaking into the house. Joshua and I prayed and searched our hearts, wondering if we'd done anything to take ourselves out from under the wings of Christ.

Then the time came for our landlords to do a *puja* for their house. Pandit, Jr. stopped by to give us an invitation. "Please be here. You don't have to come for the *puja* itself. After the *puja*, it's just a housewarming party. We'll make sure you aren't served prasad (food offered to idols)."

The puja was held in the cement paved patio. The priests sat in a circle, chanting and throwing bits of food, orange flower petals, and various powders into a fire. A yellow tarp shaded them from the sun. The droning of their voices made me dizzy.

Bob and Hazel took pictures of the interesting ceremony from a window, commenting on the priests' white clothing and how one person showed the others what to do. Meanwhile, Darshika paced like a cat who smells a dog. I stopped her.

"Are you okay?"

"I have a headache," she said.

"So do I." In fact, I felt as though invisible claws were being screwed into my skull. I suddenly realized this was spiritual warfare. Why had it taken me so long to notice? We'd prayed a prayer of protection over our home. Now we needed to get ourselves under the wings of Christ. And fast.

"Let's pray," I said. Darshika pulled her scarf over her head, and I folded my hands. "Father in Heaven, we pray that Your holy angels would be in every room of this house. Fan away the darkness, God. I claim the blood of Christ to cover us!"

For twenty minutes, we prayed. I visualized angels rushing through our home with flaming swords, kicking out corner-lurking demons. When we said amen, Darshika looked up at me, her forehead relaxed, shoulder lines soft. "My headache is gone."

"Praise the Lord!" The tightness in my skull was releasing. "Mine is better, too."

We made it through the hours of *puja*, then joined the Pandits for their housewarming meal. Afterward, we spent time in prayer before going to bed, relieved it was over. The next morning, the concrete patio looked like a parking lot after the fourth of July. Colored powder and ash were everywhere. I sighed as I surveyed the wreckage. We would keep Ashi and Arav inside until Sarala had a chance to sweep.

# 49

# HOUSE CHURCH

J oshua returned from his tour with the suggestion that we buy a car. We'd
spent our first five years in India without a car, a strategic choice we didn't
regret. But after hitching rides to the emergency room by bus, taxi, and
friends' cars, we wanted our own transportation. After all, we had two children
now and a new believer whose family lived several hours away.

We told our angel dispatchers of our need. In less than a week, we were able
to buy a car. It was used but sturdy. It was also a stick-shift. I saw this as a sign
that Joshua should drive. In turn, Joshua felt learning to drive a stick shift should
be my next offensive move against anxiety.

So I learned to drive a stick shift on winding mountain roads while dodging
ditches, flocks of sheep, stray cows, ladies with huge piles of sticks on their
backs, and school buses going the opposite direction—all in my lane. It was
terrifying. For me and everyone else.

Once, I drove into a ditch and killed the car. Just then, a bus eased around us,
slowing almost to a stop. The bus passengers were staring at me through the
windows. I heard someone shout, "It's Joshua's wife!"

"Great," I muttered. "Everyone in our village saw that."

"You're doing great," Joshua said. "I mean, you will do great. Once you get
the hang of it."

After a couple of weeks, I could drive a stick shift. We took Darshika home
with her new government card, a healed surgical incision, and the ability to read
a children's Bible. She just knew everything would be okay now, and we believed
her.

ONE DAY, Joshua commented, "You'll never guess who I saw riding a bicycle this morning."

"I give up. Who?"

"Naina."

"Seriously?" I grabbed my phone. Naina was my most independent, boundary-pushing friend. And cycling was her secret dream.

"You're cycling?!" I texted.

"Yes. I'm so happy!" Naina wrote back.

Later that day I visited her. "I'm so proud of you!"

"I'm proud of me, too!" Naina patted herself on the back. "*Shabash*, Naina! Good job!"

"Now we have to go for a ride together!"

"Yes! Abigail, I feel like I've sprouted wings. Not that it's easy to cycle here. I know people think I should stay home. But I feel better when I exercise and spend time outdoors. Even though some ladies are judgmental, others have shown an interest in learning."

"I feel those judgmental stares when I ride too. But it's better than walking. At least they only have a moment to judge you before you zoom past!"

Naina laughed, then sighed. "If only our society would treat women as people and not as property or servants. So many daughters-in-law work hard but go crazy because of poor treatment and lack of freedom."

"I have friends who complain of this exact thing," I agreed.

"I think educating and training women is the solution. I know it's hard to understand, but in India, we disrespect the weak. Educated women don't have to depend on their families for money. This gives them more power in their relationships."

Naina and I began cycling together when our husbands could watch the kids. Sometimes I visualized what would happen if Naina chose to follow Jesus. What fun, meaningful ministry we could have together. We could bike to far villages. We could pray with people.

I gave Naina a printout of some Bible verses. She kept them for a couple of weeks. Then she returned them without explanation.

---

ONE DAY when Naina and I cycled into Pahargaun, I brought home four rainbow-colored seed packets, all of them flowers. Ashi and Arav helped me plant them. We waited, checking each day for the curling green miracle to emerge. Days turned into weeks, weeks into months, but the flowers never germinated. We never knew why.

In the meantime, it seemed Ashi and Arav were wilting. I had fasted twice now, and we'd had everyone's vitamin levels tested. We all needed Vitamin D and B12, so we supplemented. I knew eggs contained vitamin D, but we'd been abstaining from eggs ever since our landlords moved in.

Kay brought her children to visit. As we sat outside watching the three older kids play, baby Elijah on Kay's lap, Kay shared a concern. "Elijah hasn't grown in two months. I've been trying not to worry. I know kids grow at different rates. But we're thinking it might be time to take him to a pediatrician."

Thus began a round of trips to the doctor, first in Pahargaun, then Chotashaher, then many hours away in Delhi. Angel dispatchers all over the world prayed for the children of the missionary families on the Parvata project.

---

ONE EARLY MORNING as Joshua and I prayed together in the *tandoor* room, I noticed his voice sounded burdened.

"Why don't we pray more specifically?" I suggested. "What is it exactly that we want God to do?"

Joshua looked up. "We want God to give us a house church. It's been five and a half years. We want people to come to church."

We'd been praying for our four-person congregation for months. Inspired by another pastor, we'd even begun holding church in the Hindi language, dressing up as though expecting guests. It was faith in action. The faith that God would bring someone to worship with us. Occasionally someone came. Rose had come once, Chayana several times. And, of course, Lars and Kay joined sometimes. But many Sabbaths, we were alone.

"Okay. Let's ask for a church."

Two hours later, I heard a knock at the door. I opened it. Six smiling women stood outside. "Do you recognize me?" One of them asked. "You gave me a cauliflower the other day."

I thought back. I'd been given three giant cauliflowers by the Entrepreneurial Tibetan Lady. I'd shared one with a Nepali woman as she walked back from working in the fields.

"Oh, yes! I remember you."

"We wanted to ask if maybe . . . if we can come to your house for church on Saturday."

Church? On Saturday? I looked around at the group of smiling women. "Are you Christians?"

They nodded. "Yes. We are Christians, and in Nepal where we're from, we go to church on Saturday. We heard you worship on Saturday and decided to join you."

"You're an answer to our prayers," I said. "Of course you can come!"

We spoke to our landlords. They were okay with it since these Nepali women were high caste. We began preparing for our first real house church.

Meanwhile, people from every caste and of every age continued to visit Mr. Pandit daily. The low-caste ones just yelled up at the house, not daring to come near Mr. Pandit's front door. It was hard on Ashi and Arav to have people constantly coming into our "yard." Visitors squeezed their cheeks or tried to take selfies with them. Once more we felt like we lived in a zoo.

I wondered if we should move again. But Mr. Pandit's family might be interested in Jesus. His wife had even bought herself a Bible. How could we leave now?

# 50

## AMBASSADOR

One morning, inspired by Kay's prayers for her friend to experience God in a tangible way, I asked God to make me His ambassador. Did He have an errand to send me on? I thought of visiting Puja. But she and Shankar lived more than an hour away.

When I finished my silent prayer, Joshua cocked his head. "I think you should visit Puja today."

I took that as God's answer. Wrapping a light jacket around a Hindi Bible, I put the bundle in my backpack and walked my bicycle to the road. As I rode down the mountain, I thought back to our experience with Chayana. After the books I'd read on spiritual warfare, would I do anything differently if I encountered a demonized person again?

I thought for miles, analyzing our experiences and praying for wisdom. But soon I grew weary of this train of thought. God is powerful over the enemy, but He is also awesome in His own right. I spent the rest of the ride singing hymns of praise rather than battle cries.

---

I SAW SHANKAR FIRST. He swaggered over to me. "Well, well, if it isn't Abigail. Nice bike."

"It's Joshua's. Is Puja upstairs?" I motioned to the communal home where Shankar and his family lived.

"We don't live in the main house with my parents anymore." Shankar paused his perma-smirk. He sounded tired. "She's out back in our new room. Feel free to visit."

Puja's and Shankar's room was sparse but clean. A poster of Lakshmi, the goddess of wealth, covered half the wall above a large bed. Puja stood when she saw me. We hugged and asked about each other's families.

"Say, do you want to buy a sweater? You or any of your friends? I've been knitting." Puja brought a colorful stack out of a metal locker. I pulled on a pink sweater. The sleeves were far too short.

Just then, Shankar came. His mouth curved into an amused smile. "Hey, that looks good on you. You should buy it. Isn't my wife a good knitter?"

"She's wonderful. But this one's a bit small." I didn't want the sweater, but I did want to help Shankar and Puja. I glanced up at their locker where Lucky's jar had sat in their old room. "How about if I take the tan one?"

"Take two." Shankar picked up a royal-blue sweater that looked like it would fit a ten-year-old. "This is a good color for you." "I thought the baby would bring us together. I guess he did in a way. We're a team now. He's very understanding, even kind. He's still away a lot for anti-corruption rallies, but now he shares about the causes he supports. And he agreed for us to move into our own room."

I was surprised. Maybe Shankar had married Puja out of duty. But the way he looked at her had changed. He was still a flirt, and culturally he couldn't show Puja affection in front of other people. But deep down, he'd chosen loyalty to his wife. "Puja, I'm so happy for you."

"If only we could get pregnant again. Then things would be good with his parents too. I'd have someone to share my life with, to talk to."

I nodded. This was how Parvata women spoke about sons. I prayed with Puja. Then I shared about the many women in the Bible who had asked God for a child. She listened, nodding and leaning forward, eyes wide. "I like these stories."

"I have an extra Bible in my bag. No pressure or anything, but if you had one, would you want to read it?"

She nodded. "I'd read it."

I handed her the Bible. "I find a lot of strength and encouragement in this."

Puja smoothed the plastic cover with her palm. "I have no problem reading a Bible. All the gods are one, you know? All the holy books are divine messages."

It was getting late, and I knew I should visit Shankar's parents before I began the steep climb to my village. Puja and I hugged. Then she walked me to her door. "We're selling walnuts. Do you need walnuts?"

"If I do, you're the first one I'll call," I said. "See you soon, Puja."

---

WHEN I WALKED into Shankar's parents' house, I saw Puja's sister-in-law Anjali sitting on a mat, elbows and knees sticking out. She massaged her forehead with her thin, bony fingers. She sighed. "Ever since I got on this medication, I feel so strange."

I sat next to her but couldn't help staring. I recognized something in her posture, the way it seemed someone else moved her head and limbs. She looked possessed.

The rest of the family sat on mats opposite ours. I asked Anjali what medication she was taking, a polite question in India. Her father-in-law locked eyes with me. "You know nothing about this kind of medicine."

"It's okay, Uncle," I said. "I don't need to know."

The patriarch suddenly leaned forward, pointing a finger in my face. "If you know of something that will fix her problem, I want to know what it is."

My heart began beating hard. "What's going on, Uncle?"

Shankar's father related the heartbreaking story of Anjali's torturous life. Staying awake for forty-eight hours at a time. Running away with her young son. Now she was under psychiatric care and psychoactive drugs to control her symptoms.

My phone rang. It was Joshua. He and the children were with Lars and Kay. I asked them all to pray. Hard. Hanging up, I said, "I don't know, Uncle. I'm not a doctor. But I know Someone who can heal anything."

After asking permission, I read them the story of the demon-possessed man among the tombs whom Jesus healed and spoke for several minutes about God's power. I didn't want to say that possession was Anjali's problem. What if I was wrong? What if I offended them?

"Let's pray," I said. As I prayed, I remembered something I'd read in one of my spiritual warfare books. "In the name of Jesus Christ, I command any demon in you to be silent unless I give it permission to speak. And I command it to identify itself."

Anjali spoke about other things for several minutes. Then she said, "The demon in me lets me tell the future."

"I believe it's true," her husband said, turning to me. "Before you arrived, Anjali told me Abigail was coming. I didn't know you were planning to visit today, so I asked, 'Abigail who?' She said, 'The singing Abigail.' Strange, isn't it?"

I said nothing but thought of singing on my bicycle on the way down the hill. I talked with the family and prayed for Anjali, but nothing happened. I wondered if something might be keeping Anjali from freedom. I asked her if she got any benefit from her "gift."

"Yes. When I go home, my dad makes whatever I want to eat. I don't have to tell him. I can affect what he does. I can change what happens."

At this, the family exploded.

"How can you say you enjoy being like this?" one of them demanded.

"Don't you see how this is ruining our lives?" another said.

Anjali hung her head. I felt for her. Although her husband was a kind, gentle man, like many married women she was not her own person, not free and independent. The demon made her feel powerful. Although loyalty was important to the Parvata, power was a core value.

I asked the family if they had tied any strings onto Anjali. Hindus sometimes tie a red string on a possessed person as a protection for the wearer and others. They said yes. I told them that the God of Heaven will not share His glory with another, so if they wished to ask Him for freedom, they should ask only Him. That way they could know for sure who gave deliverance.

Shankar's father said they would remove the strings after one month, not before. I encouraged Anjali to take time to think about her choice. Maybe she could muster up the desire to be free.

A week later, well before the month was up, Anjali ran away again and took her son with her. Over the coming weeks, I prayed for Anjali, wondering if there was anything else I could have done.

# 51

# HIDDEN THINGS

I finished my paper about spiritual warfare and included Anjali's and Chayana's stories as case studies. I felt less like an expert and more like a new soldier writing home from the front lines. But arrangements were made for our family to attend a spiritual warfare conference near Chicago to present the paper.

When we arrived stateside for the conference, I noticed several things. Cars in the United States stay in their lanes so it almost looks as though the ground is moving instead of the cars. Americans as a people live spread out with ample personal space. We breathe our own air, and our arms don't touch when we take the bus. Having space, whether personal or corporate, shapes the American worldview. We mind our own business. Even when someone dies, we give them space, leaving casseroles on doorsteps or donating sick time so coworkers can grieve alone.

Our parents came to see us. We took Ashi and Arav to a pumpkin patch for a hayride in the frigid October air. They each picked out a round, orange pumpkin, laughing as they carried the awkward, round gourds to a borrowed Radio Flyer wagon. My heart ached as I watched them enjoying my parents and Joshua's parents. I wanted more than anything to stay. But I couldn't forget India. We had to accept these blessings even if they didn't last. We had to go back.

My dad took me to buy a nice outfit to wear for my presentation. That Friday afternoon, dressed in black and gray, I stood in an academic hall full of people. I didn't have all the answers, but I could describe the battlefield, and I knew who would win the war.

---

WE FLEW BACK TO INDIA. Soon after, I got a call from Darshika.

"Once a year, all the wives fast for their husbands," she explained. "It's called *Karva Chauth*. I've prayed a lot about this, and I want to take part. I want to pray to Jesus for my husband Jahne. And I want you to be there."

"We'd be happy to come support you," I said.

"There's just one problem. The end of the fast includes a ceremony where I'm supposed to worship the moon. All the wives pour out water as an offering to the full moon. Then our husbands feed us. They give us clothes and jewelry too. But I don't want to worship the moon."

"What are you going to do?"

"I'll perform the fast. But I won't do the *puja*."

"We'll be there to pray," I said.

The day of the fast was hot. I fanned Darshika with a notebook and listened to her worries. "They want me to have a baby. But, well, Jahne works at a factory about four hours away from here. He only comes to visit one day a month."

"I see. That certainly makes it more difficult to get pregnant."

"Yeah. Could you maybe talk to my mother-in-law? They don't see any reason for me to go stay with him, and he doesn't want me to stay with him, either."

"That seems strange," I said. "In my culture . . . well, never mind. I'll be happy to talk with her."

That afternoon, I brought out three henna cones and decorated the hands of Darshika's female in-laws in flowers and leaves and curlicues. As their henna dried, I turned to her mother-in-law. "Aunty. You had your female buffalo impregnated last month, right?"

"That's right," she said. "Cost a fortune!"

"Could you have called the vet any old time to do the procedure?"

"Oh, no. Everyone knows there is a certain time for that. The cow has a time."

"Well, you know human females have a time, too. I know it's important to you to have a grandchild. Perhaps Darshika is not pregnant yet because her husband is always away."

"Ahhh." Darshika's mother-in-law nodded. "Maybe we can do something about that."

That evening, the other wives poured their brass urns of water out before the moon. Darshika sat in the house, decorated in her wedding clothes. Every few minutes she namasted towards heaven, her lips moving in prayer.

Then it was her turn. Joshua and I stood to the side like witnesses in a court. Her mother-in-law brought Darshika outside, where a full moon turned the world silver. Darshika looked up.

*God, give her strength,* I prayed.

Darshika lifted the urn high above her head. I couldn't breathe. This was her test, not mine. I could only watch.

I suddenly thought about martyrs. Movie martyrs die to heroic background music. But not real martyrs. Real martyrs hear the crackling of flames, the jeers of onlookers.

"Hurry up, will you?" Darshika's mother-in-law said.

Darshika turned away from the moon. She poured the water in the other direction and lifted her head. Aloud, she prayed, "For You, my heavenly Father."

"You're doing it wrong," someone said.

"Don't you know anything?" asked another.

On the outside, it felt anti-climactic. Darshika's husband fed her, and the fast was over. But I believed there was music playing. Secret music only God could hear.

---

THE NEXT TIME we prepared to visit, Darshika asked us to bring her sister with us. Damini lived just an hour south of us. We'd never met her before but agreed to bring her along. At the designated meeting spot, Joshua slowed the car. I kept my eyes peeled for Damini. When she saw us, she gave a tight-lipped smile.

"You must be Damini! I've been so excited to meet you!" I reached out to hug Damini, but her body stiffened. Her eyes widened as she surveyed our car.

"Here, sit in the front," I said, crawling into the back seat between Ashi and Arav. Damini sat.

"Darshika is like a sister to us. She calls us bhaia and bhabi. Since you're Darshika's little sister, you are ours, too. You can call us bhaia and bhabi if you like." I tried to help Damini feel comfortable in the Indian way by assigning each of us a familial relationship.

"Okay." Damini was nothing like her bubbly sister. For the next hour, she answered only yes or no questions. Once when Joshua got out of the car to buy mangoes, she commented, "You are so lucky."

"Oh? How is that?"

She bit into her words. "You don't have to do any work. I work all day long in the fields. Sunrise to sunset. You sit around all day and do nothing."

My lips pursed in annoyance. "Some people think that about foreigners. People have even asked me if I bathe my kids or wipe their bottoms when they poop. Of course, I work! As though I don't do dishes, sort rice, and wash my clothes. My husband works hard, and so do I."

I stopped, out of breath. *Don't be defensive*, I told myself. "So, Damini, what is your favorite time of year?"

"Spring. So many powerful devtas come. A lot of foreigners worship the devtas. Do you?"

"No."

Damini stiffened. "How can you not worship the devta? What in the world do you worship if you don't worship the devta?"

"Jesus, the Messiah."

"Never heard of Him." Damini paused. "Say, why don't you wear makeup and jewelry? Don't you think women look beautiful when they wear makeup and jewelry?"

There was a hint of accusation in Damini's tone. She was well-painted and had four piercings in each ear. A long necklace dangled from her neck.

"I think you look beautiful," I said. "You're free to wear those things. But I think God created women beautiful as they are. I try to be beautiful without a lot of extra stuff."

"Hmm." Silence.

*This might be a long trip!* I thought to myself. *God, help me connect with Damini.*

Later when Joshua got out of the car again, I leaned forward from the back seat.

"Damini, if you could do anything in the world . . . you know, since you don't like working in the fields . . . what would it be?"

"I don't think that way. I don't dream. I don't think of what could be because nothing will ever change." The bitterness in Damini's voice was a thin veil for her despair.

After we arrived at Darshika's home, we took sickles to the field to cut grass for the water buffalo. The women laughed as I bludgeoned the grass with a rusty, useless sickle.

"That sickle is just like me," Damini said with a bitter laugh. Darshika and I touched her shoulders. She continued, stone-faced, to slice through the grass and pile it in a basket.

---

THE NEXT DAY as we sorted rice, Damini's story came tumbling out. Like Darshika, she'd been forced to leave her children behind to flee an abusive husband. Now the villagers hated her. Her brothers took turns beating her. One brother had even said she should just kill herself and get it over with. I imagined myself in Damini's position and felt nauseated.

Damini longed to escape, but she couldn't read the signs to take a bus, and if she could, where would she go? I understood. A single, illiterate woman in India was very vulnerable.

Darshika interjected, "I begged those useless idols for help for years. How many times did I bruise my forehead bowing before them? And did they ever help me? My husband still beat me, still drank. My life was a wreck. They didn't even give me peace. But Jesus did. He changed everything."

Damini stared at her hands. Darshika looked at me. I shared briefly how God valued Damini enough to send His own Son to die for her. She was silent.

That evening, Damini said she wanted to go home. The next morning, we took her to the bus stop. Damini stood, staring straight ahead at the bus, her shoulders tight. Suddenly, she threw her arms around me and burst into tears.

"What is it, Damini?" I asked.

"When you came, you hugged me and put me in the front seat." Damini wiped at her eyes with her scarf. "No one hugs me in my village. Any time I go somewhere, they beat me. But it had been so long since I'd seen my sister that I had to come. Now I don't know what I'll tell them. I don't know what will happen. But I have to go back."

She began to cry again. Darshika and I wrapped our arms around her, and I whispered in her ear, "If you ever want to leave, just call us. We will help you run."

Darshika later called to tell me Damini had prayed her first prayer on that bus. She'd asked Jesus to keep her brothers from beating her. And for the first time in her life, Damini returned from a trip outside the village, and nobody laid a finger on her.

---

WE VISITED Darshika every few months. Darshika's in-laws didn't want her to live with her husband. He didn't want her to live with him either. Though they were rarely together, Jahne's parents continued to pressure Darshika to get pregnant. They began saying that her infertility was because she didn't worship their village devta. He was, they said, a particularly vindictive spirit who inflicted medical harm on uncooperative villagers.

I racked my brain for some cultural clue as to why Darshika couldn't just go live with her husband. I knew the husband-wife relationship was contractual for the Parvata. We knew couples who were close, but most just fulfilled their relational duties and sought heart fulfillment from parents, friends, or children. Could that be why Darshika couldn't live with her husband?

In the meantime, Darshika shared her growing faith with her in-laws. She prayed for them when they were sick. She always called to tell me when God answered a prayer. She often related her experiences to her favorite Bible stories. She said humans are just like the ten lepers. God answers our prayers, but only a few appreciate the healing.

Darshika often mentioned the story of Elijah on Mount Carmel. The false prophets of Baal prayed for hours, even cutting themselves, to no avail. But Elijah hadn't finished his prayer before God sent fire from heaven to devour the sacrifice on the altar.

Darshika prayed for a Mount Carmel moment with her husband and his family. We prayed too and wondered when and how God would answer our prayers.

---

ONE NIGHT, I had a dream that Darshika and I stood in a barren field. She pointed down at the dirt, a disgusted look on her face. "Look! They sold you this barren field. It's because you're foreigners. People are always cheating foreigners. You need to get your money back!"

"No," I said. "You don't understand, Darshika. The roots grow first!"

Somehow, I showed Darshika beneath the dirt. We saw roots stretching white through the dark soil like in a time-lapse movie. Then I woke up.

Darshika called later, complaining that her family would never accept Christ. They'd only agreed to her being a Christian when they didn't know she wouldn't worship their gods anymore. Ever since she'd failed to worship the moon, they'd been pressuring her to do *puja*. I told her about the dream.

"It's for me!" she exclaimed excitedly. "The dream is for me!"

But I knew it wasn't just for her. It was for me too. That evening, I got on my laptop. Though I'd always wanted to garden, I knew nothing about plants. Looking it up, I discovered it was true. The roots of a plant grow first so that long before any green shows, something is happening. Something hidden deep inside the ground.

# 52

## BEING MEAN

A shi, Arav and I were on a walk one day when a BMW jerked over to the side of the road in front of us. Out stepped a woman, wearing a loose flowery top and jeans. She strode over, smiling. Ashi and Arav got behind me.

"Hello," the woman said, and reached out to shake my hand.

"Hello," I responded, not letting go of the children. *Don't speak in Hindi,* I reminded myself. *This is family time.* I tried to continue walking. The woman moved to stand in my path.

"Your children are just adorable," she said.

"Thanks," I said. I tried to walk around the woman. She moved to block me.

"I want a picture with them."

"Thank you," I said again. "But no. Enjoy your vacation." I turned to leave.

"Come on, just one." I whirled back around.

"I said no. My children don't want to!"

"But *I* want to."

"Excuse me?" Now my Hindi switched on. "I told you, 'No.' Why are you following us? Go away!"

"Oh!" the woman exclaimed. "You speak such good Hindi!" The children and I did an about-face and marched away.

I had done it. I had faced my fear, and been rude, and told someone off, and kept my kids safe. I had won the Monster game. Even if the monster was a possibly well-meaning middle-class woman in a flowery shirt.

I just wished winning the game felt better. It never felt good to be mean. But sometimes, in this world, there are more important things than being nice.

WE DISCOVERED that many of those coming to worship with us on Sabbath mornings belonged to a secret house church that met every Sunday morning. We were overjoyed. God's Word was going forth!

Joshua visited their congregation a couple of times. Then one Easter Sunday, I visited. Ashi wasn't up to being the center of attention, so Joshua took her for a walk while I brought Arav with me. As I neared the apartment, I noticed two long sticks set on top of two cars. On the sticks sat a box covered in silver faces with their eyes closed. The idol for the devta was parked right outside the house church!

"*Jai Massih*," I greeted the group. It means, "Victory to the Savior." Some Indian Christians say it instead of namaste.

Church began. Most of the people sang, but a small group of women next to me chatted. Someone said they weren't Christians but relatives who'd been invited for the Easter service. Shortly after, someone came in and whispered something about the devta to the woman next to me. She and her friends went out to see. Soon they returned, flushed with excitement.

The pastor announced the opening song: "Come, Holy Spirit." As we began to sing, the woman next to me gasped. I glanced at her. Her eyes were closed, her face twisted. She screamed like she saw something frightening on the backs of her eyelids. All the hair stood on my arms. I knew exactly what was happening. The woman was possessed.

I rushed Arav out of the room and down the stairs. Just at that moment, I saw Joshua and Ashi passing the building on their walk. I ran to them and thrust Arav into Joshua's arms.

"What is going on in there?" Joshua asked. People around us stopped and looked up towards the room where the woman still screamed. "Deliverance session?"

"Not yet. But there will be!" I turned and ran back to the house.

Inside, the congregation was still singing. I knelt in front of the woman. The pastor tried to stop me as though the screaming were a manifestation of the Holy Spirit. I thought briefly of how shamed he'd be if I didn't listen to him. But I knew. And just like the pastor at the church four hours south had said I'd be, I was angry.

"Get out of her! In Jesus's name, get out!" I commanded. Grabbing the woman's shoulders, I shouted at the thing and said it had no right to stay. Finally, the woman gasped one more time and fell back against the wall. It was gone. Without looking at the pastor or the rest of the congregation, I left.

After that incident, we were alone again on Sabbaths. The pastor *had* thought the woman's screaming was a manifestation of the Holy Spirit. I'd shamed him in front of his followers. He told them not to worship with us anymore.

But I'd *known* what it was. Maybe it was the gift of discernment. Or maybe it was because I'd seen a devta parked right outside the church. The pastor was new to the area. Perhaps he didn't know about devtas. How could I ease his hurt pride?

Some Christian friends of Ayushi's got word of the incident and told her our denomination must not believe in the Holy Spirit. She told me she was confused and needed time to think. Then, while we were still wondering what to do about the church group, Darshika called us on the phone. She spoke in a harsh whisper.

"Bhabi, they're taking me to the temple. There's nothing I can do!"

"What?" My mind raced.

"It's about the baby," Darshika said. "That there isn't one yet, I mean. I can't talk. I have a lot to say, but not now. Just pray."

I sat down at the computer to ask our angel dispatchers to pray. I knew we needed backup. We were being attacked as Job had been. The Chaldeans and Sabeans had raided. What was next? Would our own four walls collapse?

---

WE PRAYED for Darshika and waited. I asked Joshua to buy groceries. He took Ashi with him, and returned a couple of hours later, his backpack bulging with tomatoes, onions, lentils, yogurt, flour, rice, cheese, and eggs. He looked frazzled. "The dogs in front of the Cheese Guy's shop are getting worse."

I could picture them, eight or nine dogs lounging around the cheese shop, all of them with the characteristic inbred, mangy look of street dogs. "Was Spiderman there?"

Spiderman was the Cheese Guy's pet, an aggressive dog who lavished love on his adoptive family but bit everyone else.

"No, I haven't seen Spiderman in a few weeks," Joshua said. "But one of the dogs started coming towards us, growling. I grabbed a rock and threw it. But he hardly noticed it. Pretty soon the whole pack of them were coming towards us, growling, barking."

My heart raced at the thought of the danger my family had been in. "What happened?"

"A shopkeeper noticed what was going on and ran out, shouting and throwing stuff. The dogs left. That's when I noticed I was dangling Ashi by her arm high above my head. I guess I did it automatically."

Joshua yanked a banana off a large bunch on the counter. His hands shook as he peeled it. "This has to stop. It's the fourth time in two weeks they've come after Ashi and me. I talked to several people on the way home, and everyone agrees something must be done."

I swallowed. "This has happened before? How come you didn't tell me?"

"You know how it is. The village dogs are always barking. You just keep a rock in your hand. But they were more determined this time."

Joshua was right. I always grabbed a rock or two if I was out walking and saw a dog.

"Back in the states, dogs like that get put down," Joshua continued. "Everyone I talked to agrees these dogs should be poisoned before they kill someone. They could have killed Ashi today! The Cheese Guy's worker even gave me some poison."

"Well, I'm not sure, Joshua. Let's pray about it."

WE KEPT WAITING to hear from Darshika. I tried calling, but she didn't answer. I could only imagine the temptation she faced. They would expect her to eat prasad, to bow to the idol, to listen to the devta as it spoke from the mouth of the gur.

Finally, Darshika called to tell us what happened. She walked to the temple with her husband and his family. They kept telling her, "Darshika, you have to do this. Worship Jesus, but worship our gods too!"

Outside the temple, families sat together on the ground, singing Hindu songs of praise as they waited their turn to speak with the goddess through her medium. As Darshika's family waited, she prayed, *Forgive me, God, for being here. Be with me! Cover me with Jesus's blood. Forgive me. Help me to be faithful!*

Darshika's stomach growled. Someone offered her a handful of dried fruit. "No, thank you. I'm fasting."

She silently thanked God for giving her the idea to fast. This allowed her to avoid food offered to idols without embarrassing her family. Her turn finally came. Like Naaman of old, she had to go into the temple (2 Kings 5:18). But she determined to keep the temple of her mind and body pure.

She listened as the medium told her family that she was unhappy and moody. The family, consumed by faith in their goddess, nodded. Yes, Darshika must be unhappy.

"But you can all relax now. You will hear good news soon. The girl will tell you with her own mouth just a few days from now that she is expecting a child."

As the medium tied a scarlet cord around Darshika's belly, the social pressure felt like a noose. *Forgive me, Lord,* she prayed. *Give me freedom!*

Upon returning home, Darshika cut the string from her belly. She showed it to her husband before tossing the string into the fire. "My God will answer our prayers for a child. You will see! And when He does, your mother will see that this string had nothing to do with it."

---

THE DAY TO poison the wild dogs came.

"If you have to do this, at least make sure Spiderman isn't around," I told Joshua. "It would be a disaster if he ate the poison."

"Don't worry," Joshua held a bucket of chicken innards in one hand, a bottle of poison in the other. "I haven't even seen Spiderman outside for weeks. The Cheese Guy has paid several people's hospital bills this year because of that dog. I think he finally gave him away."

"I hope you're right." I frowned. "Why doesn't someone else do this? Someone local? Someone who can't get kicked out of India?"

"Well, a bunch of people said we'd do it together. They gave me the poison and the meat. But now they're all mysteriously busy. I think they're scared of the Cheese Guy."

"Shouldn't you be scared of him, too?"

"He's a reasonable person. And those dogs hurt his business. Besides, I'll put it out at night, so nobody's pet gets ahold of it."

"Are you sure you're doing the right thing?"

"Look," Joshua said. "When there's a snake or a tiger that's killing people, the villagers take care of it. There's nothing set up in the government to handle this kind of thing. Several people have already been attacked. If we don't do something, someone's kid is going to die."

Joshua left to put out the poisoned chicken. I knew he was right. We wouldn't hesitate to kill a deadly snake or man-eating tiger. Why did it feel different when there were dogs involved?

---

THE NEXT MORNING, we were up before dawn to pack the car for one of our required visa runs. Darshika's home was on the way to Delhi, where we'd catch our flight. I was eager to see her and to pray with her. It took six hours for us to arrive, tired, dusty, and hungry. Darshika hugged us. So did her mother-in-law. We'd been there so often, their house was becoming a second home to us.

I had just set down our luggage when Joshua's phone rang. "Hello? Oh, hey Ashish! Yeah, we're just . . . wait, what happened? Oh, I'm so sorry! That's terrible, I—"

Joshua had turned pale. As I came closer, I could hear a man screaming expletives over the phone. Then he hung up. Joshua just stood there holding the phone.

"What is it, Joshua? Who was that?"

"That was the Cheese Guy."

"Oh, no. Spiderman?"

"Spiderman."

## 53

# I WOULD DIE FOR YOU

J oshua tried to call the Cheese Guy but got an earful of expletives followed by a dial tone. "He keeps hanging up on me. Ugh, why did I do it? You tried to warn me."

I could feel Joshua's regret in my stomach as if I'd been the one to place the poison. "Because you thought Spiderman was gone."

I grabbed the phone. Before the Cheese Guy could start screaming, I said, "Hello, Bhaia Ashish. This is Abigail."

He sighed. "Look, I'm sorry. I don't want to hurt you. But we have laws in India protecting stray dogs."

"Bhaia, we didn't mean to hurt Spiderman. Joshua feels terrible. He's crying."

"What hurts the most is that it *is* Joshua." I could hear a tremble in the Cheese Guy's voice. "I didn't think your husband was capable of this. Everyone knows your husband as a good man. I've seen him myself digging trash out of the ditches so our village will be clean. But now? I don't even consider him a human being. How could anyone do such a thing to my pet? We raised him since he was a puppy. He died in my wife's arms."

"Brother, I'm so sorry this happened," I said. "Joshua hadn't seen Spiderman in several weeks. He wasn't even sure you still had him."

"Look, I know my dog was bad. He bit people. He was aggressive. I know that. I've spent thousands on other people's hospital bills. But you didn't have to poison him."

"We didn't!" My voice grew louder. "The dogs outside your shop tried to attack Ashi four times. Spiderman wasn't even with them. We heard about villagers taking care of violent animals this way. We didn't know you still had Spiderman, and we didn't know it was illegal."

"Why would legality matter? You killed a living creature. For me, that is unacceptable."

"In our country, we euthanize violent animals. We feel we are stewards of God's creation, but human life takes priority over animal life."

"We believe that all life is sacred," he shouted. "Your husband will pay. I'm sorry but believe me, he will pay."

"May I ask what you mean by 'pay?'"

"I'm standing outside the police station right now. I'll report him, and things are going to go very badly for him, I promise you!"

"Listen," I said. "We don't care if you tell the police. Do what you feel is right. But we're friends. Do you think we'd live in India so far from our families if we didn't care about you and our other friends here? We didn't mean to hurt you or your dog. Believe me, we'd never do something like this on purpose."

The Cheese Guy's tone did not soften. "Your husband is not a human. He could have talked to me. He could have said, 'Ashish, we need to take care of these dogs.' I have spent my own money to have the wild dogs vaccinated and fixed. I want to take care of the problem. But in my religion, life is life. You don't just kill something, whether it's a human or a dog."

I thought back to Mrs. Opee's reluctance to kill a fly, however disease-bearing it might be. "I can see we have a cultural difference here. But listen. Joshua is a good man. He's never laid a hand on me. Never yelled at me."

My eyes stung with tears and my voice broke. "He put the poison out at night so your pet wouldn't eat it. He was trying to protect our children and the other children in the village. He didn't even act alone, yet he wants to take full responsibility."

"That doesn't make me feel better. I'm sure everyone was happy to kill Spiderman."

"Nobody was trying to kill Spiderman! Why won't you believe me?"

"What am I supposed to do, just forget that you poisoned my dog?"

"Have you ever heard of something called forgiveness?" I cried, exasperated. "It might be hard now, but you will never have peace unless you forgive. Go ahead, tell the police. But please, someday, forgive us."

There was a long pause. I wondered if he'd hung up. Then he muttered, "I'll talk to my wife. If she's okay with it, I'll drop the charges."

The Cheese Guy's wife called ten minutes later and spoke with Joshua.

"I had a dog when I was growing up," Joshua said. "She died when a car hit her. She was in a lot of pain until the moment she passed. I know how hard it must have been for you, and I feel terrible."

"We've had him since he was a puppy. He died in my arms," she said.

"Please forgive me. I made a terrible mistake."

She sighed. "Okay, I'll tell my husband not to talk to the police."

Joshua hung up. "They're going to drop the charges."

"Let's go back," I said. Joshua nodded. We gathered our few things, gave a hasty explanation to Darshika and her family, and got back in the car. We arrived at three in the morning, carried Ashi and Arav to bed, and dragged ourselves into our room for prayer and sleep.

The next morning, we got up early and walked over to the cheese shop. Ashish, the Cheese Guy, lived upstairs with his family in a sprawling, stone-worked home with picture windows in the back. It was the only house in the village to glow in the winter when the power went out because they were the only ones rich enough to own a generator.

Joshua knocked. Ashish opened the door. He was so tall he had to bend his head to look at us through the door frame. He wore a robe over a T-shirt and jeans and fuzzy slippers. When he saw us, he heaved a giant, weary sigh. "You didn't have to come. You were in Uskigaun last night. That's six hours south."

"We didn't want to let a day go by without apologizing to you in person," Joshua said. "I'm so sorry."

The two embraced. Looking tired and confused, Ashish led us to his living room. "Tea?"

The tea took an awkward eternity to arrive. We made small talk. Soon, Ashish's wife glided in, wearing a flowing oriental housecoat over blouse and slacks. She was a schoolteacher and carried herself with perfect, effortless posture.

When I saw her, I stood and walked over to her. "I'm so sorry."

We embraced. She said it was okay and sat down with us. There was a long, awkward moment of silence as their servant girl brought steaming cups of chai. Part of me wondered if it was safe to drink.

"I blame myself partially," Mrs. Cheese Guy said. "Someone told me you were thinking to put poison in the street for the strays that night. But I forgot."

"We'd been keeping Spiderman inside all day." The Cheese Guy ran his fingers through his hair. "He'd attacked several people. It costs a lot of money to pay people's medical bills. So we let him out at night only. That way there would be fewer people for him to bother."

"I see," I said. "We thought you might have given him away since we hadn't seen him in a few weeks."

"She says 'we,'" Joshua said. "But she means me. Abigail told me not to do it. She was afraid Spiderman would eat the poison."

My heart caught in my throat. I hadn't wanted Joshua to take the fall alone. Mrs. Cheese Guy sipped at her tea. "It's very painful to die that way, you know."

Joshua nodded and looked at the ground. Although our children normally squirmed and fidgeted when we visited people, they seemed to sense the solemnity of this moment and sat still. It took a second eternity to drink the tea. When there was just a centimeter left in the bottom of my cup, we took our leave.

---

JUST ACROSS THE path from our house stood a two-room cement shack. In front, a drippy faucet stuck out of the ground. Off in the distance, a yellow tarp shielded a latrine. At any given time, at least two families lived in those two rooms, usually migrant workers from Nepal laboring in the apple orchards. Walking by, I often saw children caring for younger siblings without an adult in sight.

This particular season, two little girls lived in the house. Ashi and Arav enjoyed playing with them, running around, chasing each other, growling, or laughing. Sometimes, the Nepali children would admit they were hungry or needed help to brush their hair or clean a scrape. I would feed them, braid their hair, and kiss their booboos.

One day when the water pressure was low at their spigot, the older girl came to my door carrying a bucket. "Aunty, could I bathe at your faucet?"

"Give me your bucket." I came back with the bucket, now heavy and steaming. When she saw the hot water, her eyes grew large. "Oh, Aunty, hot water!"

I invited her to use the bathroom, but she wouldn't. Her little sister stood guard while she bathed at our outdoor spigot.

Another time, the girls succumbed to temptation and stole some of Ashi's toys. I went to see their mother. "Aunty. I love it when your children visit. They are so sweet and respectful. They are welcome in our home."

"They love to visit you," she said. "Thank you for looking after them sometimes."

"It's my pleasure." I paused, unsure whether I should say anything. "Aunty, there is one thing I wanted you to know. They are so little and don't know better. But they took some of Ashi's toys without asking. If they ask for something, we will give it. But I wanted you to know they didn't have permission."

Aunty stared at me, horrified. Was she wishing she didn't have to work all day, wishing she could shepherd her little lambs onto a good path? I felt the weight of her choice, the choice between food and good character.

"Aunty, don't worry," I said. "I'm not upset. They're so little. But I was sure you wouldn't want them stealing. I told you so you can correct them."

"I'm so sorry. They said you'd given them the toys." Huddled on a nearby mat, the two girls looked pale and scared. Without glancing at them, Aunty added, "You girls are not to visit Ashi again."

"No, Aunty," I assured her quickly. "We are not mad. They're welcome to come any time."

"No. They must not visit you again."

And they didn't. A few months later, they left, and a different family with children moved in. Those children were low-caste. After a while, Mr. Pandit informed us they weren't welcome on the property. So Ashi and Arav played by themselves in the house.

---

PEOPLE all over the village gathered grass and dried it on the roads and on their roofs. It was autumn again, the sixth anniversary of our arrival in India, and almost time for Diwali, the Hindu festival of lights. People drew footprints on the ground leading from their gates to their doorways and placed candles in the windows so the goddess Lakshmi would enter their homes and bless them with prosperity.

On Diwali, I went to see Ayushi's family. I found Ayushi sitting alone on the floor in her kitchen. "Where is everyone?"

"On the roof. They're celebrating. Doing fireworks and all."

"And you?" I asked.

"I'm not. I just can't. I still want to follow Jesus, Abby."

"How are they taking it?"

"They're upset. My boyfriend and I will marry next year. Then I won't live at home anymore. This would have been my last Diwali. They don't understand why I'm not participating. I just don't believe in it anymore, you know?"

I nodded. "I know."

"I've chosen Jesus. I've made a commitment. And I'm not going to turn my back on Him."

As I walked home, I thought about Ayushi. Sometimes it seemed Satan's schemes had smashed Ayushi's hopes and distracted her gaze. Yet here she was giving up Diwali for Him. I looked skyward past the smoke from fireworks going off all around us. *Thank You for having a Plan B. For Ayushi, and for all of us.*

---

WHEN YOU ASK people to rethink their worldview, you can't help but ask yourself the same questions. Like Ayushi's family, my mother didn't believe Jesus was the son of God. There'd been times in my journey when I'd shared her doubt. But I'd always believed there was a God. And God always provided answers for everything else.

As I read and reread Scripture, I became struck by the otherness of God. We are so individual, so three-dimensional, so limited. But God? God can somehow be everywhere and know everything, yet still be personal and distinct. He is outside of time, yet He entered time. He confined Himself to our flesh, squeezed Himself into death, all to burst open the graves on a rock floating in space.

One afternoon, Joshua suggested we visit Lars and Kay. As we drove, I opened my phone and clicked play on my current favorite song, a Hindi Christian hymn with a middle-eastern flute. Below us, the fields looked sewn-together. Above us, clouds hung low and heavy with water. I closed my eyes, and the music wrapped around me.

"Is there anyone in the world unaware of Your glory?" the lyrics echoed through the car. Suddenly it all came together. The glory of God. His otherness. His awesomeness. His oneness. And in contrast, the fractured Parvata people, taught to fight and feud and lust even by their gods. *Oh, God! If only Your glory could be known in all the world. I would die for You, to make that glory known!*

---

THAT NIGHT AS I SLEPT, the sound of someone crying filtered into my consciousness. I sat up and looked at the clock. 3:00 a.m. Who was crying?

*Neenoo is crying.* I knew that voice. God was speaking to me. But it would take me another fifteen minutes and a lot of internal struggling to obey Him, climb the stairs, and join the Pandit family at Neenoo's side.

For several hours after the incident with Neenoo, all was quiet. Then he began to cry again. I took a deep breath and prepared for the discomfort of obedience. But when I prayed, I didn't feel impressed to go upstairs.

*Let them try their way,* came the answer. *They have to see that it doesn't work.*

As Neenoo cried, I thought about Jesus's statement that we must "die to ourselves" (John 12:24-26). Dying to self is the demise of your pride, your expectations, your right to control. Like me, Mr. Pandit would one day be asked to die to his pride. Would he lay it down at the foot of the cross? Only he could decide.

I knew that the death of one's pride felt like a real physical death, scary and painful. But I also knew that when you give up everything, one thing at a time, it is then that Christ can use you and replace your questions with the truth—that He is very close, and very real indeed.

# 54

# DARSHIKA'S FIRST FORGIVENESS

"Just pray, Darshika. Pray! I'll call you in a minute." I hung up the phone and turned to Joshua. "Darshika thinks Jahne will divorce her. Do you think we should go down there?"

"Maybe. What do you think?"

"We're the only family she has. If you were her actual brother, we would go."

"Then let's go."

Six hours later, we arrived at Darshika's in-law's house. The courtyard was strewn with lawn chairs, as though there'd been a lot of people visiting. Darshika's in-laws sat in two chairs, their lips curling. They were joined by his aunt and uncle, who'd helped arrange the marriage. They gossiped about Darshika, how terrible she was.

"Namaste," I said. The group smiled at us, a strained, polite smile. My smile felt forced too. Hearing them talk about Darshika like that bothered me.

Darshika saw us from the kitchen. She came out holding a wooden spoon in one hand. Grabbing my arm with her other hand, she turned me away from the chairs. "Did you hear them talking about me?"

"Yes. Are you okay? What happened?"

"I have a lot to say. Not yet." Darshika walked toward a spigot just beyond the small group. I followed. As we passed the chair sitters, they stiffened.

"I'll give her a *chalak*!" Darshika's father-in-law said so she would hear. A *chalak* was a divorce. I felt myself bristle against the harsh words.

"Hey!" Joshua put a hand on my shoulder. "Why don't you two take a walk? I think you need to calm down."

I grabbed Darshika's hand. "Let's go."

We walked past several buffalo lazing in their pens, then stood next to the stucco wall of a neighbor. We both looked around. No obvious eavesdroppers.

Darshika trembled with anger. "Bhabi, he wants to write up a *chalak* for Jahne and me. They don't want me anymore!"

"What happened?" I asked again. "Everything seemed fine. Did they find out about your divorce?"

"That's just the thing. They have no idea. I'm so confused. I work hard, but they say it doesn't count because I didn't help with the harvest."

"But you had surgery. You were told not to carry heavy things." I thought back to an article I'd read about uterine prolapse in India. Now I understood why so many women in agricultural areas suffered this condition after giving birth. They'd had to return to hard labor too soon. "Is there anything else, Darshika? Anything you could have done to contribute to the problem?"

"Bhabi, I swear I did my best. I felt so bad about not being able to work in the fields that I did extra around the house. I scrubbed their pots and pans till they shone. I cleaned under their beds and all the cupboards. But they don't care about keeping things clean. If it's not heavy lifting, it's nothing. They only care about the harvest. Jahne's father even called me a worthless prostitute."

"Hmm. You know, when Joshua and I got married, there were family cultural issues too. I mean, we're from the same culture, but our parents still do things differently. We had to talk and figure out our expectations. We had to give each other grace."

"Yeah, right," Darshika said. "Talk to Jahne's parents? Ha!"

I knew Darshika was right. An Indian daughter-in-law doesn't talk with her husband's family in the way I'd suggested. It's her job to observe. She learns what ticks off her in-laws. She alone does the adjusting.

"You need the grace of Jesus to handle this, Darshika," I said. "If you want to make it work, you must do everything in your power to adjust to their family culture, so long as it doesn't violate your conscience. I don't envy you, though. It would be very difficult for me to handle this situation. It would be difficult to forgive them."

"Forgive? Forget difficult! Try impossible!"

Despite my calm exterior, I was upset. Why should Darshika have to live with her in-laws while her husband worked several hours away? This wasn't the marriage she'd agreed to. We walked back to the house and went to Darshika's room. She got out a suitcase and started packing.

Then Jahne showed up, holding a motorcycle helmet. "What are you doing?"

"Packing." Darshika crumpled up a blouse and threw it into her suitcase. "Your dad said he's giving us a divorce."

"Divorce? Did you marry my dad? Nobody can divorce you but me. And I won't do that."

"I'm not staying here."

"Look, you just have to be flexible. It will get better." Jahne faked the nonchalant yet authoritative attitude of a cowboy, but I knew he was a little scared of me. It was time to play the part of a real Indian bhabi.

"Listen to me!" Squaring my shoulders, I stepped closer to Jahne. "Your wife is in hell here. Be a man and take her with you!" From the corner of my eye, I saw Joshua nod in agreement.

Jahne smiled but whispered his answer. "Okay, okay. Just relax!"

I knew he meant I should lower my voice. Instead, I called his bluff. "Your parents are bullying *our* Darshika. Don't you dare stand there pretending this is nothing. Your dad called your wife a prostitute. He said he will make the two of you divorce. There is something wrong, and you need to listen to your wife and fix it!"

"It will all be okay." He tried to smile away his nervousness. "My dad's just mad, see? It'll all blow over. Trust me."

"I don't trust you," I said. "You've said before you'd take Darshika to live with you. But she's still here. Everyone is pressuring her to get pregnant, but the only person who can get her pregnant lives two hours away. Talk to your parents and fix it!"

He lowered his voice further. "I can't talk to them."

I knew he was right. His parents threatened to revoke his inheritance over the smallest infraction. Suddenly, the truth became clear to me. Jahne couldn't take Darshika to live with him. He'd have to feed and clothe her, and his parents wanted the money from his job in the factory. I felt compassion for him welling up in my heart. I was trying to scare him, playing the part of the assertive Indian bhabi. But I also sensed his frustration and pain. He was stuck in the middle. He couldn't talk to his parents on Darshika's behalf because he couldn't talk to them for himself.

I softened my voice. "Jahne, your first responsibility is to this woman. You promised to give her a new life. I know it's hard, but you've got to be strong."

He stared at the floor. "I'll try."

"Don't try. Make it happen. Take her with you. Help her understand your family. At least until she's pregnant. Give her time."

"I'll take her with me."

"Do you hear that, Darshika?" I turned with the same assumed authority to Darshika. "Your husband will take you with him. Will you go?"

We all waited. She looked at me through reddened, teary eyes. That's when my plan backfired.

"No!"

"What do you mean, no?" I asked, stunned.

"I want out. I'm done."

I frowned. "Darshika, it's time for a walk. You're coming, too, Jahne. We have responsibilities at home to take care of, and you're going to walk us to our car."

"Goodbye," I said to Darshika's family as we walked past. We'd eaten nothing, a hospitality faux pas. Darshika's sister-in-law's jaw dropped as she watched us go. She held a platter of steaming teacups. I didn't let myself care.

Soon we found ourselves at our car. Darshika cried, her face in her hands. I put my arm around her. "Darshika, Jahne will do his part. But you have to do yours too. You have to forgive. Forgiveness is part of being a Christian. If you choose not to forgive tonight, you are turning your back on Jesus."

"Never! I'll never forgive them. You don't understand how hard this is. I can't. I literally can't."

"You're right, Darshika. You can't. But Jesus can. Are you willing to try? Are you willing to be willing?"

"No! I just can't." I could feel Darshika's disappointment and pain. But this was the one battle I couldn't fight for her, the battle against herself.

"We'll pray for you." With a final hug, I got into the front passenger seat.

Behind the wheel, Joshua started the car, but after a few meters, he stopped. "I have a bad feeling about this. Like if we leave, Darshika will do something drastic."

"You're right. We need to stay." We got out and walked back to Darshika's house.

---

THE NEXT MORNING, we emerged from repacking our things to discover a large group in the courtyard, including the *pradhan*, aka village chief. Joshua and I sat among them as they discussed Jahne and Darshika. After some time, the *pradhan* looked at me. "Miss, would you like to say something?"

I was surprised. Was the village chief giving me, a woman, the chance to address the group? "Yes, I would,"

I stood up. "*Pradhan*, sir, to all present I would like to say the following. When we have discord in our families, it is never the fault of one person alone. Each of us must see the part we have played in our conflicts. I believe the way to solve this problem is for each person involved to forgive the others. By forgiving, the entire family can have a fresh start. Without this step, I believe resolution is impossible."

I sat. Several of the villagers nodded their approval. So did the *pradhan*. He looked at me. "Thank you for your comments."

Then he looked at Darshika, his expression kind. "Daughter, would you like to say something?"

"Yes, sir!" Darshika stood. I held my breath, wondering what would happen, as she walked to her mother-in-law. She knelt. "I'm sorry for anything I did to cause problems."

Darshika embraced her mother-in-law and broke down in tears. Her mother-in-law patted her back awkwardly. Her father-in-law chuckled. Then everyone laughed. The implied message was that Darshika was making a big deal over nothing. *Only martyrs in films have music*, I thought again.

"We love you, child," said her father-in-law, trying to seem laid-back and gracious. "It's nothing. Nothing happened."

Darshika stood and turned to the *pradhan*. "I'm sorry for my part in this, like my bhabi said. And if it's okay, I'd like to go and live with my husband."

There was a murmur in the crowd. The *pradhan*'s secretary, a woman, spoke up. "Why should you do that? Plenty of wives live with their husband's family."

I knew she meant to imply that Darshika wanted to live with her husband to be intimate with him—a terrible social shame. The others were nodding. I felt my blood boiling for Darshika and for all women who are treated as purchases rather than people. But Darshika remained calm.

"I think it would be best for all of us if we had a break," she responded with composure. "I'll be happy to come back after a few months. But we need a break after this drama."

"Is your husband willing to take you with him?" the *pradhan* asked.

Jahne stood but avoided eye contact with his parents. "I'm willing."

"What Darshika has requested is fair," the *pradhan* said. "It is the right of this couple to live together. Why should she stay here and fight when all she's asked for is a break? Go, child, and live with your husband."

He turned to Jahne's father. "Is this agreed?"

It wasn't a request for approval but a command. Jahne's father gave another face-saving chuckle. "Of course, whatever makes them happy. I love Darshika like a daughter."

But though Darshika's father-on-law was smiling, his jaw was clenched. At that moment, I realized he'd been shamed beyond shame. My speech made him look unforgiving. Darshika's apology made him look cruel and hasty. And she'd gone above his head to ask that she be allowed to live with Jahne. This might not be the end of the story.

---

JOSHUA and I drove home in silence. After some time, I spoke up. "You know, I asked Darshika when she was able to forgive. She said she didn't feel anything until the moment she hugged her mother-in-law."

As we discussed what had happened, we realized this was the first time Darshika had ever forgiven anyone. It had been beautiful. Like watching someone be born.

"You know," Joshua said. "I hope we have a lot more ministry to do here. But if this today was the only reason we came to India, it was worth it."

"I agree. It was all worth it."

## 55

# ASHI'S ENEMIES

I knew before they said anything that Lars' and Kay's time in India was drawing to a close. Baby Elijah was still not growing. They didn't say goodbye but see you later. They were sure they'd be back once they figured out what Elijah needed. They even left their stuff at their house. But somehow when they got into the taxi and Posy waved her little hand out the window, and shouted goodbye, again and again, I knew they weren't coming back.

Around Christmas, a different group of Nepali believers began attending our house church, and once again our home was full of music and laughter every Sabbath morning. We continued connecting with people, watching for signs that the gospel had taken root in their hearts. Mr. Pandit seemed as hardened to the gospel as ever, but Sarala and Mrs. Pandit often commented that God had changed Darshika. Our God must be real if He had intervened in her life.

The following spring I found a small plot of land nearby, where the owner said I could plant a garden. This time I bought dahlia bulbs and vegetable seeds. When the "baby plants" were "born" from the earth, it was a miracle. Ashi and Arav oohed and ahhed and poked. My heart filled with joy and love for my children as they discovered each new seedling.

Did God experience joy each time I died to myself and was born again? Did He laugh when I buried gospel seeds and got to watch them being "born?" Was this why He'd brought the animals to Adam (Genesis 2:19) to see what he would name them?

In late spring, Joshua left again to lead a tour group. Our landlords planted marigolds and roses in pots around the property, warning the children not to touch the blooms. They needed the petals to worship their gods.

But the flowers were so beautiful that Ashi picked some anyway. Our landlords were angry. Neighbors told me so.

"We have our own garden," I told my children. "On Sabbath, you can pick dahlias for the table. If you want other flowers, you can pick dandelions." But soon, Ashi gave into temptation and brought a marigold bouquet into the house.

"Ashi, you must not pick these flowers," I said. "These flowers aren't ours."

"I'm sorry, Mommy." Ashi hung her head. "Will they hate me now?"

"Of course not. Listen, I know what we can do to make it right." I got out construction paper and markers, and Ashi made a card for Mr. Pandit and his family. When she'd finished coloring, I told her, "We must pay for the flowers you picked. That means it will take you a little longer to earn the stuffed dog you've been saving for. But it's the right thing to do."

I felt like a wonderful parent. Thanks to years of listening to *Uncle Arthur's Bedtime Stories*, I knew how to handle this situation. The parents in those stories turned every incident into a chance to teach their kids morals. There were many stories about paying for something stolen, broken, or lost.

We took the card and money upstairs, where I told Mrs. Pandit and Sarala, "Ashi wanted you to know she's sorry about the flowers. She earned this money doing extra chores and wanted you to have it."

The ensuing explosion caught me off guard. As though I'd committed the unpardonable sin, Mrs. Pandit demanded, "Why did you do this? It wasn't a big deal! Why did you have her apologize?" "Why did you give money?" Sarala added. Both women stood. They yelled at Ashi and me, telling us we'd done the wrong thing by trying to pay for the flowers. For the first time in a cultural clash, I couldn't save my tears until later.

"Mother," I said to Mrs. Pandit. "Listen to me. How will my child learn not to pick your flowers if I don't tell her it's wrong? How can she know the value of your flowers if I don't make her pay for them?"

"No, no!" yelled Mrs. Pandit. "Stop crying. This is all blown way out of proportion. If you make her pay for it, she'll think money solves problems. But it doesn't!"

My mouth fell open. "Mother, Ashi doesn't think that, and neither do I. You worked hard to plant your flowers, and Ashi worked hard to earn her coins. She will understand what she stole if she has to pay for it."

"It's not stealing. She's little," said Sarala.

"It's stealing no matter how old you are." I looked from Sarala to Mrs. Pandit and back again. Ashi gazed up at all our faces, looking miserable and overwhelmed. Her mother hadn't known how to fix this after all.

"Don't you dare go tattling to Joshua," Sarala said. "It's very bad to burden someone on a business trip."

"That's right," Mrs. Pandit said. "You'll cause him stress. You leave him out of this."

Ashi and I went home. I cried more and prayed. I guessed I'd caused Mrs. Pandit and Sarala to lose face. They didn't want to look like they were mad about the flowers.

I BEGAN NOTICING STRANGE THINGS. Sometimes when she didn't know I was listening, Mrs. Pandit would talk to Neenoo as she helped him toddle up the stairs to their house. "Hurry, hurry! Ashi will get you!"

The usual expression was "hurry, a cat will get you!" Cats were detested in north India, and children were taught to fear them. Did Mrs. Pandit hate Ashi? But why? Was all this just about the flowers?

Neenoo's big sister Dee occasionally came to play, but her visits changed. Sometimes she was mean to Ashi, with no clear reason. Maybe our relationship with our landlord was becoming strained, and Ashi was getting the brunt of it. Joshua and I asked God what to do and tried to coach Ashi in being sweet.

---

DESPITE INCREASING stress with our landlords, there were some bright spots in Ashi's life. She had special connections with our first landlords, especially Ajay when he was home. Also with Rose and with Joshua's friend Yog. Now there were two markers hidden in Yog's shop, one each for Ashi and Arav. Ashi would draw flowers as big as the sun while Arav drew scribbles. Yog and his sisters, who had no children, doted on ours. Ashi in particular could do no wrong.

In the evenings, eyes squeezed shut and hands folded tight, Ashi would pray for her favorite people. "Dear God, please bless Darshika bua and Yog *Taoji* (father's older brother). Please help them to turn away from idols. In Jesus's name, amen."

---

DARSHIKA CALLED. "I know he'll listen to you. Please tell Jahne that I can't go to the temple if we have a baby."

"Namaste," I said, and heard Jahne chuckle a namaste in response. He was always chuckling, trying to seem like nothing bothered him. But I knew he worried. His parents didn't like that Darshika had been living with him for the past several months. They needed the money he earned, and a wife must eat, drink, and be clothed. Darshika also insisted Jahne take medicine when necessary, allow her to bleach the floors, and eat a good breakfast. Those things cost money.

"It's not a big deal. If we have a kid, Darshika will just have to go to the temple once to do a sacrifice. I know she's a Christian, but I'm the one the devta will attack if we don't do these ceremonies."

"Jesus can protect you too," I said. "We can pray for you that you'll be free from the devta."

"No. Our devta is too powerful. I won't be safe without the sacrifice."

"You must feel so stuck in the middle between your parents and your wife, between all these religious ideas."

Jahne didn't answer, but I heard a shaky sigh. Jahne and his family didn't mind Darshika following Jesus so long as He wasn't the only god she followed. *God, show Darshika what to do!*

LITTLE NEENOO'S BIRTHDAY CAME, and we were invited upstairs for the party. I was glad. Maybe this meant we were okay with our landlords after all.

Ashi had decided to give Little Neenoo a special gift: Grandpa Dave. Grandpa Dave was a large, pink stuffed bear given to Ashi by and named after my dad. The day of the party, Ashi changed into a puffy dress. Then she sat down to have one last moment with the bear.

"You be nice to Little Neenoo, Grampa Dave. He doesn't have any bear like you, and I want him to know I'm friendly, so I've got to give you to him."

It was another perfect scenario for a bedtime storybook. Dee and Little Neenoo had stopped playing with Ashi. Now Ashi would give them her most beloved possession as a peace offering. Later at the party, Neenoo hugged the bear, and everyone said thank you. But Sarala hung him on a nail in the wall and never brought him down for Neenoo to play with.

This added insult to injury for Ashi. To hang Grampa Dave on a wall, never to be enjoyed, hurt her soul. She wilted. She said she hated India and wanted to go "home."

---

I TALKED with Kay on the phone. Kay said doctors were running all kinds of tests on Elijah but still didn't know why he wasn't growing. "We want to come back. We're praying about it. I mean, we could bring extras of all the feeding supplies. It's just . . . the germs."

"I know, Kay," I said. "Elijah can't afford to get a tummy bug, right?"

"Exactly. But we want so badly to be in India."

Kay and I prayed they'd be able to return. She said Posy, now three, talked about India all the time. She would ask when they were going "home."

"Pray for us, too," I said. "I wish Ashi felt that way about India."

"We pray for her every day," Kay said. "God will show you what to do."

---

A FEW WEEKS after Little Neenoo's party, I found a pile of yellow petals on the ground. Joshua joined me and the kids in Arav's room.

"Okay, guys," I said. "You know we can't pick these flowers. Can you be honest and tell Mommy who picked them?"

"Me," said two-year-old Arav.

"Thank you for being honest, Arav. You know Mommy will have to give you a swat, right?"

"Uh-huh." Arav sighed, resigned to his fate. He didn't cry when I swatted his behind. He even hugged me afterward, because that's what we did when we had to swat the kids.

"What are you doing?!" Sarala burst into Arav's room. The children turned to look at her, startled. I glanced out at the front door. It stood wide open.

"Arav picked some flowers," I said, ruffling his hair. "We have an agreement about that."

"No!" she cried. "No, I saw. It was Ashi. Ashi, tell them you did it. Don't let your brother take the blame."

"But I didn't," Ashi said, eyes wide. "Mommy, I didn't."

"I saw her!" Sarala jabbed a finger in the air towards Ashi. "I saw her do it!"

"But you've been in the field all morning," I said. "You just got back. How could you have seen?"

"Well, it wasn't him."

"It *was* me, Mama," Arav said, patting my hand. "I wanted to make somefing."

"Don't worry," Joshua soothed, escorting Sarala outside. "We didn't spank him hard."

Ashi sat on the floor and frowned down at her dusty toes. I didn't know what to say.

---

SOMETIME AFTER THIS, I came outside with a basket of laundry to find Ashi screaming. Mr. Pandit was holding her arm, yanking her across our veranda. He was scowling.

"Let go!" I shouted. Mr. Pandit let go. He turned and walked away.

"What happened?" I asked Ashi.

"I don't know," she wailed. "He was trying to get me. I hate it here, Mommy. I want to go home."

I held Ashi close and kissed her little blonde head. Posy called India home. Ashi called America home. If only home could be wherever we actually lived.

Joshua and I tried to help Ashi love India again. We tried to be faithful missionaries. It seemed like everything was dying. Everything was failing. Even our health. Before the month was out, both Joshua and I had MRIs for stress-related symptoms. We needed a break, and our children needed one too. In August, we called our supervisors and made plans to take our furlough three months early. We would spend autumn in India, and take our furlough just after Christmas.

# 56

# PLANS FOR OUR DAUGHTERS

One day during Arav's nap, Ashi asked to play outside. I said yes and grabbed a basket of clean laundry to fold while I supervised her. Clambering over our stone fence, Ashi walked into the field in front of our house. *Climbing fences in her silver sequined shoes,* I thought. *A perfect metaphor for my beautiful, active child.*

Ashi loved wide open spaces where she could see all around her. No one could sneak up and touch her face or grab her arm. No one could yell at her or tell her parents to spank her. I could see on her face that Ashi felt unlovable. How could such a beautiful person feel that way?

Not that Ashi was an angel. In the last six months, she'd given herself two haircuts, painted a mural on her wall with Joshua's deodorant, and sold Arav his own toys.

Arav had his own growing list of offenses. Most of his involved eating inedible things, including a burrito made of mud and a leaf. Followed shortly by a banana flavored dewormer.

But these were all normal childhood escapades. One day they'd be funny stories to tell around the dinner table. They did not obscure Arav's loving, easygoing personality, nor Ashi's helpful, compassionate one.

And Ashi had tried everything she knew to reach out to our landlords, to make up for the flowers. They'd said it was no big deal, but we heard the truth from neighbors. People began badmouthing Ashi in the community. For the first time, we truly felt the sting of *zabardasty* in the form of peer pressure.

*Maybe this isn't about flowers,* I thought to myself. *Maybe this is about power.*

Mr. Pandit lost power when Darshika shared with Sarala about God, when his wife asked me questions about my fast for Ashi, and when she bought herself a Bible. He lost power when his family questioned the Hindu narrative of reincarnation. He lost power when God freed his grandson

Neenoo of a pestering spirit. No, it wasn't about the flowers. It wasn't even about Ashi.

*God, I want out of this house,* I prayed. *Please, make me willing to stay if You ask us to. But if there is any room in your plan for us to go, make a way for us.*

I looked out again at the field. Ashi sat in the dried grass, just staring. She'd turn five the following week. *I'll throw her a party. I'll give her lots of little gifts with notes about why we love her. And the last gift will be an Indian dress just like the dresses she admires in Rose's closet.*

---

ASHI'S BIRTHDAY ARRIVED. We did everything she loved. We ate pizza, swam in a natural hot spring, and walked on the rumbly bridge. It was almost time for cake and the last gift when Naina called.

"My son wants to play with Ashi. He's been pestering me all day. Baby Davni just woke up too, and she loves to get out. Would it be all right if we came?"

"Of course!" I had planned only a small family party, but perhaps one friend would be okay. Later as our children played, Naina and I chatted.

"I'm so sorry I don't have a gift for Ashi," Naina said. "All the shops were closed on the way here!"

"I had forgotten that our daughters share a birthday," I said. "Otherwise I'd have a gift for baby Davni, too. How will you celebrate her birthday?"

Naina shifted. She looked embarrassed. "Since my husband is away again on business, I thought we'd just wait until next year to celebrate."

Joshua mouthed the words: "We have two cakes."

I play-glared at him. Joshua was easy to please when it came to food. But when I'd announced that vegan chocolate cheesecake was on the menu for Ashi's birthday, he'd insisted we buy a back-up carrot cake. I stood and walked with Joshua to the kitchen.

"Speaking of cheesecake, I talked to the Cheese Guy," Joshua said as he opened a box of birthday candles.

"I see you lived to tell about it."

"He asked me to come sit in his car. At first, I wondered what he was going to do to me in there. Then I figured, it's daytime. Too many witnesses. Anyway, we just sat and talked, and he even shared about some issues he's facing."

I smiled as I lifted my cheesecake. "Only God could turn our biggest mistake into the friendship you've been praying for since we arrived."

"Amen. Hey, are you sure about that cheesecake?"

"Have a little faith, Joshua."

Together, we carried out the two cakes. The vegan chocolate cheesecake had five candles for Ashi, the carrot cake just one for Davni. Joshua tried the cheesecake. "Hey, this isn't terrible!"

"Told you!" We laughed.

Naina looked at both of us. "I will never forget this day. It's like God arranged everything for me. Every time I come here, I just feel like something is different. I mean, I believe all the gods are the same. That there is One Supreme God but many expressions of Him. But most people just make demands of God. You ask for wisdom, not for wealth. You want to know God's will. It has changed the way I pray. I want to know what pleases God, not just give Him a list of what I want."

Ashi received her final gift, a light pink Indian dress covered in embroidery, fit for a princess. As she floated around the house, my heart swelled in worship to God. I had planned a special day for my daughter, and God had planned a special day for His.

Maybe God really would work everything together for our good.

---

MRS. PANDIT always said everything was fine, just fine. So, one evening as we often did, we went upstairs to visit Mr. Pandit's family. Sitting on mats, we chatted about the weather and the apple harvest.

Mr. Pandit sat with his arms folded and smiled, but his smile was strange. Like he was happy about something terrible. He watched us talk for a while. Then he spoke. "My wife tells me your Bible doesn't have caste in it. Is that true?"

"It's true," Joshua said.

"Well, let me explain caste in a way you'll understand," Mr. Pandit said. "I am the head. Would I put my shoes on my head or my hat on my feet? When I pose these questions to the outcastes, they shut their mouths. They know it's true."

"I assume the low-caste are the feet?" Joshua asked.

"Of course. And Brahmins are the head."

"Then what are we?" I asked.

"Ha! You foreigners? You are the stomach."

I felt like someone had punched me. We foreigners were the stomach? Mr. Pandit smirked, seeming to enjoy my discomfort. I knew exactly what he meant. Stomachs are fed. Their purpose is to take. To consume. He was saying we were blind consumers. Was this why his wife and daughter-in-law had said we tried to solve everything with money? Didn't they see all we gave? All we'd given up?

---

ONE OF THE men who had attended our house church before the possession incident called Joshua. His sister-in-law Alisha had left her baby behind and run off with a man. "We have to find her."

Joshua drove with the man all the way to Delhi to find Alisha, a beautiful, newly baptized Christian who truly loved Jesus. It wasn't hard for them to convince her to come back. A few days after she returned, I visited her.

"Why did you leave?" I asked as she handed me a cup of tea.

Alisha turned around and pulled up her shirt. There were long, ugly scars across her back. "You know my husband is not a Christian. He beats me, and sometimes I think I'll die. Once he beat me so badly I couldn't breathe. I had to go to the hospital."

"I'm so sorry," I said. "I didn't know."

"If my husband would become a Christian, everything would be okay," Alisha said. "Just look at my brother-in-law."

"Your brother-in-law is a good man," I said.

"He used to beat my sister. She beat him back too." Alisha and I shared a laugh. Her sister was a lovely blend of sweet and feisty.

"Listen," I said. "If you need to leave to live, I'll help you myself. But you shouldn't run off with a man. And you shouldn't leave your daughter behind."

"I'm ashamed that I left my daughter," Alisha said. "But this guy was a Christian. He said we were going to have a new life together. We didn't do anything, I swear. I stayed at his parents' house."

"A new life is something *Jesus* gives," I said. "Not a boyfriend. You know that."

"I know."

"If he beats you again, come to my house, okay? Bring your little girl. We'll help you in whatever way we can."

"Thank you," Alisha said.

---

WE PRAYED EARNESTLY for the pastor who'd told his contacts not to worship with us. I baked cookies for his congregation. When Joshua heard the pastor's mother was sick, he called to say he was praying for her.

Sometime after this, one of the Nepali laborers living in the cement block across from our house was attacked and needed medical intervention. Several of our Nepali friends came to Joshua to see if we would help. He drove the group to the hospital, and under conditions of anonymity, helped with his medical costs.

One afternoon, Joshua ran into the pastor, who told him, "I've heard about the way you've been helping our members and the Nepali community. Maybe there's a way we can work together. We are all working in the same field, after all."

"And the field is large," Joshua said. "We are praying for you, your family, and your members."

The pastor's congregation began attending our house church again. When Darshika came to visit for Christmas, she was thrilled to see the house so full. That Sabbath morning was emotional as she and several others shared their testimonies. Darshika had found peace and the ability to forgive. Now God had granted her request to conceive. She would have her baby that summer.

Jahne still wanted Darshika to go back and live with his parents. Darshika was reluctant. Since we were leaving on furlough after Christmas, Darshika asked to stay on with us, then housesit during our furlough. Jahne gave his permission.

---

DARSHIKA'S SISTER Damini came for Christmas. She was amazed by Joshua's camera and turned out to be naturally gifted at framing good shots.

The kids and I cut out a giant pile of paper snowflakes. Despite the drama of past months, Sarala's kids and their cousins came to help. I strung the delicate circles along with a line of LED lights all over the house. Everything twinkled, even our breath in the cool air. In the *tandoor* room, there was always someone to load wood into the stove, always someone to help sweep, always someone to talk to.

*Has India turned me into an extrovert?* I wondered.

---

THE MORNING we were scheduled to leave, Darshika stumbled out of her room, rubbing her eyes and shuffling in her slippers. "Bhabi, I had the strangest dream."

"What was it?" I asked.

"I was out walking in the fields when I saw this tall apricot tree full of ripe apricots. I was so happy to find it. I pulled out a corner of my patu and started filling it with apricots. There was a barbed-wire fence nearby. Suddenly, I saw Ashi coming toward me wearing a patu. She said, 'Bua, I want some apricots!' But she couldn't get to them because the barbed-wire fence was in the way. So I held some fruit over the fence to her. She lifted a corner of her tiny patu, and I filled it up with fruit. Then I woke up."

As we drove away, I thought about Darshika's dream. Surely it must mean that Darshika would harvest fruit while we were away from her on furlough. Surely it couldn't mean more than that.

---

DURING OUR FURLOUGH, Ashi and Arav blossomed. They began to smile at new people. I hadn't realized before how the constant face touching had made them both avoid eye contact.

As she settled into safety, Ashi opened up to me. "Mr. Pandit is a bad man, Mommy. I know he'll hurt Arav and me if we go back. I saw him touch one of my friends where you said not to. I screamed and ran away."

I tried not to let my face change expressions. But I couldn't breathe. Ashi had seen her friend molested? Was this why the Pandit family hated Ashi? Because she'd seen Mr. Pandit's true nature?

Our organization had a trauma care plan in place. Calling Bob and Hazel, I told them everything that had happened over the last few months. They immediately contacted a counselor who flew out and talked with both Ashi and me.

Joshua and I prayed about what to do. Our organization encouraged us to take some extra time to get things figured out before we returned. But furloughing wasn't easy. While we loved the time spent with family and friends, it was tiring, too. We didn't have our own home. Joshua felt purposeless. Besides, Darshika would have her baby soon. How could we just leave her there alone?

So we told our organization we were going back. They insisted we book tickets to Thailand two months after our arrival in India. Looking forward to a family break might make things easier.

Meanwhile, Lars and Kay made the decision not to continue serving in India. Instead, Lars would fly back to deal with the belongings they'd left in their house. He booked tickets to fly shortly before us.

"I just talked to our landlords," he told Joshua. "His relatives plan to move into our old house once I get our stuff out. But maybe you could stay there while I'm selling everything. That way Ashi won't have to go back to the old house. And maybe I can help you guys in some way while I'm there."

Joshua and I prayed and talked. We'd find another house, somewhere safe. And we wouldn't try to stay in India forever. We'd plan on two more years, giving us a total of nine in the field, and concentrate on handing over our fellowship group to an Indian pastor.

We tried to prepare ourselves, mentally and physically, to go back. But the day we told Ashi we were returning to India, she turned in on herself like a flower in darkness.

# 57

## THE ONE QUESTION

At the airport two months later, it seemed thousands of people jostled past as we walked toward security. Our furlough was over, and we were on our way back to India. Arav held my hand and clomped in his new shoes. Ashi yanked on my other hand before pulling away. "Grandma Follows!"

Joshua's mom scooped her up. Ashi broke down in an animal-like sob, grabbing her grandma's neck and holding on tight. I tried to be in the moment of pain yet help everyone transition to joy. "It's time to go, sweetie. We'll see Grandma Follows again soon."

"No. I don't want to go!" Ashi cried. "Grandma, Grandma!"

"I know, honey." I tried to unlock her limbs. Mrs. Follows looked torn as though she didn't want to let go either. I could see pain and fear on her face. Would everything be okay? Had I heard God right? Had I ever?

Ashi looked at me, face red. Then I started sobbing. "It's okay. It's going to be okay."

Ashi let me take her in my arms, and we all went through security. After boarding the plane, I broke down again. The image of Ashi's face stared at me even when I closed my eyes. I saw something in her face that I had hoped I'd never see. Distrust.

And she was right. I should have protected her better. I should have insisted we move to a different house the moment I sensed something was wrong. If only I'd lidded the pot the day she was burned. If I'd kept her with me the day she was poisoned. If I'd been rude for her earlier. If I'd understood the culture better and sooner.

*God, why am I not a better mother?*

When we landed for our first layover, everyone in the plane stood. I noticed a familiar-looking woman with a pixie cut and two kids a few rows ahead of me. We chatted while waiting for the plane to deboard. It turned out she was a member of Joshua's parents' church who happened to be on the same flight for the first leg of our trip.

In the airport, Arav ran around in circles. Ashi sat on a window ledge and glared out at the airplanes. The woman from my in-laws' church appeared again. Herding her two children towards us, she said, "We should have prayed with you. Kids, these are real live missionaries going to tell people about Jesus. Let's pray for them."

I don't remember what she said, but I remember the impact that it had. It was a glimmer of hope. Of all the airplanes leaving Seattle that day, God placed this angel dispatcher on ours. Maybe He still was the God who sees.

---

WE RETRIEVED OUR CAR, and Joshua drove us to Pahargaun. I went over my plan in my head. Lars and Kay's old home would be our temporary safe house. Then God would provide us with a more permanent home where our children would be safe. Darshika would have her baby. We'd have better boundaries and be more assertive. I'd win back Ashi's confidence, and her heart would heal. By the time we left India in two years, everyone would be okay again. God had called us. He would come through. He always had.

Lars met us at his and Kay's old house. He had three weeks to pack, sell, or give away their belongings. Darshika arrived by bus, hugging everyone and laughing as she dabbed at her tears. An orange tunic stretched tight across her swollen belly.

Darshika and I cleaned until Lars and Kay's house shone. We emptied shelves. We scrubbed corners. Lars sold things. The kids ran around in circles and bickered. Joshua house-hunted. One place seemed promising. It had a large lawn, something I'd rarely seen in India. There were three bedrooms and an actual living room with windows. Two rooms with outside entrances stood just to the left of the house.

*One for Darshika, one for church group storage,* I thought.

Just then, a tall, gangly man walked in the gate, greeted us shortly, and entered one of the outside rooms. Joshua and I looked at each other, then Joshua stepped closer to the landlord. "Who is the gentleman who just arrived?"

"He's a good friend of mine," the landlord said. "He stays in that room there."

"So are you renting the whole property? I mean, is he planning on staying here?"

"Yes, yes, I'm renting the whole property. Just not that room."

I looked at the house. It was like a dream come true. The kids rushed past me, playing tag in the sweet-smelling grass. Surely God had provided this place. He would make it available.

We told the man we'd rent the house only if we could have the entire property. He said he'd call us, and we left. Over the next few days, I drew floor plans like an architect with OCD, imagining where we'd put our things in that house.

The kids were bored and naughty, and I knew they needed a routine. Time-outs and chore charts work when you're in your own home. But we were floating, lost in a sea of other people's homes, other people's schedules, other people's rules.

I thought of the millions of refugees forced to flee their homes each year, some running from religious persecution. Many faced the same threats Ashi had described. I thought of how many times Darshika had run away in the night. Refugees can't just go home. Darshika could go home but at the cost of her faith and the future faith of her child.

I knew my troubles were light and temporary compared to those of refugees. We had food. We had clothing. We weren't cold at night. For these things, I was thankful. But it was still hard.

If only I could get us into a house, I could help everyone transition. We'd be stable. Nobody would go crazy. We would not detonate.

"MOMMY! I NEED YOU." I walked into Posy's old room where Ashi and Arav lay in their sleeping bags on the floor. Ashi had dragged her mat to the middle of the room.

"Mommy's here. You're safe, Ashi. Go to sleep." It had been two hours since I'd put the children to bed. Arav had long since slept, but not Ashi.

"I need you and Daddy. I need you now."

I called Joshua. Ashi instructed us. "I need one of you on this side and one on the other. Someone's going to try to steal me. You have to be my walls."

We normally wouldn't have, but we obliged this time, lying down one on either side of our daughter. Ashi fell asleep between her walls. We waited until her breathing slowed, then eased ourselves off the floor. Lars was asleep in his room when Joshua and I trudged into the living room. I cried and hugged my knees.

Joshua listened for a few minutes, standing above me. I knew he felt the weight of being a "wall" even more than I did. He was the dad, the protector, the one to comfort me when I comforted the children. I felt myself withdrawing. I couldn't burden our families back home. I couldn't burden Joshua by saying more. So I just sat.

Joshua disappeared, emerging a moment later with his bicycle. He set it up as a stationary bike in the living room.

"You're going to ride *now*?" I wailed, offended.

"No. You are."

"I don't want to."

"Ride." He pointed to the bike. "You need this."

I stood up. Because I trusted Joshua. And because something in me knew he was right. I cried and rode and rode and cried, channeling all the energy of my fear and anger into my legs. I must have looked ridiculous. Joshua brought a still-unsold electric fan and set it up to cool my face. Finally, exhausted in every way possible, we slept.

SEVERAL NIGHTS LATER, Darshika began to pace, grimacing. I placed my hand on her taut belly. "Darshika, what is it? Are you in labor?"

This was not Darshika's first labor. It could go very quickly. I looked at my watch. Less than a minute after the first, Darshika had another strong contraction.

"I'm taking her to Pahargaun," I told Joshua. "I don't think we have time to get to Chotashaher."

I helped Darshika to the car and sped to the mission hospital in Pahargaun. Several of the nurses recognized me. They escorted Darshika to a room and commanded her to lie on her back.

"I have to pee," Darshika said.

"You must pee on the bed," a nurse said, grabbing a bedpan.

I frowned. "Seriously? That seems a little extreme. She just has to use the restroom. Please let her empty her bladder. It's better for labor."

"No," the nurse repeated. "We are not allowed to let patients use the restroom during labor. We don't want any babies born in the toilet."

Meanwhile, two other nurses were trying to get Darshika to lie down. Another yanked at her sweater. They likely wanted to take her blood pressure. "Lie down! Lie down, I said! If you don't obey, I'll tie you up with ropes."

"Bhabiiiiiii," Darshika cried, lunging to grab on to me. Suddenly, I didn't care how anybody felt but Darshika. Who was going to advocate for her if I didn't? I stood up straight, anger welling up in my chest.

"You are treating this person like an animal. Have some respect. If you're not even going to let her go to the bathroom, I'm taking her home. I'd rather help her have her baby in the car than stay here!"

Grabbing Darshika's hand, I helped her towards the restroom. Just as she was pulling up her pants, the doctor came. She checked Darshika's progress. "False labor. You can go home."

Of course it was false labor! I should have waited longer, but after a two-hour labor myself, I'd feared we wouldn't make it in time. As a frazzled Darshika yanked her sweater on, one of the nurses stepped forward. "Listen, I'm sorry. You said her contractions were close. We thought she'd have her baby in the toilet."

"I understand." I smiled, joining the face-saving game, though I still felt angry. "I'm sure you've had it happen before."

"We have," another nurse said. "And I've been kicked in the face by women during labor. You have to be tough on them. Tough and strict. Otherwise, they go crazy."

This time I allowed myself to relate. "I'm sure you've had some crazy experiences. May God bless you as you work to help people."

Darshika and I walked back to the car, avoiding a pack of dogs leering at us from their dumpster diner. Darshika heaved herself into the front seat. "I knew you wouldn't let me stay there. They wouldn't listen to me. I knew you would rescue me."

As we drove home, we processed the event, how wrong it had been. I knew it had reminded Darshika of her two older children who'd been born "like dogs" in an unlit room behind the tandoor. She'd had only her own patu to clothe them.

---

"I GOT a call on the house with the yard," Joshua said a few nights later. "He says the friend stays. I told him we weren't interested."

"Oh." I went through the motions of putting the kids to bed, reading to them, singing to them. I was a good actress, pretending everything was fine. But it wasn't. It had been five months since we'd had our own home, and the horizon was nothing but a straight, gray ocean of displacement.

I used to wonder how Israel could doubt or forget God after He'd rescued them with miracles they could *see*. They'd heard His voice and seen His brightness in the pillar of fire and the pillar of cloud. But then, so had I.

Darshika slept. Lars and Joshua strategized in the kitchen. I knelt on the floor, anger welling up in me. The room was silent as death, and only an artificial orange light penetrated the night.

"How could You?" I asked, hissing the words through clenched teeth. "I trusted You to provide, and You didn't. I put every single thing I have on the line. Everything I care about. I've given You my children. I've surrendered. And You are not coming through! We don't even have a place to live. Maybe the Son of Man had nowhere to lay His head, but I have little children!"

Somewhere in the back of my mind, I knew Ashi could have been truly hurt by Mr. Pandit. I knew God had prevented worse from happening. But her physical safety didn't guarantee her emotional safety. What if Ashi would not be okay in her heart? In her mind? And what if it was my fault?

I was an experienced questioner. But my belief in God had always been my rock, my starting place. When my mother converted to Judaism, I'd read the Bible from cover to cover, searching for Him. When we encountered other viewpoints, other religions, big questions, I looked straight into the face of my beliefs. Though it terrified me, I didn't flinch. If it was all a lie, I wanted to know. If it was the truth, I would follow it anywhere.

I thought back over my few years as a mother. I'd fasted and prayed with one request—that God would protect the hearts and minds of my children. Now Ashi was living the very life I'd worked so hard to keep at bay. We were nothing but an emergency, and Ashi would learn to be anxious.

Just like me.

Had I imagined the miracles? The dreams and impressions? Was it all just a big coincidence? Was I a fool, putting my family through this unstable hell for nothing?

"Oh, God," I bit out the words. "Are You even real?"

## 58

PARABLE OF PAIN

After that, we practically moved into our car. Of course, we slept at Lars' house. But if someone had a small errand to do, everyone came along, and we went as far as possible. The kids looked out the windows at the patchwork fields. I had time to think without wondering if they were being abducted or damaging each other.

As I thought, I prayed. *God, if You are there, why are You so silent? I don't understand. I surrendered everything. This is the one thing I asked You for, the one thing I really cared about—mental stability for my children. I believe. Help my unbelief! Even more than my unbelief, help my kids.*

I thought of Mary. Had she wondered why the census came so late in her pregnancy? Had she wondered why God didn't provide an inn? Yet Jesus was born where He was supposed to be born. In Bethlehem, as was prophesied hundreds of years before. I thought of Abraham, who was asked to sacrifice his only son, his gift from God.

*I don't see it, God. And I don't feel it. I just hope You're there doing something. I don't know if it's okay to ask You this in the midst of my doubt, and I don't even know if it makes sense. But God? Take Jesus instead of Ashi. Please. I have nothing more to give. He is all I have to offer. He is my ram in the thicket.*

ONE DAY, Joshua said he'd found a house. "Two issues. It's in our old village. And it's not finished."

"Are you serious? How is that going to work?"

"Just come see."

We got in the car again and drove over the bridge, past the Cheese Guy, past the path to our old house. There on the other side of the village from Mr. Pandit was a trail leading through the fields.

"Mina and Manu own it," Joshua said. "They've been working on it for several months."

Mina and Manu were good people. Joshua had spent a lot of time in Manu's shop discussing religion, politics, and purity. I had prayed with Mina many times. While they were not open to Christianity, we appreciated their honesty and kindness.

As we walked along the trail, it turned from mud to rough cement. Rounding a corner, we saw several bushy apple trees. Something resembling a yard stretched around a one-story cement house. Manu joined us and began pointing out the amenities, which included a primitive two-story cow shed, three cows, and a wrinkled old man.

Manu gestured to the man. "This is Peanut. He will care for the cows so you won't have to do anything."

"Brother, is it possible for us to rent everything? Even the cowshed?" I peeked in the door. There was a living room with large, clear glass windows. I could already see our wool carpet in the middle of the floor. There was also a small kitchen and three bedrooms.

"It's not possible," Manu said. "My mother wants the cows to stay. But Peanut will come and care for them."

"I don't know if this will work," I side-whispered to Joshua.

"I think it could work," Joshua whispered back. "There's a yard. Peanut seems harmless enough."

I didn't know whether Peanut was harmless or poisonous, though he seemed gentle enough. Manu must have sensed my discomfort. "Peanut's a good guy. He takes care of the cows, that's all. He won't bother you. Or your kids."

"Sister, are you sure you don't want to move in yourself?" I asked Mina. "I know you designed this house. It's your home."

"It's no problem," she said. "We want you to have it."

"Besides, we could use the money," Manu admitted. "When you leave, we get the house back. Stay here as long as you want. We know you'll take care of it."

We agreed to rent the house.

---

WE HADN'T SPOKEN to our old landlords since our arrival and knew we'd have to have a conversation before moving. I drew the short stick and went by myself when I knew only Mrs. Pandit would be home.

Aunty probed. I said she and I were fine. I didn't say, "Everyone else in your family are bullying my small child, and your husband is a predator."

When other villagers asked me why we were moving, I only said we liked the new house. But people gossiped. "Something happened. The Pandit family must have done something. What did they do?"

One day, an old man stopped Joshua as he walked down one of the narrow dirt paths by our new house. "It's good you moved. Mr. Pandit is a bad man."

That night, I went online and signed a petition for the government of India to remove the statute of limitations on childhood sexual abuse. And I prayed for Ashi's friend, who had long since moved away.

---

OUR HOUSE CHURCH members helped us move. On our very first night in the house, we discovered the living room windows couldn't be opened. Joshua added another item to a growing list of projects. Fix windows in living room. Striding into the kitchen, he gestured to the area where cabinets should have been. "I'm going to build shelves. Let's have open shelving. That way we avoid mold."

We decided to build bunk beds and have one room dedicated to homeschooling. Joshua would build a couple of desks for the kids and stairs going up to the roof so we could hang our clothes to dry. We'd buy a cord of wood for winter and stack it against the house.

"This living room is huge. It'll be a great place to have church," I said. "We can use the homeschool room for the children's Sabbath school."

"What about Darshika?" Joshua asked.

"I've been thinking about that. If Jahne is willing to bring her to live with him after the baby is born, she'll go. If not, she wants to stay. She knows his parents will force her and the baby to bow to their idols."

"Maybe she and the baby should have the homeschool room."

"I think we need space," I said, surprised at my directness. "I think we need to be able to be 'us.'"

"What about Darshika?"

"I'm working on a plan for Darshika and the baby. I'll tell you soon."

---

WE GOT a call from our supervisors, Bob and Hazel. "Would you like us to come help for a week or two?"

"Yes!" We couldn't pretend we didn't need help. We needed help with the kids and the house projects, not to mention Darshika's impending delivery. Lars offered to stay a couple of extra weeks, too, until Bob and Hazel could come.

---

IN THE MIDST OF PACKING, moving, making excuses about why we were moving, driving to appointments, buying stuff from Lars and inheriting other stuff, and driving up and down the mountain, Darshika's water broke. I recruited Lars to take Darshika and me to Chotashaher so Joshua could stay with the kids.

At the hospital, we were shown to a private room, which I think I appreciated more than Darshika did. To her, the kindness and the privacy were frosting on the cake of second chances. By late afternoon, Darshika had only experienced a few weak contractions. Dr. Wonderful instructed the nurses to induce her.

Several hours later, Darshika was in the delivery room. Dr. Wonderful glided in the door, snapping on a pair of white gloves. "Oooh, I'm here for the good part!"

I laughed. *This doctor loves her job. She loves these women.* What a blessing Dr. Wonderful was to the Parvata.

Just then, I looked down at Darshika and felt my smile vanish. She lay there, head tilted back, the whites showing around her black-brown irises, staring at me as though it was the last time she'd ever see me. My heart pumped a burst of adrenaline into my veins. Was Darshika going to die?

"You can do this, Darshika," I told her. "You're almost there. The baby is almost here."

Finally, the baby was born. Dr. Wonderful handed him to the pediatrician, Mr. Dr. Wonderful. "It's a boy!"

Darshika collapsed onto the bed and closed her eyes. She cried. I cried. The doctor beamed. Many days later, we talked about that moment. "What were you thinking? Right before your son came?"

"I was remembering. When I was fourteen, right after I got married, I helped with some of the births in the village. I saw three women die during childbirth. Three. When I was in labor, I saw their faces in my mind. I thought I was going to die. But then I looked up at you, Bhabi. It's the strangest thing. I saw you above me with light glowing all around your head, and suddenly I knew I wasn't going to die."

---

THAT NIGHT I didn't sleep much. In between moments of helping Darshika with the baby, I listened. A woman across the hall was nearing her moment. Every three minutes she screamed, a panicked, startled cry. She finished out each contraction with a moan. The words of Jesus suddenly rushed into my mind:

Nation will rise against nation, and kingdom against kingdom. There will be famines and earthquakes in various places. All these are the beginning of birth pains. (Matthew 24:7-8)

This was it. The answer to my question so many years ago. The trials and pain of the past few years were birth pangs. Pain with a purpose. It is pain that comes faster and faster, the rests shorter, until you don't think you can do it anymore. And then the miracle.

Think you can't stand it? That is the last step before a baby is born. The last step before a spiritual breakthrough. The dark night before Jesus comes and the shadows vaporize into a fading memory.

At that moment, I felt God draw near. And I understood God's parable of pain, the message hidden in the pangs of childbirth: *Keep pushing, girl, you're almost home!*

*Beloved, do not be surprised at the fiery ordeal among you, which comes upon you for your testing, as though something strange were happening to you; but to the degree that you share the sufferings of Christ, keep on rejoicing, so that at the revelation of His glory you may also rejoice and be overjoyed.*

1 PETER 4:12-13

# 59

## A QUESTION FOR GOD

Joshua called on the phone. "Can you come? You need to get away. It's been two days."

"I know. But the baby's jaundiced. It's going to be several more days before Darshika can take him out of the hospital."

"What can we do so you can leave?"

"I don't know. She needs an attendant. Let's pray."

Jahne arrived later that day. He grinned, silent and silly, over the boy who looked just like him. I hoped the baby would steal his heart and make him want to keep Darshika with him.

"Darshika? Jahne? I am going now," I said.

Darshika looked up at me, mouth open. I ignored her pleading eyes. "I must go care for Ashi and Arav. Jahne, take care of Darshika and your baby. You'll have to get whatever they need. The nurse will show you where the pharmacy is."

Joshua and the kids were waiting outside in the car. Ashi and Arav cheered when they saw me. We drove to a park and walked down to the river. Shedding our socks and shoes, we waded in. I looked around. For some reason, there weren't many people at the park. I could see all around us. The shallow, sandy river stretched before us, the grassy park behind us. I felt safe.

"Maybe we can do this," I said to Joshua.

"Yeah. I think maybe we can."

---

LARS BROUGHT DARSHIKA and Jahne back to his house. The couple and their new baby lived together like a little family in Posy's old room. But after a few days, Jahne had to go back to work. He wasn't willing to take Darshika with him. She could either stay with his parents or not be with him at all.

"Go to my parents' place as soon as you're able," he said. "They will do a ceremony for the devta to protect the child. And me."

"I can't," Darshika said. "I'll do anything you ask but that."

So Jahne left. Then it was Lars's turn to leave. He'd take a taxi to the airport in Delhi, and we'd drive Darshika to our new house. We prayed together. Lars brought Joshua in close for a back-slapping man hug.

Joshua started crying. I looked up at those men, two brothers forever bonded in service to God and to each other, and I cried too. Darshika wailed. The baby slept. The kids peeked in and asked why everyone was crying. Ashi rushed to my side and tried to wipe away my tears. Arav hugged my leg.

And so Lars left his old house, his old friends, India, and us.

---

PUJA SQUATTED on the ground and tossed a handful of dried mint leaves into a pot. Pouring in sugar, she stirred. Ashi and Arav bounced on her bed. Joshua and I tried to stop them, but Puja and Shankar told them to continue.

Shankar motioned to our son. "Hard to believe our Arav would have been that big." He'd taken to calling Lucky "Our Arav." Shankar's cocky half-smile was still there, but his face had grown older, more serious. There were lines around his eyes.

"I'm sure you still miss him," I said, "Even though you didn't get the chance to know him."

I thought about how Indians don't have baby showers. It's not just to protect from the evil eye but to ensure a mother doesn't bond with an unborn child. As though you could avoid the pain of grief if you could keep your heart from loving.

"We've been going to doctors," Shankar went on. "It's expensive. They say she needs an operation. That her tubes were damaged by the miscarriage. I don't know."

"I see. I've had a friend who had that operation. It's invasive." I thought of Darshika's scar, which stretched across her entire abdomen.

We drank mint tea and talked. Shankar tried to sell us walnuts. Puja showed us some sweaters she had knitted. Shankar told us about the various anti-corruption rallies he'd been a part of and how glad he was to be a member of the Congress party. Ashi and Arav sat on the floor, sipping the sugary mint tea, quiet for the moment.

"What do you feel is the gist of your political party?" I asked, knowing that Congress was the opposing party to that of the current president of India.

"We believe in religious liberty. We believe people have the right to choose what they believe. The BJP? They'd force everyone to be Hindu."

My heart burned in my chest, and I gave Joshua a quick look. Could this be an opening? Would we be able to share with Shankar and Puja?

"What do you think about that?" Joshua asked.

"It's why I'm in the party," he said. "I don't believe in this Ghar Wapsi stuff. It's wrong." Ghar Wapsi. Homecoming. It referred to the Hindu extremists who forcibly converted Christian and Muslim children to Hinduism.

"Religious liberty is important to us too," Joshua said. "Our church even has an organization that helps support freedom of religion all over the world."

"That's important," Shankar said, "Some people want everyone to be a part of their religion. But all the religions are the same. They all give the same essential message. I feel it's wrong to pressure people."

"We think so too. That it's wrong to pressure people." I took a deep breath, praying before I went on. "But there's one point I disagree with. I don't believe all religions have the same essential message. The Quran says to slay idolators. The Bible calls idols an abomination to God. How can that align with the Bhagavad Gita or any of the Hindu scriptures?"

Shankar shook his head. "Look, it's like this. The gods give messages to men, and as they come from the mouth of the gods, those messages are pure. But man wants to justify himself and his own religion. So he changes the divine message to make his way seem right. Look past the humanity of the writings, and you will find the divine."

"I don't believe that," I said. "How can something be the truth and a lie at the same time? I believe truth exists. God is reaching out to mankind, trying to tell us what it is."

Shankar shook his head. "No, that is wrong."

I stared at Shankar. At that moment, I felt something inside me change, as though the burden of reaching Shankar and Puja had slipped off my heart. Joshua and I had planted a seed. It was up to God now.

I smiled. "We agree on one thing. We agree that freedom is important. You have every right to believe what you do. And we have the right to believe as we do. And because we're friends, we can have conversations like this and it's still okay."

The tension broke. We talked about other things. Ashi and Arav got restless, and it was time to go. As we drove home, I thought about Shankar. He wasn't a perfect person, but he was a good man, a man God could use. We'd done our best to share. Shankar could open his eyes and see the lavish love, mercy, and worthiness of the One True God. Or he could keep the golden imitation. It was up to him to decide.

---

JOSHUA and I moved into the living room so Darshika and the baby could have our room. One night I had a waking dream that someone was breaking into the house. I could see them, and screamed, thinking it was real. Then I heard Joshua's voice. "Abby, I'm here. I'm here."

I forced myself to breathe. *It's only a dream. Remember, this is just sleep apnea and stress and a bad dream. Just breathe. You're almost to the other side.*

The next afternoon, Joshua sat beside me in the living room. "I've been praying, and I think I've gotten myself to the place where I'm willing to leave if we need to."

"I was just thinking how I'm willing to stay," I responded. "I guess surrender is the important thing. It's whatever God wants now."

"Maybe we need to ask Him what He wants," Joshua said. "We always ask Him to help us stay here in India. To help us reach people. Maybe we should ask Him to show us His will."

There on the cement floor, we knelt and laid everything at the feet of Jesus. If He said to stay, we'd stay. If He said to go, we'd go.

*Only don't let us stray from Your will,* I prayed.

---

THE KIDS WERE ecstatic when Bob and Hazel arrived. Hazel read to them. Bob joked with Joshua. They surveyed the growing list of fix-it projects necessary to make our unfinished house livable.

"Shall we get started?" Bob asked.

"I have one project that's not on the list," I said. "A room for Darshika."

Everyone followed me outside. I pointed to the cowshed. "Just hear me out. The building is sturdy. The upstairs room just needs a good scrubbing."

We walked up the ladder. I pushed the door open with my shoulder, disturbing a pile of trash on the floor. Out wafted a musty, mousy smell. "I know it looks scary, but if we clean and paint it and put some ruffly curtains in the window, it could be cute."

Bob looked around. He was catching the vision. "We could replace the ceiling and maybe polish the floor. This is good wood."

"The cows below will heat the room in the winter," I said. "People have likely lived here before."

Darshika creaked up the steps and peered into the room. "I used to live here when I worked for Manu's mom."

She was open to living there again, but then Darshika could live anywhere. I wanted to surprise her with a TV-worthy miracle transformation, so we kept her away during the next several weeks of whirlwind activity. Bob and Joshua manned the power tools, sawing, gluing, hammering, and drilling. They finished a ladder for the main house first so we could dry our clothes on the roof.

Meanwhile, Hazel and I gathered bag after bag of mouse nesting, dirt, and dust from Darshika's room. We took down the old ceiling and bought wood laminate to insert in its place. Bob and Hazel painted the walls Darshika's favorite color—pink. We scrubbed the floor and put down more laminate. I sewed two mint-green curtains for the window.

The day came when we revealed the room to Darshika. She ran her hand along the walls. She touched the curtains. Then she turned to us. "I can't believe it's the same place. It's beautiful!"

---

AFTER A POSTNATAL CHECKUP IN CHOTASHAHER, we visited Pastor John and Martha. Martha held Darshika's baby, cooing and snapping her fingers at him, so Darshika could eat. Everyone was in a festive mood. It was good to get out of the house and forget our building projects for a while.

"I don't know what I'd do if it weren't for Bhabi," Darshika said. She gave a short laugh. "Probably die!"

"Don't say that," I said, with a halfhearted laugh, unsure what else to say. I glanced at Martha. She frowned.

"Your bhabi is right!" she said in a loud, stern voice. "You should never talk like that."

Darshika's eyes grew wide. "Why, sister? I was only joking."

Martha softened her voice but maintained an authoritative tone. "In our Lord's Word, it says that out of the same mouth should not come blessings and curses. You must never speak like that again. It's not becoming for a Christian. You must put all your faith in the Lord. What if your bhabi had to leave for some emergency, not of her choosing? God brought her into your life. And He will find another way to care for you if she has to leave."

Martha's sermon was not just for Darshika. The thought of leaving the Parvata people was painful. I knew how much the gospel was needed in India. I understood the social, political and worldview factors that made following Christ difficult. A gospel harvest, a church-planting movement, was going to take time. How could I just leave?

I thought back to a comment Mr. Pandit's son had made, one others had echoed. "How nice that your God gives you a break each week. Our gods never let us rest." God is the Creator, the author and finisher of faith, the beginning and end of His own work. He is the God who gives rest. Had I forgotten?

I thought of Kay, the way she didn't hurry, the way she sought to fulfill God's expectations rather than everyone else's. Yet God had used her to help Saachi. And me.

That night, Joshua and I prayed. We felt on the verge of burning out, felt our children wilting in our arms. We'd been praying for wisdom. Logic said to go home and get the help and stability we all needed. Yet we knew that God sees beyond what we see. If He asked us to stay, He would provide all the healing and stability we needed. We just had to know His will.

This time we wouldn't ask our angel dispatchers or families for advice. We'd ask God to show us Himself. We put out a secret fleece and waited, each of us straining our mental faculties to be neutral about God's answer. But after so many years of putting aside my will for God's, I'd seen a pattern. What God wanted was so often the opposite of what I wanted. That's why, though I tried to be neutral, I thought I knew. I thought He'd do a miracle again. I thought we'd stay. Maybe forever.

# 60

# GOD'S ANSWER

That night after the kids went to bed, Bob and Hazel came to pray with us. They spoke peace and wisdom as we awaited God's answer. "We're your supervisors. But we won't try to convince you either way. We just want to give you the support you need to make your decision."

I watched, thinking I would see God fix everything again. But all I saw was a dry fleece that should have been wet and then a wet fleece that should have been dry. The decision was mine, and I knew it. I would be the one to make the call.

I'll never forget the day I told Joshua, lying on our bed sans pillow and staring up at the ceiling. Tears streamed out the corners of my eyes. "I'm sorry. I'm so sorry."

"Why?" he asked. "What's wrong?"

I closed my eyes. "Joshua, I'm sorry because I don't want to hurt you. And I know how disappointed you'll be. This is your dream. But we have to go home."

There was a pause. "Okay, Abby. Let's go home."

"What about the church group? And Darshika? What's going to happen?"

"I don't know."

We made the decision on a Friday afternoon. We told Bob and Hazel, who said they understood. That Sabbath we told Darshika. The grace and acceptance of her reaction caught me off guard. Though she cried a little, she said she understood. "God's got me."

"Pray with us," I said. "We need to figure out a way for you to stay here until you're able to live with Jahne. We don't want to leave you alone. Ayushi says it isn't safe for you to stay here by yourself. And we need to figure out how to keep the church group going. We don't have all the answers, but we believe God is leading."

The following Sunday morning, Joshua and I woke up early. We walked outside and gazed out at the fog moving through the apple trees. I sat on the makeshift sawhorse Joshua and Bob were using to build stairs, shelving, fencing, and desks.

"What are we going to do next?" Joshua asked.

"I don't know," I said. "It doesn't make sense. It seemed so clear we were supposed to come back to India. And clear that we should rent this place and fix it up. Do you think we're making the wrong decision to leave?"

"We asked for a sign, Abby. And God gave us that sign. It was clear."

"So we're leaving."

"Yeah. There goes a year of rent."

"Well, Darshika can stay here. Maybe she can keep the church group going."

"I don't know. Will Jahne let her stay here if she's by herself? Is that even safe?"

"Maybe not."

"Well, whatever we do, we should do it quickly. We fly to Thailand next week, and it only makes sense to fly home from there."

"We have to say goodbye to a lot of people."

"I'm tired."

"So am I."

"What are we going to do with all our stuff?"

"Let's pray."

"Dear God," I began. "You've given us so much. You've blessed us more than we could have imagined. We have this house. We have Darshika and a church group. God, it seems like You've released us from this calling. But we need You to confirm Your will again. We'll stay if You call us to stay and go if You tell us to go. We need Your blessing to move forward in peace. If it is Your will that we leave India, show us today what to do with Darshika and the church, and this house. Amen."

Two hours later, Joshua's phone rang. "Hello? Namaste, Barnabas."

My ears perked up. Barnabas was a Christian friend of ours who worked at our denomination's mission in Delhi. I got up and followed Joshua, who was already pacing around the living room. He wasn't making sense so far. "What? Really? I mean, I—yes!"

"What's going on?" My heart pounded. Something told me God had answered our prayer.

Joshua put his hand over the mouthpiece. "Barnabas says there are two young men who want to come and do ministry in our village. They have a stipend but nowhere to stay."

At his words, all the hair on my arms stood at attention. Joshua was speaking again on the phone. "Yes, sir. We can provide accommodations. In fact, God has already provided them!"

He listened a while longer before hanging up. Then he stared down at the phone. I couldn't take the suspense any longer. "What happened?"

Joshua put the phone down and turned to face me. "There is a group from 1000 Missionary Movement in Delhi right now. They've been fasting and praying since Friday about where to go. Two of them felt impressed to come here."

"Friday? That's the day we made our decision to leave!"

"Exactly."

"When can they come?"

"In two days."

"I had no idea we were fixing this house for someone else!"

Joshua and I hugged each other, then ran outside and bolted up into Darshika's room. We told her the story a mile a minute, and we all hugged and laughed.

"This will be perfect," Darshika said. "I'll cook for the Bible workers, and everyone will see I'm taking care of your guests and your house for you while you're gone. I'll be safe with the Bible workers here, and Jahne will see that I have to stay to take care of your property."

The three of us knelt. We thanked God for His provision and care. As we prayed, I remembered my question from several weeks before. *God, are You there?*

*Yes, I am.* As He'd done for Daniel of old, God had sent an answer the moment I asked. It had just taken several weeks to unfold.

Not a soul on earth, not even our parents, knew we were leaving except Darshika, Bob, and Hazel. Darshika didn't know anyone in Delhi, and Bob and Hazel didn't speak Hindi.

But God on His heavenly throne had known all along.

---

I SAT on the end of Darshika's bed and folded baby clothes. "Are you still interested in getting baptized?"

Newly named Baby Enoch stirred. Darshika picked him up to nurse him. "Yes. You know I want to follow Jesus."

"Would you be interested in getting baptized before I leave? No pressure. I just thought if you wanted to, we could have your baptism along with the baby dedication."

"I've thought about that. But I have a lot on my mind right now."

"Oh?"

"Whatever I do will affect Enoch. What if I make myself a target by doing something so public? Don't get me wrong. I want to follow Jesus, and I'm willing to follow Him one hundred percent. But if I die, who will teach Enoch about the true God?"

"Are you worried you'll be killed if you get baptized? Do you think Jahne would do that?"

"It's not Jahne I worry about," she said. "Christians in India have been murdered. Pastors, their wives, and families. People who did nothing wrong. I just imagine them pounding down my door, killing me and taking Enoch to 'reeducate' him."

I knew Darshika was talking about Ghar Wapsi, the same movement Shankar didn't believe in. The movement that forcibly converted Christians and Muslims in India to Hinduism. It was the same movement that had brought our taxi driver friend Amul back to Hinduism after being a Christian for ten years. I thought of his daughter's subsequent demonic possession and his search for help from the goddess Durga.

"I understand. This isn't my decision. It's yours. And Christ taught us to count the cost. That's a good thing to do, not a betrayal of your faith. You shouldn't do anything you aren't convinced and convicted about. Never do something for me, Darshika, only for Jesus. You just keep praying about it and let me know what you decide."

"I *will* get baptized," Darshika said. "But I won't be ready to do it before you leave."

That night, Joshua and I knelt on the carpet with our children. "Kids, Mommy and Daddy have been praying and talking. And we've decided it's best for our family to move back to the U.S."

"Why?" Ashi asked. "Is it because of me?

I pondered Ashi's question. Was it because of her? Ashi's need for safety and peace had motivated us to pray and seek the Lord's will. But ever since Joshua and I made the decision, we could see it was time, not just for Ashi but for all of us. Could it be that Ashi and Arav were barometers, telling us that our family needed something?

"No, honey," I said. "It's just time."

I expected the kids to react with joy or sadness. I guess they were used to being dragged all over the face of the earth. It must have felt normal to them.

"I like 'Merica," Arav said. "Gramma and Grampa's in 'Merica."

Bob and Hazel promised to pray. Then they left, and we began work on our impending transition. Between selling things and giving things away, we tried to visit people. Most reacted as though we'd told them we were going on vacation for two weeks. Some cried. Others asked if they could have something they'd seen in our house.

Then we visited Ajay's family. They fussed over us and worried. They wanted to know if something was wrong. We said no. They told us to come back to visit. Lovelina asked me to come for her wedding. I promised I would. We took pictures with them. They cried real tears.

"You know," Joshua said as we walked back from their house. "I know sometimes it might feel like people here don't care. I'm sure some people just see us as a good connection. But not everyone is like that. Ajay's family cares. A lot of people do."

"I was thinking the same thing," I said. "I don't want to be jaded about our experience here. We came here to give. You can't give expecting to get something. We tried to love people from our hearts. We were sincere."

"And we did our best. Didn't we?"

"I hope so."

# 61

## LAST DAYS IN OUR VILLAGE

The Bible workers arrived in pleather jackets and bright white smiles. They were new theology graduates, thin, on fire for God, ready to witness. They fit into the chaos with grace. Darshika set herself up as their big sister. They took turns holding the baby for her while she washed their clothes and cooked for them.

The day of the baby dedication, a big crowd came to help shuck peas, peel garlic and potatoes, and grate tomatoes. I decorated our living room with colorful balloons taped high up the wall. We spread out my tablecloths on the floor.

Martha and Pastor John came with several families from their house church. The two Nepali groups were there, and Ayushi came. A brand-new missionary family from another organization came too.

Everyone talked and laughed. We sang and had prayer. The pastor gave a beautiful and inspiring talk about raising Enoch to follow Jesus. It had happened. I had seen the first Christian Parvata baby dedication.

---

THE NEXT MORNING, I visited Darshika in her pink room. She sat on her bed in a patch of light coming through the green silk curtains, folding laundry.

"Hey," I said.

"Hi, Bhabi," she said.

"How's Enoch?"

"Cute and perfect."

I lifted a pair of Enoch's tiny socks to fold. "Listen, I wanted to tell you I'm sorry."

"Why? What happened?"

"Because we're leaving. I know this is difficult for you."

"Bhabi." Setting down a blanket, Darshika leaned towards me and put her hand on her heart. "Listen. I watch you with your kids, you know that. They're wilting, okay? And look at you. It's like you're reaching into the water and lifting out a drowning flower. If only I'd had a mother like you to rescue me when I got into a bad place. If only I'd had a mother like you to keep me from drowning. No, Bhabi. don't be sorry. You're a good mom. You take your flowers and go plant them where they can flourish."

"But what about my seedling? I care about my seedling too."

"I know. But your seedling has been planted now. God's got your seedling."

"I can't help but remember your dream," I said. "The one with Ashi behind the barbed wire fence."

"Me, too, Bhabi. Me, too."

---

THAT SABBATH, the two church groups gathered together in our living room. There was a rainbow of color and texture. Embroidered tunics and sequined tunics. Flowery scarves and solid scarves. Tight cotton *churidar* pants and billowy *patiala* pants. Our flowery wool rug. Woven, scrap-fabric cushion coverings from Lars and Kay. My two acrylic paintings of mountains, which I would leave with Darshika. A few leftover balloons from Enoch's baby dedication.

"*Jaisa mata sambhaltihain,*" someone sang. It was a favorite Hindi gospel song. "Just as a mother cares for her little ones."

"*Vaisa Yeshu salmbhalega,*" the group sang the response. "In the same way, Jesus will take care of me."

The words brought tears. Darshika and I clung to each other and cried and laughed and sang and cried more. Darshika had often called me Bhabi Ma, which means, "my older brother's wife who is like a mother to me."

Ajay was home on vacation and came by that evening. I introduced him to the new Bible workers. I told them how small he'd been when I first met him and pointed out that he was taller than me, now. Ajay smiled and didn't say much, but he looked like he was going to cry.

---

THE FOLLOWING morning was our last day in Kushigaun. Naina rode her bike to meet me. We sat on the roof and cried. She said she hoped my God would provide whatever we needed.

Then people started coming. I was surprised at who came and who didn't come. Chayana came but didn't know what to say. Tripti didn't come. The Nepali Christians came. Ayushi came and stayed for hours. The Momo Lady didn't come. She was out of town. I prayed for everyone, telling God I wanted to "*somf*" them into His hands. The word is something like entrust or give or commit. It is the word Jesus used when He said, "Into Your hands I commit My spirit."

Then it was time. We hugged Darshika again. The Bible workers strode with their fresh energy up to the taxi with our suitcases. I took Ashi and Arav's hands, and we walked the path to the taxi. On the way, someone I'd never met before asked me why we were leaving. I didn't know what to say, so I told her the kids had to go to school in America.

I had pictured the moment of leaving the mission field many times. But this wasn't how I'd pictured it. I'd pictured Isaiah 55:10-13:

> As the rain and the snow come down from heaven, and do not return to it
> without watering the earth and making it bud and flourish, so that it
> yields seed for the sower and bread for the eater, so is my word that
> goes out from my mouth: It will not return to me empty, but will
> accomplish what I desire and achieve the purpose for which I sent it.
> You will go out in joy and be led forth in peace; the mountains and
> hills will burst into song before you, and all the trees of the field will
> clap their hands. Instead of the thornbush will grow the juniper, and
> instead of briers the myrtle will grow. This will be for the Lord's
> renown, for an everlasting sign that will endure forever.

I'd pictured wind on that day. Wind turning the apple orchards into an orchestra of joy, each leaf proclaiming that Christ had got the victory and there was a church in Kushigaun. I'd pictured Brahmin hearts blooming like apple blossoms, filling the air with praise.

But this day was windless. Everything felt normal. And though God's Word had gone forth, I would not be here to see it accomplish His purpose.

I looked past the shops up the hill. There were many people I hadn't had the chance to say goodbye to. People whose weddings I'd attended. Whose babies I'd held. Whose medical cards I'd deciphered for them. Rose was visiting family. Puja lived too far away to visit. Would I ever see them again? Any of them?

I climbed into the car. Ashi and Arav were already looking at books in the back seat. I had no idea what would happen in the future. I didn't know what would happen in India or in my little family. I only knew I was being called somewhere else to do something else. I knew I was being called to let go of something that was never about me in the first place. It was something I didn't start and something I couldn't finish. I had been a part of something God had been doing all along. It was His from the start. And He would finish it.

So I had peace when we left. The peace that makes no sense.

## 62

# ONCE UPON A TIME

W e flew to the United States and settled into a rental owned by our mission organization. I bought a big piece of black card stock and hand-lettered the words, "Home is wherever I'm with you." I taped it to the wall between pictures of family and friends from India and America.

There were over fifty churches within driving distance of us, several of which were Adventist. We chose one with a nice Sabbath school for the kids.

I'll never forget our first Sabbath at that church. I held it together for the first few praise songs. Then we sang one about missions. I burst into tears. Black women in big hats handed me tissues from the pews behind and in front of me.

"It's okay, honey. Just tell Jesus everything," one woman said. "He's listening."

Ashi attended a Christian kindergarten. Both Ashi and I worked with wonderful Christian counselors who helped us process what we'd seen and experienced in India. Our organization asked Joshua to work in the office, creating witnessing materials for the Parvata people. I helped sometimes too.

There were bike rides and church socials and trips to the lakeside with friends. I felt the way I'd longed to feel in India. Normal. Comfortable. I enjoyed things I'd never appreciated before like clean spinach and frozen strawberries.

But I missed India too. In India, people were not always rushing off to work. In India, people lingered and listened. I hoped I could be that kind of person even in the U.S.

Ashi's fear and pain faded. Instead of the poisoning, she remembered when God told me to check on her in the night. Instead of the landlords who hated her, she remembered the neighbor who gave her a flower every time she walked past his house. And she prayed for Yog, her *Taoji*, her dad's older brother, that he would turn away from idols.

ONE DAY BARNABAS CALLED, our friend from the mission in Delhi. He said they'd been praying for the Parvata project and wanted to build a church in our village.

"Do you realize what this means?" Joshua exclaimed as he hung up. "If they build a church, they will keep it staffed with people who can work among the Parvata. Indian people who will understand them better than we do."

"This is another miracle!" Having a local worker take over our project was something we'd only dreamed of. But God had done in mere months what we'd thought would take years.

I called Darshika. She had tried again to live with Jahne's parents, but they had bowed Enoch's little head to the ground before the family idol, and he had gotten sick. So she was back in the pink room with the mint green curtains. Since Jahne wasn't willing for her to live with him, he visited her once a month.

Darshika said everyone liked the Bible workers: Ajay, Yog, even Jahne. She promised to visit Naina and Ayushi herself. I felt a pang of longing. But I also felt tired. I needed rest.

As I hung up the phone, I thought about our decision to leave. I'd thought following God's will meant doing the opposite of what I wanted. But Christian obedience is not animism. It isn't completing a sequence of rituals. God wants the hard heart work of staying yourself while following Him.

And that is exactly why I told God no. I told Him I'd never be a missionary again. I didn't have it in me to do it again. To learn another language. To squeeze myself into another culture. To love another people group.

*Feel free to do what You always do,* I prayed. *If anyone can take a tired, shriveled old heart and make it new again, it's You.*

THAT SPRING, I shared a song with our congregation. "I wrote this song after we returned from being missionaries in India. I was inspired by a Bible verse, Psalm 126:6, which reads, 'He who continually goes forth weeping, Bearing seed for sowing, Shall doubtless come again with rejoicing, Bringing his sheaves with him.'"

As I adjusted my guitar strap, I looked out across the pews. Several returned missionary families sat in the congregation. I went on. "When I first read this verse, I immediately pictured the tears of the sowers dripping down their faces onto the ground. Their tears watered their seeds. Without the suffering of the sowers, the harvest would never have happened."

I clipped on my capo and began to fingerpick. The strings vibrated against my fingers on the fret. I looked down at my lyrics and sang.

TO GROW SOMETHING HERE
By Abigail Follows

*They went through so much just to buy the land.*
*And those newlyweds, they used to press the plow by their own hands.*
*It was with joy they spent their last just to buy the seed.*
*As they threw it wide, they couldn't help but dream.*

*"Wouldn't it be beautiful*
*To grow something here?*
*To labor hard together*
*For a harvest every year?*
*Everything will bloom*
*As in faith we persevere.*
*Wouldn't it be beautiful*
*To grow something here?"*

*Now silent in their grief, they walk the barren rows.*
*They don't ask, "What happened here?" They both know.*
*And as drought grips the earth, their tears fall to the ground.*
*They walk home wondering, "What are we gonna do now?"*

*It would have been beautiful*
*To grow something here,*
*To labor hard together*
*For a harvest every year.*
*Now nothing's gonna bloom.*
*But didn't we persevere?*
*It would have been beautiful*
*To grow something here.*

*Well, those two, they kept walking, kept on crying over what they thought*
    *they'd lost*
*Little knowing their tears soaked into the ground on which they walked.*
*Then, one day, purple clouds came with a ripening rain,*
*And beneath them stretching out there stood a ready field of green.*

*Wasn't it beautiful*
*To grow something here?*
*We'll labor hard together*
*For a harvest this year!*
*Everything will bloom*
*As in faith we persevere.*
*Wasn't it beautiful*
*To grow something here?*
*Wasn't it beautiful*
*To grow*
*Here?*

It was a song of faith, not of sight. And as I sang it, I saw the other missionaries in the room wipe their eyes. Someday it would be true. Someday God would make it true.

---

SIX MONTHS LATER, Joshua and I sat on the couch in our living room. Ashi and Arav played tag with a group of other missionary kids on the lawn.

"I'm ready to make a decision," I told Joshua. "I know we've been counting the cost this week. Looking at all the difficulties of cross-cultural missions. But I *want* to want to go."

"There are hundreds of potential pastors at the seminary nearby," Joshua said. "But this week there were only three families at our organization's orientation. Just three families ready to be missionaries. I know He moved us out of India, but I don't feel released from my original calling."

"Neither do I. I also sense a calling. Both to be a missionary myself and to support you in your call."

"This time we're going to rely on God so much more because we've done this before. We realize that it isn't about us. It's about Him."

I nodded. I thought about the Jesus Teacher, the first person to plant a gospel seed in Darshika's heart. He never saw it grow. But he knew the One who caused buried apricot seeds to rise up green in the spring. I hoped that when the Jesus Teacher left Anderagaun village he knew his sacrifice was not in vain.

"We'll be different this time," I said. "We know God's ways are way beyond just what missionaries can do. All we have to do is obey and watch Him work out His plans."

"There's something else," Joshua said. "I want you to know that *I'll* be different too."

"What do you mean?" I asked.

"Abby, you tried to build our home. You tried to have boundaries. For years I didn't see that boundaries and home-building are important to missions. I thought that if we became Parvata, we could reach the Parvata. But now I realize we have to have boundaries or we'll burn out. All of us. We have to be ourselves. We have to trust God to do what He said He would do."

"We'll both be different, Joshua. And we'll keep being different because when you follow Jesus, you don't stay the same." I smiled at my husband. Both of us were far from perfect. But Joshua followed God. And because of that, I knew I could follow him anywhere. Whether or not he knew where he was going.

"Does this mean we've made a decision?"

"Let's pray."

"Dear God, thank You for Your leading and guidance and grace. We accept Your call. Please continue to confirm Your will. Send Your Holy Spirit ahead of us to prepare people to receive Christ. Send them dreams and visions. Send them questions. And use us in whatever way You see fit. Amen."

---

A FEW WEEKS after our prayer of acceptance, I was again wrestling with our call to be missionaries in another country. I wanted confirmation. Just one more fleece.

*God, I hear You calling me to give my anxiety into Your hands. It just feels so unsafe to stop worrying. I guess I have to wait until heaven to be free of anxiety. But You are strong enough to handle this weakness. Please, Lord, confirm Your call again.*

Unbeknownst to me, around this time a friend and former missionary was writing me a letter. I received it a week later: "Have you not heard God calling you in the night? If He has called, then faithful is He! We cannot afford to waste time nor energy on past experiences or fears. Some feel one must ruminate or figure it all out. It really boils down to trusting our Father's heart."

---

WE TOLD the children we planned to be missionaries again. They were excited, sad, intrigued, and scared all at the same time. As were their parents.

One day Joshua took Ashi to a local thrift store, where she bought an old CD by *Go Fish*, a Christian band that performed children's gospel music. Later, I slipped Ashi's new CD into the car stereo system. It was raining. The beat of the windshield wipers and the blast of the heater made the car feel cozy. Most of the songs were your typical silly kids' song.

Then came the last one: "You Are Mine." The lyrics talked about how a lot of changes happen in life, but it's okay because God goes with us and takes care of us. We are His, and He loves us.

I glanced at Ashi in the rearview mirror. "Ashi, I think Jesus sent you this song."

"I think He did too, Mommy," she said. "This is just what I needed to hear."

At that moment, I remembered the shepherds who used to cross the roads of Kushigaun with their hundreds of sheep. They always wore wool clothing in earthy colors and whistled to tell the sheep where to go. Once I saw a broad-backed shepherd stride up the road with his flocks behind him, a baby lamb riding in the pocket of his coat.

The lamb peeked out of the pocket, wide-eyed with wonder at the world. The shepherd glanced back at his flock and whistled a melodic line. Then he walked forward, shoulders back, a smile on his face. And the sheep followed.

*I trust You, God,* I prayed. *Lead on.*

# EPILOGUE
## OUR MINISTRY NOW

After spending one year in the United States, our family did launch to another closed-access country to be missionaries. And we did do things differently. For starters, we weren't afraid to buy cooking utensils!

While we still make an effort to bond with the people of our host country, we are careful to maintain family boundaries. We give ourselves permission to take regular breaks and have fun, even when it doesn't seem like we've "accomplished" anything. As a result, we and our children are better able to rest in the faith that Jesus is the one to reach the unreached. He is just generous enough to use us flawed human beings to help Him do it.

At the time of the writing of this book, we have been in our second country of service for two years.

Despite doing a few things differently the second time around, we don't have many regrets from our first years in India. Bonding did make a difference. It helped us to understand the Parvata people. It made sharing Jesus with them possible and makes us informed angel dispatchers now.

We still recommend that new missionaries stay with locals when possible, learn as much as possible about their culture, and strive to reach proficiency in the language as quickly as possible. We are in favor of temporarily sacrificing comfort for the sake of bonding with a people group. But we also recommend taking breaks and doing what it takes to maintain the personal or family identity.

We learned a lot from Lars and Kay who, though their first priority was to make themselves a home, still bonded with and ministered to the Parvata people and years later still sometimes referred to India as "home."

God is still leading me in the slow, steep path out of anxiety. But the view along that path is inspiring. I can only praise Him for the healing potential He placed within our minds and bodies. I can only praise Him for the Holy Spirit, through whom that healing is available to each of us.

For our first three years in India, Joshua and I were together almost 24/7. We like to say we squeezed ten years of marriage into three, with the same number of ups and downs. While this was difficult at the time, we learned a lot about relationships and enjoy the fruits of that hard labor now.

Ashi and Arav still bring joy and energy to our home no matter where we are. It is challenging to help kids navigate a culture their parents are just beginning to understand. But we thank God for the chance our children have to be exposed to other ways of thinking. And we praise Him for His love and leading in their young lives.

Even from our new country of service, we keep in touch with our Indian friends. Jahne visits Darshika often and attends church with her when he does. But Jahne still wants Darshika to live with his parents and do as they say. She wants to live with him and worship God. We continue to pray for Darshika as she stands alone in her faith.

One of the Bible workers who replaced us was eventually hired on as a full-time pastor. Although he struggled with illness and loneliness, God blessed his ministry. He continues to work with many of the same people we did. We pray that one day an ethnically Parvata pastor of any denomination will serve in that mountainous area.

Some years after we left India, missionaries from another organization entered our village. One of the first people they met was Naina, who later told me, "Your God brought someone just like you to tell me about Him!" Amen!

India continues to be listed as a country of particular concern by the United States Commission on International Religious Freedom. In their 2020 report, they mentioned in particular anti-conversion laws and the Ghar Wapsi movement.

> While the constitution protects the right to proselytize, ten states have anti-conversion laws criminalizing conversion using force, allurement, inducement, or fraud, but many use vague language that can be interpreted as prohibiting consensual conversions . . . Authorities predominately arrest Muslims and Christians for conversion activities. To date, however, there are no known convictions for forced conversion. Hindutva groups pursue mass conversions through ceremonies known as ghar wapsi (homecoming), without interference from authorities. Empowered by anti-conversion laws and often with the police's complicity, Hindutva groups also conduct campaigns of harassment, social exclusion, and violence against Christians, Muslims, and other religious minorities across the country. Following attacks by Hindutva groups against religious minorities for conversion activities, the police often arrest the religious minorities who have been attacked.
>
> "INDIA USCIRF-RECOMMENDED FOR COUNTRIES OF
> PARTICULAR CONCERN," US COMMISSION ON INTERNATIONAL

FREEDOM, ACCESSED FEBRUARY 7, 2021, HTTPS://WWW.
USCIRF.GOV/SITES/DEFAULT/FILES/INDIA.PDF

In the past five years, persecution in India has increased significantly. To learn more about the persecuted church worldwide, visit opendoorsusa.org, where, as of 2021, India was listed as the tenth most difficult place to follow Jesus.

Please join us in praying for the religious liberty situation in India. Pray for Darshika, the Momo Lady, Lovelina, Yog, Tripti, Bimla, and the many others you have read about in this book. You are not powerless. You can be an angel dispatcher, inviting God to send angels where they may not otherwise be welcomed.

Finally, I want to thank you for reading our story. May it deepen your compassion and love for the Indian people, and inspire you to go with God on your own adventure.

Love,

Abby

PS. If you have been blessed by *Hidden Song of the Himalayas,* please consider helping others find it by leaving a review on Amazon. Thank you so much!

# GLOSSARY OF HINDI TERMS

Bahu - daughter-in-law

Betho - sit down

Bhabi - older brother's wife

Bhabi ma - older brother's wife who is like a mother to me

Bhagavad Gita - one of the best-known of the many portions of
    Hindu scripture

Bhai / bhaia - brother

Bua - father's sister

Bindi - a dot worn on the forehead by married women or as jewelry
    by unmarried women

Boori atma - literally, "bad spirit"

Chalak - divorce

Devta - a village-level demi-god

Dhanyavad - thank you

Dharm - religion / duty

Didi - elder sister

Ghar Wapsi - a campaign facilitating the conversion or
    reconversion, sometimes by force, of Christians and Muslims to
    Hinduism

Greh - astrological bad fortune

Gur - medium of the devta

Jai - victory

Jai Massih - victory to the Savior; a Christian greeting

Janeo - a string tied around a Brahmin man's chest, signifying his
    entrance into adulthood

Kajal - black eyeliner applied as a protection against the evil eye or
    as makeup

Karma / karm - the sum of a person's actions in previous and current lives, which affects what happens to them now and in the future

Kuvari - a virgin

Mela - a village festival

Momos - a savory, East and South Asian dumpling

Pakoras - a spicy fritter made of fried and battered vegetables

Patu - a wool wrap worn as a dress or used as a blanket

Pradhan - elected village chief

Prasad - food offered to idols

Puja - the Hindu form of worship / respect for the divine

Rakhi / Rakhi Bhandan - a Hindu festival celebrating the bond between brothers and sisters

Sehali - a close female friend of a girl or woman

Shauk - interest or hobby

Somf - to commit into someone's care

Tanda - cold

Tandoor - wood stove

Taoji - father's older brother

Tilak - a paste applied to the middle of the forehead for various purposes

Yatra - a religious pilgrimage

Zabardasty - force or peer pressure

## About the Author

Abigail Follows has lived on three continents and understood the life stories of friends in three languages. She has been a cross-cultural missionary for 11 years. Abigail lives wherever God leads with her husband, two children, and cat, Protagonist. You can find her online at www.abigailfollows.com.